The Future of Knowledge

ALSO AVAILABLE FROM BLOOMSBURY

Reflective Teaching in Primary Schools, Andrew Pollard and Dominic Wyse with Ayshea Craig, Caroline Daly, Sinead Harmey, Louise Hayward, Steve Higgins, Amanda McCrory and Sarah Seleznyov
Reflective Teaching in Secondary Schools, Andrew Pollard and Caroline Daly with Katharine Burn, Steve Higgins, Aileen Kennedy, Margaret Mulholland, Jo Fraser-Pearce, Mary Richardson, Dominic Wyse and John Yandell
Leadership for Sustainability in Higher Education, Janet Haddock-Fraser, Peter Rands and Stephen Scoffham
Transforming Teacher Education, Viv Ellis and Jane McNicholl
Transforming University Education, Paul Ashwin
Transforming Education, Miranda Jefferson and Michael Anderson

The Future of Knowledge

The Role of Epistemic Insight in Interdisciplinary Learning

EDITED BY

BERRY BILLINGSLEY, KEITH CHAPPELL AND SHERRALYN SIMPSON

BLOOMSBURY ACADEMIC
LONDON • NEW YORK • OXFORD • NEW DELHI • SYDNEY

BLOOMSBURY ACADEMIC
Bloomsbury Publishing Plc
50 Bedford Square, London, WC1B 3DP, UK
1385 Broadway, New York, NY 10018, USA
29 Earlsfort Terrace, Dublin 2, Ireland

BLOOMSBURY, BLOOMSBURY ACADEMIC and the Diana logo are trademarks of
Bloomsbury Publishing Plc

First published in Great Britain 2024

Copyright © Berry Billingsley, Keith Chappell and Sherralyn Simpson, 2024

Berry Billingsley, Keith Chappell and Sherralyn Simpson have asserted their right under
the Copyright, Designs and Patents Act, 1988, to be identified as Editors of this work.

Cover design by Matt Beard
Cover image © Evgeniy yes and Rawpixel.com via Shutterstock / Arrows via Adobe Stoc

This work is published open access subject to a Creative Commons Attribution-
NonCommercial-NoDerivatives 4.0 International licence (CC BY-NC-ND 4.0, https://
creativecommons.org/licenses/by-nc-nd/4.0/). You may re-use, distribute, and
reproduce this work in any medium for non-commercial purposes, provided you give
attribution to the copyright holder and the publisher and provide a link to the Creative
Commons licence.

Bloomsbury Publishing Plc does not have any control over, or responsibility for, any
third-party websites referred to or in this book. All internet addresses given in this
book were correct at the time of going to press. The author and publisher regret any
inconvenience caused if addresses have changed or sites have ceased to exist, but
can accept no responsibility for any such changes.

A catalogue record for this book is available from the British Library.

Library of Congress Cataloging-in-Publication Data

Names: Billingsley, Berry, editor. | Chappell, Keith, editor. | Simpson, Sherralyn, editor.
Title: The future of knowledge: the role of epistemic insight in interdisciplinary learning
  / edited by Berry Billingsley, Keith Chappell and Sherralyn Simpson.
Description: London; New York: Bloomsbury Academic, 2024. | Includes bibliographical
  references and index.
Identifiers: LCCN 2024010730 (print) | LCCN 2024010731 (ebook) | ISBN
  9781350383913 (HB) | ISBN 9781350383906 (PB) | ISBN 9781350383937 (eBook) |
  ISBN 9781350383920 (ePDF)
Subjects: LCSH: Interdisciplinary approach to knowledge–Forecasting. |
  Interdisciplinary approach in education–Forecasting. | Epistemics. | Learning,
  Psychology of. | Teaching–Methodology.
Classification: LCC BD255 .F88 2024 (print) | LCC BD255 (ebook) |
  DDC 001–dc23/eng/20240325
LC record available at https://lccn.loc.gov/2024010730
LC ebook record available at https://lccn.loc.gov/2024010731

ISBN: HB: 978-1-3503-8391-3
  PB: 978-1-3503-8390-6
  ePDF: 978-1-3503-8392-0
  eBook: 978-1-3503-8393-7

Typeset by Deanta Global Publishing Services, Chennai, India
Printed and bound in Great Britain

To find out more about our authors and books visit www.bloomsbury.com and sign up
for our newsletters.

Contents

List of Figures viii
List of Table ix
List of Teacher Resources and Notes x
List of Contributors xi
Preface: The Future of Knowledge *Berry Billingsley, Keith Chappell and Sherralyn Simpson* xviii
Foreword *Renato Opertti* xxii

Introduction: Creating the Future of Knowledge in the Age of GenAI *Berry Billingsley*   1
Chapter Summaries and How to Read This Book
Keith Chappell, Berry Billingsley and Sherralyn Simpson 9

Part I Epistemic Insight, Epistemic Agency and Multidisciplinary Enquiries 17

Statement of support *Alona Forkosh Baruch* 19

1 Cultivating Epistemic Agents as Critical Consumers of Information *Berry Billingsley and Sean Durbin* 21

Part II Planning to Teach with Big Questions 39

Statement of support *Overson Shumba* 41

2 Igniting Primary School Students' Curiosity: Exploring the Impact of Co-Created Epistemic Insight Teaching on Learner Agency *Sherralyn Simpson* 43

3 Big Questions about Humanity's Place in the Cosmos and Epistemic Insight Pedagogy among University Trainee Teachers *Maureen Kanchebele Sinyangwe* 59

4 Big Questions – And Their Value in Extra-Curricular Activities That Teach Epistemic Insight *Laura Hackett* 69

Part III What Is the Epistemic Insight Future of Knowledge Initiative? 81

Statement of support *Richard Cheetham* 85

5 Future Libraries' AI Focusing on Motivations to Learn: A Technologist's View *Ted Selker with additional creative input and expert knowledge from Berry Billingsley* 87

6 Research Co-Creation and the Development of Epistemically Insightful Curricula *Finley I. Lawson, Mandy Dhaliwal, Michelle Lawson and Henry Coates* 99

7 How Can We Educate Future Generations to Effectively Respond to Global Challenges and Live Sustainably? Developing Agentic Learners through an Epistemically Insightful Curriculum *Agnieszka J. Gordon and Sherralyn Simpson* 117

Part IV The Future of Knowledge and Higher Education 137

Statement of support *Rama Thirunamachandran* 141

8 Dancing with the Digital: An 'EI' Workshop Designed to Bridge Disciplines and Spark Students' Epistemic Creativity *Lee Hazeldine, Karl Bentley, Angela Pickard and Allan Callaghan* 143

9 The Nature-Knowledge-Values Framework –
A Pedagogical Tool for Teaching NOS in Tertiary
Education *Klaus Colanero and Kai Ming Kiang* 155

Part V Language, Technology and Inclusivity 175

Statement of support *John Bryant* 177
10 Building a Smarter Search Engine *Aryn Litchfield* 179
11 A Sociocultural Understanding of Epistemic Insight Towards an Imperative of Interdisciplinary Teaching and Learning *Dana L. Zeidler* 192
12 Get Ready, Steady, Allez? ¡Vamos! *Martin Pickett* 205

Part VI Science, Imagination, Interdisciplinarity and AI 217

Statement of support *Nidhal Guessoum* 221
13 Science Education, Interdisciplinarity and Critical Thinking *Nidhal Guessoum* 223
14 Philosophy and Artificial Friends *Greg Artus* 237
15 Library Perspective Closing the Book, Continuing to Grow . . . *Keith Chappell* 250
16 Teacher Notes and Resources 256

Index 281

Figures

1.1	The Discipline Wheel	28
2.1	The Discovery Bag	46
2.2	Thinking like a scientist ('Why did the Titanic sink?')	51
2.3	Thinking like a historian ('Who sank the Titanic?')	52
2.4	Sparking primary students' interest in science	54
6.1	Research ecosystem development	108
6.2	Development of students' understanding of disciplinary methods to tackle a shared question	112
7.1	The blind men and the elephant	123
7.2	Example wind turbines	125
7.3	The Bubble Tool	127
7.4	Gus Speth's quote	131
8.1	Sensor technology made available in the workshop	146
8.2	Dancing robot example	147
8.3	Students participating in a discussion	150
9.1	Diagram illustrating the Nature-Knowledge-Values thinking framework	161
10.1	El Discipline Wheel in the foreground of the search engine	184
10.2	Selecting disciplines to search 'How can we live with water better?'	185
12.1	Role of the linguist in the design team	209
12.2	El Discipline Wheel (adapted)	212
12.3	Example view from a driverless car	213

Table

1.1 Assessing Students' Work 30

Teacher Resources and Notes

Teacher resource: The Epistemic Insight curriculum framework (two formats)	264
Teacher resource: Why do spinners spin? Essential experiences in science card	266
Teacher resource: Why did the Titanic sink? Essential experiences in science cards (science card)	268
Teacher resource: Who sank the Titanic? Essential experiences in science cards (history card)	270
Teacher resource: Why is the sky blue? Investigating big questions card	272
Teacher resource: How do clouds stay up? Essential experiences in science card	274
Teacher notes: Why did the spaghetti break (bridging questions)	276
Teacher notes: Why is the sky blue? – Search engine	278

Contributors

Greg Artus is a lecturer in Philosophy at Imperial College London, UK. He has published articles on machine ethics and the phenomenology of lockdown. His research interests include machine ethics, Wittgenstein, philosophy of mind, phenomenology and process philosophy.

Karl Bentley was an engineer in the petrochemical sector for over two decades prior to becoming a primary school teacher for ten years and then moving to academia where he now teaches across a range of ITE courses. His degrees cover the humanities, education and science and complement his experiences across education and industry giving him a unique view of how the epistemic insight can help students and others to look beyond domain boundaries in tackling the big questions that present-day life throws at us.

Berry Billingsley specializes in science education and leads the LASAR (Learning about Science and Religion) Research Centre, as well as the Epistemic Insight Initiative based at Canterbury Christ Church University, UK. Berry's first career was with the BBC, where she produced and presented television and radio programmes including BBC World Service's 'Science in Action', BBC TV's 'Tomorrow's World' and BBC Education's 'Search out Science'.

Allan Callaghan has a background in professional software engineer and secondary school teaching. In 2018, he started assisting Christ Church, UK, with initial teacher training and in 2020 was appointed Subject Tutor for Initial Teacher Education for Secondary School Computing teachers in Kent. In 2021, he was appointed Lecturer in Computing with the School of Engineering, Technology and Design.

Keith Chappell holds doctorates in biology and in theology and has published widely on the interaction of science and religion, the biology of pollution and in the sociology of religion. Keith researches sociology at the University of Sunderland and teaches religion, politics and society at the University of Leeds. He is an associate fellow at the Edward Cadbury Centre at the University of Birmingham and also the LASAR Research Centre at Canterbury Christ Church University, UK. Keith has a deep interest in the implications of current technological and social changes for society, religion and science.

Henry Coates is an early career teacher in geography and French in a comprehensive school in Kent. He has implemented a whole year-group approach to the development of students' epistemic insight through combined humanities and MFL (Modern Foreign Languages) programme and is committed to understanding how curriculum innovation and interdisciplinary learning opportunities can support all students achieve their full potential by supporting students' engagement and aspiration.

Klaus Colanero is a lecturer for the General Education Foundation Programme of the Office of University General Education, the Chinese University of Hong Kong. He holds a PhD in physics from the Chinese University of Hong Kong (MPhil, L'Aquila University, Italy), a masters in logic, philosophy and history of science from the University of Florence (Italy), and a postgraduate diploma in education from the Education University of Hong Kong. His main research interests are education to the nature of science, science and values, and transdisciplinary education. He is also actively involved in research on the foundations of quantum physics.

Mandy Dhaliwal is an assistant headteacher in a Girls' Grammar School in Kent, UK, where she has led the development and implementation of the epistemic insight curriculum in the school. Prior to this, she worked in several different middle management positions and has extensive experience as a middle leader and has worked as a SENCO, Head of Department and Head of Sixth Form. She is actively involved in the training and development of new and early career teachers and works with Kent School Teaching hub as an ECT support tutor which involves the delivery of the new early career framework to both early career teachers and ECT mentors.

Sean Durbin is a distinguished scholar of contemporary religion. His research interests include religion and politics, religion and society, and new religious movements, studied from an anthropological and sociological perspective. From 2014 to 2019 he was editor of the journal *Relegere: Studies in Religion and Reception*. Dr Durbin has held positions at Macquarie University, the University of Newcastle, Australian Catholic University, Canterbury Christ Church University, the University of London and Manchester Metropolitan University.

Agnieszka J. Gordon (https://orcid.org/0000-0002-5752-7087) is a research fellow (consortium lead) and project manager at the LASAR Centre, Canterbury Christ Church University, UK. Agnieszka's background is quantum chemistry and as such she has over twenty years of experience across STEM teaching and learning in higher education both in Poland and the UK. In the last three years Agnieszka has worked on educational research on the innovative teaching and research project, Epistemic Insight Initiative, enhancing teaching across Initial Teacher Education multi-institution consortium she led, as well as other STEM-related research and teaching projects. As an active STEM ambassador, she is passionate about inspiring the younger generation about STEM and STEM-related careers. Prior to LASAR, Agnieszka was an associate professor in quantum chemistry at the Faculty of Chemistry, University of Wroclaw, Poland, and honorary research fellow at the School of Chemistry, University of Edinburgh, Scotland.

Nidhal Guessoum is an Algerian astrophysicist who received his MSc and PhD degrees from the University of California at San Diego, USA, and spent two years as a researcher at NASA's Goddard Space Flight Center. His research focuses on gamma radiation, mainly from the Milky Way Galaxy, but lately from other sources in the universe as well; he has had an ongoing collaboration with colleagues at the Centre d'Etude Spatiale des Rayonnements in Toulouse, France. For the past decade or so, he has been at the American University of Sharjah (United Arab Emirates), where he chaired the Physics Department for a few years and presided over the Faculty Senate.

Laura Hackett is a qualified early years teacher and has been in education for ten years, with experience of primary and secondary schools as a TA, teacher and researcher. Laura has an MA in Early Years Education.

Lee Hazeldine is a senior lecturer in education and a research fellow for the Epistemic Insight Initiative at Canterbury Christ Church University, UK. Lee is a former learning consultant with experience in educational training and leadership. He has a PhD in Philosophy, a PGCE, an MA in Cultural Representation and a PGCert in Social Science Research Methods. He has been the lead for the Epistemic Insight ITE strand and has instigated a range of student and tutor research-informed/research-engaged initiatives, including scholarship days, cross-curricular workshops and Knowledge Lab interdisciplinary interventions across schools and faculties within a higher education setting. Lee has a range of research interests and has published in the areas of epistemic insight and cross-disciplinary learning, digital and blended learning and rhizomatic learning. Lee is currently supervising doctoral students in the field of cross-disciplinary education.

Kai Ming Kiang is a senior lecturer of General Education Foundation Programme in the Office of University General Education at the Chinese University of Hong Kong. He obtained his PhD degree in Mechatronics Engineering from the University of New South Wales, Australia, in 2007. His research interests include science education and machine learning. In particular, he is interested in bridging the history and philosophy of science with science education. He is also actively involving in popularizing science and general education in Hong Kong Cantonese media.

Finley I. Lawson is an educational development lead with the School and College Engagement Team, at Canterbury Christ Church University, UK. Prior to this he was the lead research fellow for Outreach and Schools' Partnership at the LASAR Research Centre, where he led the 'Permeable Walls' research Strand for the Epistemic Insight Initiative. He has a PhD in Theology and over ten years' experience working in educational support and tutoring across primary and secondary schools in England.

Michelle Lawson is a headteacher in a Girls' Grammar School in Kent, UK, where she has developed a research-engaged approach to staff CPD, empowering staff to take an epistemically insightful approach to their teaching. Prior to this she has extensive experience as a senior leader and teacher in comprehensive and selective secondary schools in the south-east of England. She is part of curriculum advisory groups including acting as a council member for Ken SACRE (Standing Advisory Council for Religious Education) and serving on the Initial Teacher Education Partnership Group at Canterbury Christ Church University.

Aryn Litchfield holds a first-class BA in Philosophy, Religion and Ethics and an MA distinction in Philosophy. Aryn's current research interests include virtue epistemology, philosophy of science, philosophy of religion and artificial intelligence. Aryn's research explores areas that seek to progress human potential and development, especially strands that focus on technology such as artificial intelligence and the potential existential risks and enhancements such technology poses to human ontology and way of life.

Angela Pickard is the director of the Sidney De Haan Research Centre for Arts and Health, UK, in the Faculty of Medicine, Health and Social Care. Angela is a dancer, choreographer, practitioner and academic. She became the first Professor of Dance Education in 2021. She brings with her a wealth of knowledge in arts research, particularly dance and movement practices, and a passion for exploring the value and relationship between arts and physical, psychological, social and artistic outcomes.

Martin Pickett studied BSc International Business and Politics with Modern Languages at Aston University, UK. Having used his five main languages in business LANACOS and ERASMUS, he did teacher training at Christ Church Canterbury University and studied epistemic insight. His PhD at the University of Portsmouth combined his interests of education and psycholinguistics to understand individual learner motivation to speak a foreign language. For more than twenty-five years, he has worked as an international educational consultant and teacher, currently at Saint Olave's Grammar School, Orpington.

Ted Selker is known for demonstrating and testing new ways of using technology and designing products. He works to create and guide strategic emerging technology opportunities. Ted has helped create many companies and is a founder of Moto Carma. Ted lectures internationally on innovation/invention, design and user experience. Ted currently holds adjunct professor positions at several universities. He has been a professor at CMU and MIT Media Lab. Prior to joining the MIT faculty, he gained the title of IBM Fellow where Ted directed the User Systems Ergonomics Research Lab. He has served as a consulting professor at Stanford University, taught at Hampshire, University of Massachusetts at Amherst and Brown Universities, and worked at Xerox PARC and Atari Research Labs. Ted's innovations have contributed to products ranging from medical devices to notebook computers to operating systems. Ted's work has resulted in numerous awards, patents and papers and has often been featured in the national and international press.

Sherralyn Simpson is a research fellow (primary schools lead) at the LASAR Centre, Canterbury Christ Church University, UK. Sherralyn has a teaching background in Further Education and has successfully transferred this experience to work and collaborate with teaching professionals and their students in schools and universities. Through professional development opportunities for teachers and interactive 'hands-on' science and big questions student workshops, Sherralyn has introduced and explored the epistemic insight pedagogy, its tools and exciting activities in a range of educational settings. Sherralyn is also a qualified Careers Development professional and has engaged with teaching and learning activities as a STEM ambassador.

Maureen Kanchebele Sinyangwe is the deputy director in the Directorate of Research Postgraduate at Kwame Nkrumah University in Kabwe, Zambia. She is also a lecturer and researcher in pre-mathematics, mathematics and mathematics education in the School of Natural Sciences. She has a history of teaching in primary, secondary and higher education in Zambia. Maureen is passionate about contributing towards improving the quality of education especially in areas of mathematics and researching into the various aspects of mathematics and mathematics education with a special interest both in supporting and empowering learners, student/trainee teachers and serving teachers in their continuing learning and development in the field. Other areas of research interest include, but not limited to, STEM/STEAM/STREAM; Health Education including HIV/AIDS and mental well-being. Maureen has been introduced to epistemic insight pedagogy and is exploring it.

Dana L. Zeidler, PhD, is Distinguished University Professor of Science Education in the College of Education at the University of South Florida, Tampa, Florida, USA. He has developed an international research programme in the field of science education centred on socioscientific Issues – taking a sociocultural approach to teaching and learning about how moral and ethical issues can be a means to foster the formation of epistemological sophistication and character in the pursuit of scientific literacy.

Preface
The Future of Knowledge

Berry Billingsley, Keith Chappell and Sherralyn Simpson

Imagine an education system where students are not just passive consumers of knowledge, but active creators and critical thinkers. Where exams are not simply testing students' abilities to memorize and recite facts but also examining students' understanding of how different disciplines approach the world, and how working with different disciplines can engage our imaginations and broaden our perspectives. Add to this a global conversation about the importance of epistemic insight in education and society, and an ambitious research agenda that investigates ways to bridge disciplines and compartments that are currently apart. These are some of the ingredients and aspirations that guide this book.

What is epistemic insight?

Epistemic insight refers to the ability to think critically about knowledge. It's about understanding how different disciplines create and organize knowledge, their different strengths and weaknesses and how they can work together to address different types of questions.

A leap of epistemic insight corresponds to the 'aha!' moment associated with sudden shifts in perspective and the deep connections that can arise when we look across the walls between disciplines and engage in interdisciplinary inquiry. To develop epistemic insight, we can build and strengthen interdisciplinary and collaborative approaches to learning and research, both within and across educational levels and contexts.

This book

This book is firstly the outcome of a large-scale research agenda in education which sought to design, test and implement strategies that help students of all ages to become wise and compassionate epistemic agents. An epistemic agent is someone who understands the nature of knowledge, and our initial research was about mapping out the ways that this understanding can be developed and applied by students at different points in their studies. Why? Well, the agenda motivating the research was that too many students in England and internationally are carrying out schoolwork and university projects only to pass tests rather than because they can see any intrinsic value in the work they are doing. That claim is not new, nor is the research that says what needs to change, and yet the challenge still remains. So how do you make change happen? The pivotal factors in this case have been a university that was well placed to make big changes happen, sufficient grant income to share our vision and create new resources and a team of specialists who you can meet for yourself as many are the authors and co-authors of chapters.

The Epistemic Insight Initiative

The Epistemic Insight Initiative was launched in 2017 collaboratively with the Association for Science Education and has received funding from the Templeton World Charity Foundation, the Royal Academy of Engineering, the Science and Technology Facilities Council and other organizations (Billingsley and Hardman 2017).

The initiative brought together a consortium of universities and educators to develop and test innovative teaching strategies that promote epistemic insight. In the early days, the focus was on creating strategies that are effective in schools in England, but the remit soon widened as the application of epistemic insight became apparent as an international strategy.

The Epistemic Insight 'Future of Knowledge' Initiative

This book is not simply a report of the research we did; this book is motivated by work we are doing to share our key findings and consult widely on what happens next. For example, when we started our research, artificial intelligence was only beginning to be a topic of public interest and now it is a dynamic to be considered across the education ecosystem and where questions about the future of knowledge are explored. This book contains chapters that focus on the findings of our research in schools; it also reports on exploratory research to build on these foundations to establish a dialogue about education and the future of knowledge.

The body of knowledge we produced for the Epistemic Insight Initiative has prompted a new agenda. It's called 'The Future of Knowledge'.

Guiding the reader

Readers will have many reasons for accessing this book and we offer some examples in our introduction. The puzzle that motivated us is this: Suppose schools achieve the dream of a more joined-up, multidisciplinary approach to education and for students to develop the epistemic insight they need to appreciate science and other disciplines and wanting to make a positive difference in the world – so what? What changes then? Is the purpose of becoming 'epistemically insightful' only to give students a more joined-up and meaningful engagement with knowledge in school? Suppose becoming epistemically insightful is a journey that continues, then what does it look like at universities where students, scientists and other scholars create and co-create knowledge that is transformative in the world? 'The Future of Knowledge' is a research and education agenda that explores these questions.

This leads us to the first of many comments about our agenda, in this case by Renato Opertti, the senior expert at the International Bureau of Education, UNESCO.

Reference

Billingsley, B. and M. Hardman (2017). 'Epistemic Insight and the Power and Limitations of Science in Multidisciplinary Arenas', *School Science Review*, 99(367): 16–18.

Foreword

Renato Opertti

The Epistemic Insight Initiative on the Future of Knowledge offers a superlative reworking of the nature, purpose, contents and strategies of education. The 'EI' strategy for transforming the curriculum, pedagogy, teaching and learning helps us to see what is needed to achieve the UNESCO vision of educating new generations for sustainable, fair, inclusive and peaceful futures. We need to explore, test, expand and share renewed ways of collaboration and integration among knowledge areas and disciplines to equip all learners to competently face disruptive challenges at present and in the future. Epistemological rearrangement of knowledge is crucial for strengthening the relevance of education, and for connecting the curriculum and pedagogy to societal opportunities and challenges. This is a pathway that brings together experts and practitioners from many different areas and fields, to realize the aspiration of better futures for our own and future generations.

Renato Opertti, senior expert at the International Bureau of Education, IBE-UNESCO.

Introduction

Creating the Future of Knowledge in the Age of GenAI

Berry Billingsley

We are a society that is dependent on knowledge and on citizens, teachers, tutors and scholars who are wise about how knowledge works. At the same time, huge and rapid changes are happening to the ways that we can create, apply and communicate knowledge. Some educators have been heard to say that it's impossible to keep up with the pace of change as we move from one seismic event to the next. In a couple of decades, the number of people who are online globally has multiplied many times over. In parallel, the amount of knowledge, information and misinformation we can access online has multiplied massively too. There are students and teachers/tutors who say that they haven't been to a physical library for years.

This book aims to identify opportunities and solve problems for educators, students and scholars, focusing on the role and co-construction of a term we call epistemic insight. Epistemic insight means 'knowledge about knowledge'. Students and scholars are epistemically insightful when they can talk knowingly about the value of looking at real-world questions, problems and opportunities through a range of disciplinary lenses. In other words, our claim is that if students, scholars and other citizens appreciate how disciplines work and how they can work together, then this will boost their capacity to be wise and compassionate in a complex and changing world.

Underpinning this claim is the idea that these different disciplinary lenses can bring a range of perspectives to an enquiry whenever there are complex decisions to make. Furthermore, some of those disciplinary perspectives are ones that you might expect to see in play and some others may surprise you. 'Surprise' is one of our favourite prompts in the research we carry out, and many of our workshop evaluation surveys begin with the question 'What surprised you?'.

Working out good questions to showcase how disciplines work takes time but once they exist, they can be shared. Teachers will only agree to incorporate them into lessons, however, if they agree that understanding how disciplines work is an important learning objective. Throughout primary school and for the first few years of secondary school, students generally study a prescribed range of subjects. For many students in school, learning makes more sense once teachers explain that different subject disciplines are associated with different ways of thinking and the value of bringing together ideas from different parts of the curriculum. Young students have commented in post-intervention interviews that they are surprised by how many disciplines there are and the different ways they add to our overall understanding of the world. Many students develop subject preferences, and their interest in other subjects can be increased by seeing how disciplines can interact. History deepens our understanding of science by giving us stories about how and why scientific ideas change; and geography can provide context and illustrations which aid our understanding of literature. But working across all these permutations takes time, and we recommend focusing at first on two types of questions.

Big questions and bridging questions

First, there are big questions which showcase the opportunity for many disciplines to work together, such as 'What makes me, me?'. Second, we recommend what we call bridging questions which are questions contrived by the teacher to show how two contrasting disciplines compare. An example of a bridging question is, 'Why did the Titanic sink?'. This case study is useful in two ways. It showcases the different ways that science and history each interpret the question and their different methodologies for working out an answer. It is also a useful case study to demonstrate that we get a more complete explanation when we look at both disciplines together. Looking at what we find out historically by looking at letters and testimonials, the explanation that stands out is that the Titanic struck an iceberg because the captain chose to take the ship closer to the North Pole than was originally planned. However, if we investigate using scale models and a scientific methodology, we can observe that once the hull was torn open, the bulkheads were not tall enough to prevent water from flowing between the lower deck compartments and that's why the ship filled with water and then went down. These case studies and many more are discussed in the chapters to come, along with students', researchers' and teachers' roles and reactions.

The significance of GenAI

The question of how much influence scholarly disciplines should have in shaping our education system(s) is controversial. The arrival of GenAI creates new reasons to ask the question. For decades, physical walls around buildings and geographical barriers of distance kept scholars, teachers and learners in different departments and countries working apart. Cognitively we also naturally form and think in compartments with language and location as two of the drivers that traditionally shape compartments and tell us which compartment we're in. At school, these cognitive compartments for subjects can be created and strengthened by the organization and activities of school – so that a word like 'science' has an associated language, textbook, teacher, slots in a weekly timetable, classroom and a smell that seems to waft up from the benchtops and cling to the lab coats on pegs by the door. But now that classrooms and seminars can be online, resources, ideas and perspectives from different disciplines, professions, countries and spaces can be just a click or two apart. Does this mean that the walls that used to contain disciplines will soon fade away? Or as we will argue, does it mean that their roles and questions about their boundaries are important, and that education and the future of knowledge will benefit if knowledge creators and workers are equipped with this epistemic insight.

This book is timely (do all editors make that claim?) because it coincides with the next seismic leap for education, science, business and many other areas of life – GenAI Chatbots like Bard, Bing Chat and ChatGPT. GenAI, or more fully, Generative Artificial Intelligence, is a branch of artificial intelligence where an AI generates responses to a user's questions on a case-by-case basis. But what has made GenAI really seize the public's imagination is the arrival of chatbots on our phones and laptops that can 'talk' in something like natural language. Artificial intelligence has been supporting scientific work and boosting the functionality of technologies in our lives for many decades. But the GenAI chatbots gave artificial intelligence a persona and an apparently human language interface.

'Ask me anything' is the opening invitation of one of the chatbots currently in use. If you put a question into a traditional search engine, what you get is a list of webpages. Because the AI that powers a chatbot can handle a complicated query with several parts, it can serve as a tool that boosts how quickly we can construct an interdisciplinary approach: a single carefully constructed question can enquire after several disciplines at once. That matters in the context of our compartmentalized education systems because seeing across different disciplines is something which most people find difficult to do. If you ask a science teacher to compare and contrast science and history or an arts specialist to explain the point of science, this calls for a kind of interdisciplinary knowledge – or epistemic insight – that is far from universal. In other words, we could see the arrival of GenAI as a factor and tool that will lower the walls around disciplinary compartments and/or we could see it and employ it to boost our abilities to combine disciplines by making the walls more apparent.

Which brings us to the crucial question of language and how to frame the question.

Now we have entered an age where an AI can perform this research for us, dipping into each of the disciplines in turn and then producing a multifaceted answer that can be constructed to fit a bespoke format that is specified with the request. For example, if we take the idea of a sunset as a phenomenon that can be explored through multiple disciplines, then we can word a question for an AI chatbot that asks, 'how would each of physics, history, philosophy, theology, the arts and biology explain why a sunset is beautiful' – and then, since we are interested not only in answers but also in how disciplines work, we can add this to the prompt and ask not just for an explanation in each discipline but also how we know. The epistemic insight tools and frameworks we devised for use in education can bring even more clarity to what makes each discipline distinctive – by imposing a common rubric on how the disciplinary perspectives are presented. This rubric says that disciplines have preferred questions, methods and norms of thought which is intended as a stepping stone that works in this context rather than a full account of each discipline.

Taking the big question entered by the user as the overarching driver, the results are given for each discipline in terms of its preferred questions, methods and norms of thought.

> **User:** use the epistemic insight framework that different disciplines have different preferred questions, methods and norms of thought to explain why a sunset is beautiful through the lens of each discipline
>
> **Bard:** Absolutely! Let's dive into the diverse interpretations of a sunset's beauty through the lens of different disciplines:
>
> 1. **Physics:**
>   - **Preferred questions:** 'How does light interact with the atmosphere to create the colours of a sunset?' 'What physical processes govern the changing appearance of the sky?'
>   - **Methods:** Observation, measurement, data analysis, modelling and simulation of light scattering and atmospheric phenomena.
>   - **Norms of thought:** Emphasis on quantitative data, objectivity and rigorous theoretical explanations.
> 2. **History:**
>   - **Preferred questions:** 'What cultural meanings have different societies associated with sunsets throughout

history?' 'How have artists and writers depicted sunsets in various eras?'

- **Methods:** Archival research, analysis of artistic and literary representations, comparison of cultural symbols and interpretations.

- **Norms of thought:** Focus on context, interpretation and understanding the cultural and historical significance of aesthetic experiences.

3. **Philosophy:**

    - **Preferred questions:** 'What constitutes beauty? How do we perceive and appreciate the aesthetic qualities of a sunset?' 'What does a sunset tell us about our place in the universe?'

    - **Methods:** Critical thinking, logical analysis, philosophical discourse and reflection on the nature of beauty and experience.

    - **Norms of thought:** Emphasis on reasoned argument, abstract concepts and questioning the fundamental nature of things.

4. **The Arts:**

    - **Preferred questions:** 'What emotions and moods does a sunset evoke? How can I capture the essence of a sunset in my artwork?' 'What techniques and materials can best convey the beauty of this natural phenomenon?'

    - **Methods:** Artistic creation, experimentation with visual language, expression of personal interpretation and emotional response.

    - **Norms of thought:** Subjectivity, creativity as experimentation and prioritizing emotional impact and artistic expression.

5. **Biology:**

   - **Preferred questions:** 'How does the human visual system respond to the colours of a sunset?' 'What biological mechanisms contribute to our appreciation of beauty?' 'Does a sunset's beauty serve any evolutionary purpose?'

   - **Methods:** Neuroscience, cognitive psychology, studies of human perception and colour preference, evolutionary theories of aesthetics.

   - **Norms of thought:** Integration of biological and psychological explanations, focus on understanding the underlying mechanisms of perception and aesthetic experience.

Gazing at a sunset, we're transfixed by a spectacle that transcends physics. Its beauty ignites curiosity, evokes emotions and inspires contemplation, weaving a tapestry of understanding through diverse lenses. Each discipline, with its unique 'epistemic insight', contributes a singular thread to this rich fabric, revealing facets of the sunset's magnificence.

Sense-making with AI and the structure of knowledge

In some education systems, walls around subject disciplines have reached a point where they have become invisible and yet are fundamental to shaping how a subject is taught. In many schools, the timetable has become a structure or map that is familiar to students, with its individual subjects juxtaposed in time with no connections to a bigger picture – just to exams at the end.

As students move towards the last years of school and into Higher Education and/or their many different professions, new reasons emerge to share with them the value of being epistemically insightful when addressing real-world opportunities and problems. For decades we have raised students who have learnt to think and work in boxes. Now we have not only the motivation but also the means to encourage students to notice and question the boundaries around disciplines. In the age of GenAI, the skills, insights and pedagogies we offer here are arguably essential bridges between what we can now do online and where to begin/supplement developing students' epistemic insight through library lessons, hands-on learning and other traditional and modern teaching strategies that reinforce these skills. There will be some who say that boundaries are unnecessary now that any piece of knowledge can be connected to any other through threads discovered by an AI. There will be some others who highlight the importance of disciplines as a primary means to understand knowledge itself. The position developed in this book is that having a technological boost which transforms a time-consuming task into an activity that takes seconds is an incentive to re-ignite aspirations we put on hold as well as a reason to look for and progress some new opportunities too. Programmes about AI and epistemic insight will, we hope, help to support students, educators and scholars using GenAI for research. This will include ways and reasons to ask questions about the sources and methods behind knowledge while having in mind that different disciplines have their own characteristic strengths and limitations.

Knowledge is essential for human flourishing and so too is aiming for a society of people who can create, apply and communicate knowledge wisely and compassionately in their everyday lives. This book will address that challenge locally, nationally and globally through examples and case studies of epistemic insight in action. We hope you will agree as you explore the case studies provided that they all point to and evidence one big idea. This is that being able to appreciate the distinctive natures of different disciplines and the ways that disciplines can work together will continue to be essential in a rapidly changing world.

Chapter Summaries and How to Read This Book

Keith Chappell, Berry Billingsley and Sherralyn Simpson

How to read this book

Telling the reader of an academic text how to read a book feels like giving guidance to a *Tour de France* rider on how to pedal a bicycle. So, we won't. What we will do is share our hopes and vision regarding how the book might be used and by whom.

The first thing to say is that, like the future of knowledge itself, we hope readers feel free to access the content in any way that suits them. This may be in a linear fashion, reading from beginning to end and building up a broadening and ever deeper picture of the future of knowledge as you go through each of the chapters. Alternatively, you may wish to select individual chapters, or in some cases parts of chapters. Both of these approaches are built into the design of this book and we encourage you to use the book as you see fit. Each chapter stands alone as a complete work in its own right, and yet is complemented by the chapters around it. You may, for example, wish to recommend a particular chapter to students as part of a course reading list. Chapters are structured to provide theoretical context but also practical application in the form of case studies, teaching guides or activities. Because of this, you may find some aspects of theory revisited more than once in different chapters. If you are reading in a linear way, feel free to move over repeats rapidly. If you are visiting only one or two chapters, then this is unlikely to be an issue.

As you move through the chapters you will see referenced a range of Epistemic Insight Initiative pedagogical tools such as the Discipline Wheel, the Bubble Tool, the Epistemic Insight Framework, alongside key terminology such as big questions, the nature of science, disciplines, co-creation and real-world problems. At the back of this book, a Glossary, teacher resources, notes and investigation cards are included to help provide further explanation and are available for use in the classroom or at home.

Also, as you read through the chapters it is apparent that we have not attempted to impose a rigid style on each author. This would, in many ways, be contrary to the whole ethos of the book. The diversity of approaches taken here is the product of different disciplines, different perspectives and different cultures and yet we see a remarkable convergence and agreement. We see this as modelling the very arguments we make throughout the book. Only through recognizing the diversity of ways of knowing and the knowledge that we gain can we fully explore the future of knowledge at a time when we risk a single perspective overwhelming this vital diversity.

We also see this book as part of an ongoing and vital conversation about knowledge, AI and epistemic agency. Progressing through the chapters and the statements you will also recognize questions arising and challenges for future research. It is, perhaps, something of a cliché to say that good scholarship isn't about good answers but, rather, about good questions. Cliché or not, however, it is true, and we hope that this book represents a multifaceted piece of work that sets the scene for future developments in understanding knowledge and education in the context of fast-moving technology. Again, we invite you to treat it as such and to join the debate. For researchers reading this book, we hope it stimulates further exploration of the future of knowledge.

Chapter summaries

In the following chapters we explore the future of knowledge from a diverse range of perspectives, drawing on interdisciplinary insights and experiences. These are divided into six main sections, each with a particular focus but thematically linked to epistemic insight (EI) and how curiosity, creativity and critical thinking within and about disciplines might contribute to how we gather and use knowledge in the future. For some, the perspective taken is that of scholars, for others as educationalists or practitioners. The perspective is also international, as the future of knowledge is necessarily global and has no boundaries. This means that our explorations can search for ways of knowing what matters to people in diverse places and settings. In the chapters and statements contained in this book, we have perspectives from the Middle East, Africa, Europe, Asia and North America. Each contains unique insights rooted in local perspectives and also remarkably common concerns.

Part I: Epistemic insight, epistemic agency and multidisciplinary enquiries

In **Part I**, the goal of transforming education is linked to the need for learners to be agentic in their attitudes and activities around knowledge. Epistemic insight is a leap of understanding, but how does what is happening inside learners' minds link to what is happening in the external world? The term 'epistemic agency' is introduced as the way to cultivate and evidence gains in epistemic insight alongside an acknowledgement that learners will need activities and problems which encourage them to engage with knowledge in a multidisciplinary way. In her statement at the beginning of this part, Alona Forkosh Baruch links this approach to the UNESCO development goals. In an increasingly knowledge-centred economy, goals like sustainable development and reducing poverty depend on informed and critical engagement with knowledge. If students lose their sense of agency in school and learn to absorb 'facts' without questions, then their capacity to generate and question knowledge is likely to be diminished in all areas of life. In Chapter 1, the value of epistemic agency is explored in the context of older students and assessment by Berry Billingsley and Sean Durbin. Developing this theme in Chapter 2, Sherralyn Simpson uses the metaphor of fire over cultivation as she considers igniting curiosity in primary school students. In this chapter, she provides practical advice for teachers and encourages them to use the notion of 'thinking like a scholar!' to light the fire of curiosity in children. Scholarship is not something that is the preserve of an elite but is something open to all, with the rewards this brings to individuals and society. The LASAR (Learning about Science and Religion) centre designed the Epistemic Insight Initiative having discovered the value of scholarship and multidisciplinary approaches in education while researching students' interest in how science and religion relate. In understanding how different disciplines approach knowledge, the language used and by role modelling scholarship, even very young children can find themselves acting as epistemic agents.

Part II: Planning to teach with big questions

Part II of this book considers the role of 'Big Questions' in epistemic insight. These big questions come in two key forms. The first are those that can be used pedagogically to stimulate interdisciplinary thinking and epistemic insight. The second are the big ethical questions associated with complex world problems and how epistemic insight and agency are crucial in attempting to address these. In Chapter 3 Maureen Sinyangwe places big questions in the very concrete context of the Zambian educational system, specifically that of Initial Teacher Education. Here we have an excellent example of how we can take universal lessons from a specific example. Anyone who has been involved in the training of student teachers will recognize the challenges and opportunities presented at this stage of education and how it can become a pivot point for influencing pedagogy at all levels. Using big questions and big challenges at this stage can provide a new perspective for teachers in training, enhancing their own epistemic agency and, subsequently, that of their students. Laura Hackett picks up the theme of using big questions in Chapter 4, this time with primary school children during extra-curricular activities. When you are eight years old who isn't going to be taken with questions such as 'Can we bring dinosaurs back?' or 'Is there life on Mars?'? Before you know it, you find that you are drawing on multiple disciplines to think about whether we can, and whether we should, answer these questions. She presents a picture of how quickly students can become deeply engaged with epistemic and ethical questions, and how they drive each other.

Part III: What is the Epistemic Insight Future of Knowledge Initiative?

In **Part III**, Chapter 5, Ted Selker anticipates the future library and its role in shaping the next generation of learners. Perhaps you haven't visited a library recently or given thought to what the library is about to become. Technologist Ted Selker opens our eyes to his predictions for the future library, where access to impossibly huge mountains of information are managed and shared by AI-assisted guides. Ted explains that students, armed with curiosity and critical thinking, can navigate this vast digital landscape, asking better questions and gaining more diverse perspectives than ever before. But to take advantage of the new knowledge landscape they will need an appreciation of the pitfalls of insular thinking. As an internationally acclaimed designer of technology-driven solutions, Ted is well placed to describe the tools and strategies that will empower future learners to navigate the vast and ever-changing future landscape of information. Ted highlights the dangers associated with digital echo chambers and the importance of learning from multiple disciplines, using epistemic insight as a compass. In doing so, this chapter provides further evidence for the book's central argument: that the future of knowledge lies not in passive consumption, but in active exploration, critical questioning and epistemically insightful collaboration across disciplines.

In Chapter 6, the authors Lawson, Dhaliwal and Lawson develop the idea of the agentic, curiosity-driven student to examine what it looks like and what it can achieve across a secondary school curriculum. To create concordance across subjects and levels, they begin by identifying the centrality and importance for students and society of big questions and multidisciplinary approaches to questions. They embed this in robust pedagogical theory and present a remarkable case study of implementation of the new approach in a large secondary school. They are honest about the challenges and the learning associated with this, allowing those that follow to stand on their shoulders. This chapter is an excellent starting point for any senior leadership team seeking to develop epistemic insight in their school. In the final chapter of this part, Agnieszka J. Gordon and Sherralyn Simpson apply this model to one of the greatest challenges facing not only education but humanity generally. Sustainability is a priority for transnational organizations such as the UN and OECD, which recognize in turn that success is intimately linked to education. Through encouraging epistemic agency and interdisciplinary thought, they demonstrate how new ways of thinking can be central to addressing challenges that transcend traditional notions of disciplinarity in the sciences, humanities and arts. Agency, they argue, can transform the understanding of knowledge, how it is used and how we as humans can face current and future challenges, some of which are nothing short of existential.

Part IV: The Future of Knowledge and Higher Education

Part IV turns to higher education, again bringing together big questions, societal challenges and epistemic agency. Here we explore how this potentially most flexible, and yet often conservative, branch of education can benefit from a new pedagogical perspective which can shape not only teaching but also research. In an excellent case study, Chapter 8 explores what happens when you bring together computer scientists and dance students to explore the nature of dance, the foundations of knowledge and what it is to be human. Not only are existing questions answered in novel ways, but entirely new questions come to light. In Chapter 9, Klaus Colanero and Kai Ming Kiang examine how interdisciplinary thought is critical in the understanding of the nature of science and how this can be taught.

Part V: Language, technology and inclusivity

In **Part V** Aryn Litchfield takes on the giants of technology in Chapter 10 by making a case for a new type of search engine. By building on popularity as a key component of searches, current search engines narrow answers down to a few repeated themes. The risk is that when we ask a big question of artificial intelligence, then the most popular becomes the 'correct' answer. The authors suggest a different model in which questions are reframed by users and search engines to seek interdisciplinary insight into big questions. The themes touched on here are explored more deeply by Dana L. Zeidler in the following chapter, where he considers the sociocultural context of the limited perspectives we often have when answering questions. He argues that such limitations result in a 'pedagogical moral imperative' to reconsider how education works and how it will engage with the future of knowledge. In Chapter 12, Martin Pickett takes us back to school and engages with rapidly evolving ideas linked to AI and autonomous vehicles. Here he argues that we need to think in different ways and in different languages if we are to avoid excluding large sections of the global community and to avoid limited worldview to one that trammels thought as well as the progress of driverless cars.

Part VI: Science, imagination, interdisciplinarity and AI

In our final part, **Part VI**, we concentrate on science, how it is to be taught and understood in a world of rapid discovery and innovation. Nidhal Guessoum explores the nature of science and science education and whether the aims of both are being met through current pedagogy in Chapter 13. He then reports on his own experiments in using science fiction to support the education of astronomers. This has not been without its challenges, but it has achieved some notable successes and facilitated epistemic insight and agency among students and teachers alike. Greg Artus takes a philosophical approach in Chapter 14 to consider ethical and practical issues relating to the rise in the use of artificial intelligence companions, or 'artificial friends'. From an interdisciplinary perspective he considers whether these products can actually be friends in any meaningful way and also explores the ethical issues surrounding the motivation for using artificial friends, even if they could be considered to be friends. This is more than simply the old debate about 'can we' do something and 'should we' do something. It is about whether the thing we are doing is, in fact, what we think it is.

In Chapter 15 we reflect on the big picture of the future of knowledge and look back to how we used to engage with learning – libraries. We argue not for dusty rows of books but a mentality that says it is not only allowable but desirable to wander into strange parts of the world on knowledge and see what it has to offer our many and important questions.

Chapter 16 includes a selection of teacher resources, notes and a glossary of terms to help support practical understanding and development of epistemic insight pedagogy. These 'hands-on' resources offer easily accessible classroom activities, to inspire curiosity and agentic teaching and learning.

PART I

Epistemic Insight, Epistemic Agency and Multidisciplinary Enquiries

Key ideas

1. **Epistemic agency:** The authors say that the ability to actively engage with knowledge is crucial in a knowledge-driven world. The goal identified in this book is for learners to become wise and compassionate epistemic agents, a goal which resonates with UNESCO's educational goals to promote inclusion and sustainable development.

2. **Curiosity-driven learning:** The authors point to the benefits of activities that spark curiosity and build students' understanding of scientific enquiry as ways to establish agentic learning from an early age.

3. **Multi-disciplinarity:** The idea is that engaging with knowledge across different disciplines not only enriches understanding but also empowers learners to view knowledge as dynamic and interconnected.

Statement of support

The LASAR Epistemic Insight Initiative, focusing on the question: 'What is the future of knowledge?' tackles the underlying issues related to curricular and pedagogical aspects of education. The concept of epistemic insight and its translation into practical modes of transforming teaching and learning, and consequently the educational setting altogether, aligns with UNESCO's Sustainable Development Goals, as well as with the components of the Learning Compass. Both are aimed to improve education by verifying inclusion, equity and equal opportunities, and democratization of education, thus empowering new generations of citizens supporting global interests. The multidisciplinary nature of the initiative, not only in terms of content but also in addressing social-emotional components, attests to the essential needs of the knowledge society. Epistemic knowledge is rarely incorporated in education, even in cutting-edge programs, while in this initiative, it is the pillar. It addresses the need to rethink about the nature of knowledge, rearrange bodies of knowledge accordingly, and by this – to reinvent education in a way that makes it a powerful means to improve society at large in a digitally saturated era. Translating the goals of the initiative into practice, that is, the six projects, shows feasibility to realize its goals.

Alona Forkosh Baruch, Professor, Levinsky – Wingate Academic Center, Tel-Aviv, Israel

1

Cultivating Epistemic Agents as Critical Consumers of Information

Berry Billingsley and Sean Durbin

Structure and agency in the social sciences

The terms structure and agency are used as shorthand in the social sciences for social structure and individual agency. One of the founders of sociology, Émile Durkheim (1858–1917), thought of social structures as something akin to the skeleton of a body or the frame of a building – ways of acting and thinking that are general throughout societies which act as constraints on its members. Agency, on the other hand, is conceived of as the active elements within a society. It is the ability of individuals or groups to make things happen and exercise their own self-determination within the constraints and opportunities of a given social structure (Stones 2007).

In the social sciences, structure and agency are paired together as part of a long-standing debate and point of focus that can be summarized in brief as: When it comes to shaping human behaviour, what is more important: social structure or individual agency? In other words, do we as individuals have more of a role in shaping our own behaviours and outcomes? Or does the social structure in which we find ourselves, with its various constraints imposed upon us that limit the choices we are able to make, have more influence on our behaviours and opportunities (Stones 2007)?

In the end, a good place to be is probably somewhere that achieves a balance of both. But there are reasons to say that we should be moving now towards greater individual agency and a new view of what we want to see in terms of social structure. The days when we could rely on having a group of students physically present in a classroom, lecture theatre or exam hall ended with the Pandemic. And even before then, the proliferation of electronic devices that connect to the internet meant that students became accustomed to finding their own pathways and chasing their own interests. Many students, but not all, enjoyed the flexibility. That puts pressure on classrooms to work creatively with students who vary in their experiences around agency and capacities for self-directed learning.

The OECD recently published a brief that focuses explicitly on student agency as a positive force and mindset to instil in students. They define student agency as

> the capacity to set a goal[,] reflect and act responsibly to effect change. It is about acting rather than being acted upon; shaping rather than being shaped; and making responsible decisions and choices rather than accepting those determined by others. (OECD 2018b)

As they put it, 'Education has a vital role to play in developing the knowledge, skills, attitudes and values that enable people to contribute to and benefit from an inclusive and sustainable future' (OECD 2018a: 4). A vital part of this encourages students to develop their own agency throughout their education and in everyday life.

> Agency implies a sense of responsibility to participate in the world and, in so doing, to influence people, events and circumstances for the better. Agency requires the ability to frame a guiding purpose and identify actions to achieve a goal. (OECD 2018a: 4)

Educators are critical to enabling agency in students by recognizing learners' individuality (agency), as well as 'wider set of relationships –

with their teachers, peers, families and communities – that influence their learning' (structure) (OECD 2018a: 4).

A specific type of agency is referred to as epistemic agency. The concept of epistemic agency relates to the idea that we can be active, rather than passive, in relation to our beliefs (Setiya 2013). Put differently, as we are using it in the context of this chapter, epistemic agency is the ability to reflect on how we come to know certain things, while also acknowledging the power and limitations of our knowledge. Although this concept at first might seem like a high-level philosophical debate best relegated to the academy, it has direct relevance for educators and learners of all ages.

There is resonance here with the advice by Elgin (2013: 148) that 'we need to educate students for epistemic autonomy' and that 'Students should learn to think of themselves as epistemic agents – that is, as personally responsible for what they believe . . . and why it is important to be able to do so'. In this respect, encouraging students to become epistemic agents is about encouraging them to become both *critical thinkers* and *critical consumers* of information. Being a critical consumer of information is particularly vital in our digital age due to the proliferation of misinformation, 'fake news' and the blurring and unstable distinction between social media and credible sources of information that shape our understanding of the world. Further as other research has demonstrated, 'Teachers' epistemic agency is crucial in fostering pupils' epistemic agency in the post-truth world' (Heikkilä et al. 2020: 13). With this in mind, what might a critical consumer of information look like and how can we, as educators, help to cultivate them?

Inspiring students to cultivate epistemic agency by building their epistemic insight

Epistemic insight is defined as knowledge about knowledge and is described as the 'aha' moment when a student makes a connection or discovers an application that boosts their understanding of how knowledge works. These 'aha' moments are typically in the context of student agency where a student is in the process of doing, saying or changing something in the real world. In this respect, when a student develops agency in their own learning, they not only influence how and what they will learn, they also are more likely to be engaged with their learning. At an event dedicated to the Future of Knowledge, organized by the LASAR Centre and held at the Royal Society of Chemistry in London, we were joined by Dr Suzanne Dillon, the governmental representative for Ireland and chairperson in the OECD Future of Education 2030 project. Here is how Dr Dillon (2022) explained student agency to an audience at that event:

> In a classroom where student agency is encouraged, students feel they have a purpose in learning, they can direct their attention to that purpose and they can be engaged and excited by it, and above all else they can learn that by asking questions and continuing to question their understanding of the world – and that's at the core of flourishing.

Thus, inspiring epistemic agency in students is not simply about getting students to 'take responsibility', it is about inspiring them to think beyond their exams and tests so that their questions, interests and intellectual curiosity transcends the classroom and follows them wherever they find themselves in the world.

Uncritical scientism

To counter potential risks to student agency we can look for situations that lead to passivity and an uncritical acceptance of a particular idea or claim. In the Epistemic Insight Initiative, we have instigated the concept of 'Uncritical Scientism'. Uncritical scientism is a term coined from another term, scientism, and we explain where they differ shortly. Scientism is the exaggerated trust or belief that the methods of the natural sciences are superior for all forms of investigation, and 'that science provides the only valid route to knowledge and that nothing exists beyond the material universe' (Stenmark 2018).

One example we can see of the proliferation of scientism in popular culture is the use of scientific claims in advertising that 'prove' the superiority of a product (see Pitrelli, Manzoli and Montolli 2006), or the use of a scientific expert to promote a product due to their culturally constructed authority as experts. Among the various things missing in these uses of science-as-proof and science-as-authoritative truth claims is an expectation that the methodology or expert is available to be examined. In other words, what is frequently missing here is any kind of interest or debate about how experts arrive at their conclusions, and both why and to what extent conclusions arrived at in this way are credible (Elgin 2013).

Uncritical scientism is a term we use when we analyse student interviews and comments and find examples that look like scientism. The definition of uncritical scientism is tailored to an educational context because we are interested not only in students expressing a scientistic view but also in whether they appreciate that in scholarship, other positions exist. Our interest in epistemic agency as an agency that pushes against the walls of a social structure stems in part from interviews with students about their experiences and attitudes in science classrooms. Our analysis of these interviews raised concerns that pedagogical pressures to get the 'right answer' during practical work might be leading students towards an exaggerated view of the powers of science; further, these and other studies gave a basis to say that the rush to cover a lot of content quickly was dampening the capacity of the classroom to encourage students to ask questions, particularly any questions that might be deemed to be 'off-topic' (Billingsley et al. 2018).

One of the indicators we use to say that students are developing epistemic agency in the context we use it is when they begin to recognize and express how science and other disciplines can contribute to solving real-world problems and big questions. In countries like England this is an indicator of agency because it demonstrates how students are moving beyond the siloed spaces of their school subjects. By connecting different academic disciplines, students are exercising their agency, in that they are not responding based on what they think the answer is or following the model learnt in school (i.e. what is the answer for the exam?) but are expressing their own ideas and understanding of how disciplines work.

In this respect, it is also important for educators to build students' epistemic agency by encouraging them to test the boundaries of knowledge domains in their classrooms. On top of that, due to the empirical nature of the scientific method, and the popular conception among students influenced by scientism, many students assume that knowledge and facts are settled, rather than areas of debate and inquiry.

Epistemic insight is designed to get students to move beyond this kind of thinking. One of the things that students begin to understand when they start to develop epistemic insight is that knowledge and the reasons we value knowledge can change over time. In the future they will change again and to see why, we can consider the evolving roles of technology as a partner and instigator when changes happen. 'What does it mean to be good with knowledge?' 'What does it mean to be smart?' 'Can an artificial friend alleviate loneliness?' As we start interacting with emerging technologies more frequently, such questions and epistemic puzzles will become further intertwined with these technologies, determining how we approach them and influencing outcomes. Thus, inspiring epistemic agency in students is not simply about getting students to 'take responsibility', it is about inspiring them to think beyond their exams and tests so that their questions, interests and intellectual curiosity transcends the classroom and follows them wherever they find themselves in the world.

Inspiring students to think beyond their exams also requires educators to become role models for this kind of thinking. This doesn't mean diminishing one's own discipline. Rather, it involves demonstrating and modelling a form of epistemic humility to students that shows an understanding of a discipline's strengths and limitations when it comes to answering different types of questions. Again, this can be done by asking, 'What makes a question a good one for science?' or 'what makes a question a good one for sociology?'. When educators encourage students to think this way, it models an epistemic humility. Acknowledging that one kind of question is a good one for sociology but not for science does not diminish the value of science, it merely demonstrates an understanding of science.

Epistemic insight and learner agency

The context of the Epistemic Insight Initiative, epistemic insight, is about instilling knowledge about knowledge in secondary school students so that they can not only strengthen their understanding of science as a discipline but also begin to see how a range of academic disciplines interact and work together to understand and solve big questions. This activity can become agentic by presenting students with a Discipline Wheel (Figure 1.1) and a big question, inviting them to unpack the question through the lenses of three or four different disciplines of their own choosing. To assess the activity, we can ask students to explain their choices. As students become more familiar with the disciplines, their choices are likely to become more insightful. As such we can say that students are applying epistemic insight and demonstrating epistemic agency when they begin to recognize and express how science and other disciplines can contribute to solving real-world problems and big questions. In countries like England this is an indicator of agency because it demonstrates how students are moving beyond the siloed spaces of their school subjects. By connecting different academic disciplines, students are exercising their agency in that they are not responding based on what they think the answer is or following the model learnt in school (i.e. what is the answer for the exam?), but are expressing their own ideas and understanding of how disciplines work, interact with one another and address big questions from different angles.

The value of this multidisciplinary mindset was asserted in a 1951 lecture by the Nobel Prize-winning physicist Erwin Schrödinger:

> it seems plain and self-evident, yet it needs to be said: the isolated knowledge obtained by a group of specialists in a narrow field has in itself no value whatsoever, but only in its synthesis with all the rest of knowledge and only inasmuch as it really contributes in this synthesis toward answering the demand, 'Who are we?'

Schrödinger's quote presents a scientist's view on the nature and role of specialist knowledge that students can discuss. Although Schrödinger was himself a physicist, this statement can be applied to many disciplines.

Capturing these ideas into a set of intended outcomes gives us a guide for examining epistemic insight – presented here in the format of an essay assignment in Higher Education:

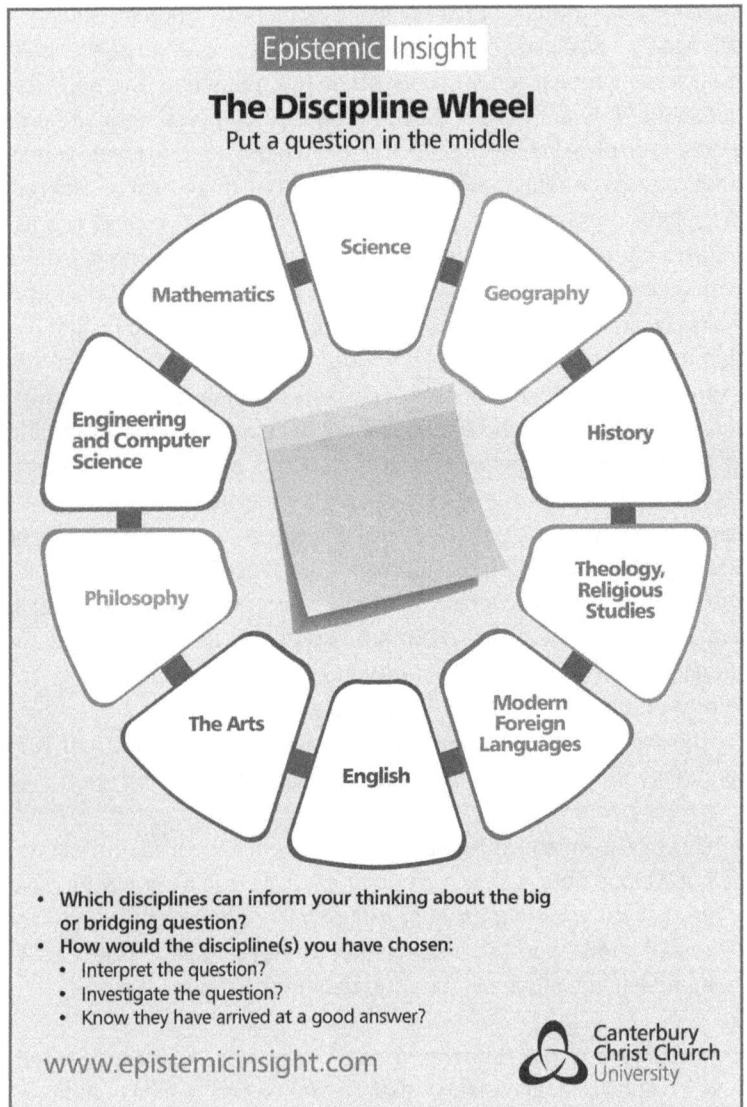

FIGURE 1.1 *The Discipline Wheel (Poster format).*

Workshop: Students to cultivate epistemic agency by designing a robot pet

Having considered the ideas above, we will now outline a way to see them in action in a workshop on artificial friends. In this workshop students are given the design brief to design a robot pet to be a companion for Maisy, an elderly person who is lonely.

Meet Maisy

- Maisy Smith is an eighty-year-old retired lawyer. She lives on her own in a small downstairs flat and she is sometimes lonely and sometimes a bit confused. Her family visit every other week.

- What kind of robot/robotic technology, if any, would you recommend for Maisy?

Four rival companies

In this situation there are four rival companies that want to provide a robot friend for Maisy.

- **Smart-tech** propose 'invisible technology' – which will seamlessly integrate with Maisy's life and needs.

- **Electromate** propose the answer is 'Daisy', an off-the-shelf electronic person who loves the company of old people and who has a nursing qualification.

- **Dare-to-dream** propose 'Charlie'. Charlie is the robot you adopt and teach to be the perfect companion for Maisy. When Charlie first moves in, they can do nothing and know nothing but Charlie gradually learns from you – your values, your beliefs. Once you are happy that Charlie is ready – you can introduce Charlie to gran.

- **Design your own friend** propose that you can design a robot that meets all the exact specifications you require. They even claim that their robot friends are so realistic.

TABLE 1.1 Assessing Students' Work

	Disciplinary Application and Rationale	Subject Knowledge	Critical Thinking	Written Communication
1st	The disciplines chosen to solve the problem are appropriate and the work demonstrates an excellent understanding of them, their preferred methods and norms of thought. There is a clear and strong rationale provided for the why the specific disciplines have been chosen, as well as a comprehensive understanding of the strengths and weaknesses of each one to address the problem.	The work shows a breadth of knowledge and understanding of the key concepts and issues, through engaging with and interpreting a wide range of relevant sources. Knowledge is used to build and support highly effective arguments.	Analyses key ideas, information and arguments. Interprets meaning and makes connections. Identifies and critically evaluates key arguments and statements, deciding on their credibility, strength and relative significance, drawing convincing conclusions.	The essay has a clear and engaging structure, taking the reader on a journey from the introduction to the conclusion. The writing style is appropriate; key terms are used with fluency. There are no, or very few, errors in spelling or grammar. Referencing is used consistently and matches the style taught in the course.
2:1	The disciplines chosen to solve the problem are appropriate and the work demonstrates understanding of them, their preferred methods and norms of thought. There is a clear rationale provided for why the specific disciplines have been chosen, as well as an understanding of the strengths and weaknesses of each one to address the problem.	The essay shows an understanding of key concepts and issues, drawing on a range of relevant sources. Knowledge is used to build and support effective arguments.	Analyses key ideas, information and arguments. Identifies relevant arguments and statements, deciding on their credibility and strength, drawing reasonable conclusions. Shows some understanding of the relative importance of arguments.	The essay has a clear structure, and the arguments are easy to follow. The introduction outlines the essay effectively and the conclusion summarizes the arguments. The writing style is appropriate; key terms are used correctly. There are few errors in spelling or grammar. Referencing is mostly consistent and matches the style taught in the course.

2:2	The disciplines chosen to solve the problem are acceptable and the work demonstrates a basic understanding of them, their preferred methods and norms of thought. Some rationale is provided for why the specific disciplines have been chosen, with no major misconceptions. Some understanding of the strengths and weaknesses of each one to address the problem is provided.	The essay shows an understanding of key concepts and issues, with no major misconceptions. Beginning to apply this knowledge to build and support arguments.	Begins to analyse ideas, information and arguments. Identifies some arguments and statements and attempts to evaluate their quality. Not yet showing understanding of the relative strengths and weaknesses of arguments.	The essay structure could be made clearer to better guide the reader through the arguments. The writing style can sometimes be informal. Occasionally key terms are not used when it would be appropriate to do so. There are some errors in spelling or grammar, but they do not get in the way of communicating the content. There is some consistency to the referencing.
3rd	The disciplines chosen to solve the problem are acceptable and the work demonstrates a basic understanding of their preferred methods and norms of thought though there are some misconceptions. Some rationale is provided for why the specific disciplines have been chosen, with some misconceptions about their suitability. Better understanding of the strengths and weaknesses of each one to address the problem is needed.	Shows a developing understanding of key concepts and issues, with some misconceptions. Not yet applying this knowledge to build and support arguments.	Begins to analyse ideas and information. Describes statements and arguments while not yet evaluating them.	The grammar, spelling, style and structure of the work need improving in order to communicate ideas to the reader. The essay has no or a limited introduction and conclusion. Key terms and references are not always used correctly.

Either on their own or in groups, students should work to consider which robot friend they think is best for Maisy and present a rationale as to why. Some things they should consider are any risks, benefits and other questions or issues they might have. Depending what school age this is being pitched to, you may also want to ask students to consider some of the ethical questions or issues that might arise when making a choice like this. This is because an important part of developing epistemic insight and epistemic agency also includes engaging with ethics and ethical frameworks that are important for decision making. A key part of epistemic agency involves making decisions and being able to advance an argument for making a particular decision. To enhance the quality of their arguments, students will benefit from having introductions to some of the main ethical frameworks – most likely consequentialism, duties and rights, and virtue ethics – another reason why it is important for them to engage with a wide range of disciplines.

With this in mind, we propose that students engage with the Discipline Wheel to answer a series of different but related questions:

- Which disciplines might I want to consult to determine which robot friend to use/develop and why?

- What are the ethical issues involved in creating an artificial or robot friend that I need to consider? Which disciplines can help understand and weigh up these ethical issues?

- Having considered which disciplines helped the students understand and weigh up the ethical issues, AND which did not, ask the students to consider further the importance of understanding disciplines and how they interact.

For more advanced students, it may be helpful to have them consider some additional big Questions including whether a robot can be conscious, whether a robot can be kind or more generally, 'Whether a robot can be a person?'.

Case study: Workshop at RSC, 28 September 2022

During an hour session, a cohort of sixth form students (aged sixteen to seventeen) were introduced to working with and across disciplines to extend and deepen their thinking about people's experience of loneliness, and the potential use of artificial intelligence to alleviate loneliness.

Initially, introductory presentations were given by researchers at Imperial College London. Students were encouraged to consider the challenges and opportunities of seeking to understand what friendship and commitment mean to humans, and the potential impact of encouraging people to make friends with a machine, that is, in principle, incapable of friendship and commitment. Researchers also drew students' attention to the design of a designed 'friend' – to what extent should this look like a fellow human, and what might be the impact of a human building a 'friendship' with a near-perfect simulation of a human? Importantly, concerns arise over the 'data' collected by a robot friend – when a human shares personal details, fears and secrets with an AI 'friend', who owns this information? Students listened carefully to issues that offered interesting and perhaps new perspectives on popular films and TV series they may have seen involving androids interacting in human communities.

Building upon the introductory session, having identified potential ethical concerns about creating human-like artificially intelligent devices to 'cure loneliness', students' attention was then brought to an industry which is being introduced in health care (e.g. robots that help young children manage their type 1 diabetes, and robot caregivers for the elderly) and education (e.g. interactive robots that are used for academic and social learning). The second part of the session was focused on students engaging with a tool – the Discipline Wheel – which has been developed to raise people's capacity and sense of agency to *work with* knowledge.

In response to the 'starter' question, 'what are the qualities of a good pet?', students were generally in agreement that a pet should be 'caring', 'friendly', 'loyal' and 'obedient'. We also discussed 'why have a pet?' – and students briefly shared their own experiences of the companionship they had with their pets. We also explored the responsibilities that are intrinsic to being a pet-owner, through a commitment of time and money to ensure their pets remain healthy and happy. When asked about a handheld digital pet that was popular in the late 1990s, most students were familiar with these and one student admitted they still owned a Tamagotchi (and checked it regularly to administer to its digital needs, hoping to keep it 'alive' for as long as possible). These digital pets have endured the 'toy' market for almost three decades – however, the capacity of this device's interaction is limited to a small screen with icons and simplistic 'character' representations. One of the key appeals of this digital 'pet' is the ease of its maintenance. Food, walks, healthcare, sleeping spaces – all of these elements of 'pet care' are managed in a handheld form that can be taken anywhere.

Although entertaining, a small digital pet has limited capacity for any meaningful interactions. On the one hand, this lack of meaningful interaction could avoid any of the ethical issues raised by the philosophers at the beginning of their workshop. On the other hand, for busy contemporary lives, with perhaps limited access to the space and time required for the care of 'flesh and blood' pets, a technologically constructed and artificially intelligent pet (it could be argued) could offer a valuable contribution in a person's life to alleviate their loneliness. This was then the hook that we used to pique students' epistemic curiosity and agency, so that they might think about the various questions that might arise from the design and use of a robot or animatronic pet that mimicked the real thing.

Students were now prepared to use a Discipline Wheel to investigate the question, 'What are the design criteria for a robot dog pet?'. The scene was set – each table group of students was on a committee to build a design brief for a research and development project that would prepare the way to production of this new product. (Note – this element is vital – placing students in a simulation that prepares them for professional roles, where they will be applying and integrating knowledge and skills acquired through education and their life experiences, is a vital part of building their capacity as 'future-ready' citizens (OECD 2018c)). For this session, students were given blank Discipline Wheels. An important element of this activity was to encourage students to consider and select the disciplines that they felt would be particularly useful to inform their judgements regarding 'criteria' in using science and technology to create a robot pet (as a 'solution' to the problem of loneliness – having established the value of humans' interactions with pets).

Student discussions of their initial ideas were aided by working with the structure of the Discipline Wheel. This tool, designed to enable students to consider a question through different disciplinary lenses, enabled students to shift their conversations from potentially opinion-laden 'this is a good/not good idea' to being agential when *working with* knowledge domains. Students' use of the Discipline Wheel enabled them to discuss the complexity of relationships between design processes, functionality and use of materials, as well as identify key issues that needed consideration when programming the range of responses and activities that an artificially intelligent pet dog would (or should) need to possess. This activity enabled students to consider both the intentions and potential consequences of design and programming features.

The disciplines students added to a blank A3 Discipline Wheel included computer science, the arts, psychology, English, history, geography and design technology/engineering. Significantly, students were 'thinking like a' linguist, psychologist, programmer, visual designer and a business entrepreneur. One group made a list of key features vital for a successful 'output' of a robot pet dog – these included

1) Fluffy (recognizably a 'dog')

2) Affordable

3) Capacity to learn and adapt

4) Biodegradable

5) Personality

It's interesting to note that there were criteria included that aligned to biological 'real' dogs: 'doesn't run away and truly loves you' and 'can be taught tricks, so it is a full experience.' As students were discussed these criteria, it was clear that they were exercising their agency by cognitively engaging with experiences of human persons and the significance of our interior emotional 'landscape' – insights gained through the design of this epistemological activity. It was also interesting to observe the elements of 'problem-solving' that could be addressed by a robot pet dog. Students included the following: 'it can call 911 if AI spots an emergency', 'you can manage and adapt the dog to your life', 'artificial fur can't trigger allergies', 'to be able to understand and communicate in languages (both verbal and non-verbal)', although there was some debate about whether it should speak (and whether this would lose the point of it being an 'animal'), and it should have two modes 'design coded for regular and helping mode'.

It should be emphasized that the role of the teacher/educator here is vital in facilitating these learning conversations. As students were discussing and adding ideas to their Discipline Wheel, their attention was drawn to another issue for them to consider (encouraging them to apply that which is familiar to concepts which are new). At one point, students were asked to pause and consider the interactions between humans and their pets. If a human were to mistreat their robot pet dog, should it be programmed to *not* respond or defend itself? What might be the unintended consequence of this safety design feature, in regard to how a human develops a sense of responsibility for their actions through the responses of those we engage with, and the potential impact of establishing patterns of behaviour through the algorithms programmed into the 'character' of a robot pet dog.

Another 'smaller' question was brought to the attention of students – to what extent might the geographical environments of customers purchasing a robot pet dog affect design criteria for the structure, hardware and software (temperature, humidity, levels of dust, etc.)? While students were keen to engage with this activity, it was important for the teacher/educator to extend their thinking beyond that which was immediately accessible and 'obvious'. The dialogic approach using epistemic insight pedagogy presents opportunities that complement learning programmes in school, enabling teachers and students to work together to navigate the relationships between knowledge domains through this 'problem-solving' activity.

What makes an activity like this 'successful'? While the role-play is hypothetical, students are working with issues that are evident in the real world. Working with interdisciplinary activities and tools enables students to connect their classroom-acquired knowledge with the experience of addressing real-world challenges and opportunities they are likely to encounter as they enter adulthood. As students select and work with knowledge from different domains (and the preferred language and methodology associated with these domains), they build the capacity to analyse the strengths and limitations of these disciplines to address issues. The insights and skills-building gained during this activity are transferable to a range of future challenges and opportunities that students may encounter in their professional and personal decision-making processes within and beyond education.

References

Billingsley, B., M. Nassaji, S. Fraser, and F. Lawson (2018). 'A Framework for Teaching Epistemic Insight in Schools', *Research in Science Education*, 48: 1115–31. https://link.springer.com/article/10.1007/s11165-018-9788-6.

Dillion, S. (2022). *Interview Recorded at the Future of Knowledge Exhibition Organised by the LASAR (Learning About Science and Religion)*. London: Research Centre at the Royal Society of Chemistry, 28 September.

Elgin, C. Z. (2013). 'Epistemic Agency', *Theory and Research in Education*, 11(2): 135–52. https://doi.org/10.1177/1477878513485173.

Heikkilä, H., H. Hermansen, T. Iiskala, M. Mikkilä-Erdmann, and A. Warinowski (2020). 'Epistemic Agency in Student Teachers' Engagement with Research Skills', *Teaching in Higher Education*. https://doi.org/10.1080/13562517.2020.1821638.

OECD (2018a). *Education 2030: The Future of Education and Skills*. Paris: OECD Publishing. https://www.oecd.org/education/2030-project/about/documents/E2030%20Position%20Paper%20(05.04.2018).pdf (accessed 3 March 2023).

OECD (2018b). *In Brief – Student Agency for 2030*. https://www.oecd.org/education/2030-project/teaching-and-learning/learning/student-agency/in_brief_Student_Agency.pdf.

OECD (2018c). *Student Agency- OECD Future of Education and Skills 2030*. www.oecd.org. https://www.oecd.org/education/2030-project/teaching-and-learning/learning/student-agency/ (accessed 8 May 2023).

Pitrelli, N., F. Manzoli, and B. Montolli (2006). 'Science in Advertising: Uses and Consumptions in the Italian Press', *Public Understanding of Science*, 15(2): 207–20. https://doi.org/10.1177/0963662506061126.

Setiya, K. (2013). 'Epistemic Agency: Some Doubts', *Philosophical Issues*, 23: 179–98. https://doi.org/10.1111/phis.12009.

Stenmark, M. (2018). *Scientism: Science, Ethics and Religion*. London: Routledge.

Stones, R. (2007). 'Structure and Agency', in G. Ritzer (ed.), *The Blackwell Encyclopedia of Sociology*. https://doi.org/10.1002/9781405165518.wbeoss293.

PART II

Planning to Teach with Big Questions

Key Ideas

- **Big questions:** Encouraging students to grapple with big, open-ended questions that cut across disciplines, like 'Why do life and the universe exist?', 'Can a robot have a sense of curiosity?' and 'Why does water matter in our lives?'

- **Interdisciplinarity:** Working with the 'Discipline Wheel' to bring science and other disciplines together to build a richer, more meaningful explanation of the world.

- **Teacher education:** Winning hearts and minds by equipping teachers with the knowledge and skills and explanations they need to nurture epistemic insight in their own classrooms.

Statement of support

I am a professor of science education and coordinator of the UNESCO Chair on Mathematics, Science, Technology and Engineering for Sustainable Development (MaSTED) at the Copperbelt University in Zambia. I see the Epistemic Insight Initiative for Human Flourishing as a major innovation for transforming curriculum and pedagogy.

The EI Initiative develops a sound approach by which to engage learners and teachers in interrogating big questions and difficult issues through the lenses of different subjects, thus enabling insights into the role and value of different knowledge sources. The EI Initiative, through the Discipline Wheel, helps breakdown the 'insulation' among school subjects and hence, helping learners and teachers gain holistic and multidisciplinary perspectives of understanding and knowing.

Multidisciplinary understanding and ways of knowing are needed in preparing, starting early in their education, for sustainable futures and for tackling intricacies and uncertainties resulting from global issues including climate change, pandemics and conflict. I see too an opportunity, in the African context, for the EI Initiative to transform the predominant passive transmission type learning to become active, interactive, engaged and explorative. The EI approach will excite and make learners and teachers in history, languages, religious education and in science lessons, to name a few, think like practitioners in these fields.

Overson SHUMBA, Professor and UNESCO Chair on Mathematics, Science, Technology and Engineering for Sustainable Development (MaSTED) at the Copperbelt University in Zambia

2

Igniting Primary School Students' Curiosity

Exploring the Impact of Co-Created Epistemic Insight Teaching on Learner Agency

Sherralyn Simpson

Introduction

The impact of the Covid-19 pandemic on education has been significant across the globe, with more than 1.5 billion students affected by school closures (UNESCO 2020). In response to the unfolding disruption to education, the Epistemic Insight Initiative launched *Essential Experiences in Science*, an exciting practical science enquiry and multidisciplinary research project, which responded to contemporary big questions, often highlighting real-world problems and opportunities through cross-disciplinary investigation. This accessible and inclusive resource featured a Discovery Bag which contained a series of science and big question investigation cards and equipment, easily transferable between school and home. The intervention offered questions focused on science enquiry such as 'Why do spinners spin?' while other investigations such as 'Why is the Sky blue?' explored the interaction of science with other disciplines, developing an understanding of the value of a range of disciplines by recognizing how 'science has some similarities and some differences with other ways of knowing' (Billingsley 2022). The participatory nature of these practical workshop activities aimed to remove barriers to learning by considering diverse learning needs and different contexts.

Through its promotion of equitable access to science and knowledge-based collaboration, this approach is consistent with the increased prominence of the 'Open Science' model and is particularly pertinent when responding to global crises, as experienced during the pandemic alongside other present and future world issues (UNESCO 2021). Essential Experiences in Science utilized the Epistemic Insight Framework, a pedagogical and learning approach that incorporates a series of learning objectives that value multidisciplinary enquiry (Billingsley et al. 2018). Trainee teachers and teaching practitioners expanded their pedagogical awareness of how to cross-disciplinary boundaries, supported by innovative training and development opportunities with access to a range of Epistemic Insight Initiative (EI) tools and resources available to download free on the Epistemic Insight Community found on the open science repository Zenodo .org. This platform offered an opportunity to engage with, share and collaborate with our research, thereby recognizing the important role of trainee teachers and experienced educators in generating their pedagogical knowledge base.

It is argued that through co-creation of pedagogy, teachers are ideally placed as 'insiders' to test out and reflect upon classroom teaching and learning consequently, they are not passive objects of the research (Cochran-Smith and Lytle, 1993).

As such, a series of positive impact illustrations demonstrate how our pedagogy supported primary school teachers to facilitate gains in students' epistemic agency. They explored the nature of scientific knowledge by 'thinking like a scientist', before developing students' awareness of how science relates to other ways of knowing, for example when 'thinking like a historian'. Sharing and critically engaging with the investigation cards in such a practical way can expand the research knowledge base, enhance pedagogy and make accessible new and exciting research opportunities. This research offers opportunities for children in other nations and international contexts to experience practical science with big questions through the Discovery Bag resources, recognizing the value of an equitable multidisciplinary education as ascribed by the OECD (2019) learning compass. As such, epistemic insight invests in students' curiosity about their world, and offers strategies to navigate cross-disciplinary boundaries and an openness to different views and perspectives.

Unpacking the Discovery Bag

The Discovery Bag (Figure 2.1) offered an inclusive resource for schools through its exciting practical science enquiry and multi-disciplinary activities which responded to contemporary questions and real-world opportunities and challenges.

The resource featured a series of accessible, age-appropriate 'hands-on' science and big question investigations which are designed to fit different contexts, intending to expand student agency. Within the Bag there are a series of investigation cards with equipment, aimed to engage primary students, supported by guidance for teachers, easily transferable between school and home. Fundamental to this innovative pedagogical approach is the exploration of big questions, defined in the Epistemic Insight Initiative glossary as 'complex [inviting] enquiry through many disciplines . . . which . . . seldom have simple agreed-upon answers' (Billingsley and LASAR 2023). When students are first introduced to these big questions, we concentrate on the nature of science enquiry, through, 'Why do Spinner's spin?', before exploring the knowledge interaction between science and other disciplinary perspectives, within 'Why is the Sky blue?'. This question explores how science encourages us to investigate ideas about the natural world, initially through the power of observation. The investigation then goes beyond science to consider 'Why do we need colour?', a question which acknowledges how different disciplines

FIGURE 2.1 *The Discovery Bag.*

understand the experience of colour, for example communicating colour through Art.

Fundamental to the pedagogical approach is the Epistemic Insight (EI) Curriculum Framework (version 2 is available to view in the Glossary). This framework provides a sequence of learning objectives that encourage student curiosity in big questions through three specific categories which explore the knowledge interaction of science with other disciplines (Billingsley et al. 2018). As such, multidisciplinary perspectives are considered essential when responding to the challenges and opportunities in today's fast-evolving society, for example finding ways for experts to work together to achieve a sustainable global society. Hence, LASAR's research-based pedagogy acknowledges UNESCO's holistic rationale of integrating science with social dimensions as fundamental for solving world problems (2019).

The EI framework can be applied whenever students commence their epistemic insight journey. As a 'starter' for Key Stage 1 and 2 or later in their school career, students are guided through the framework to advance their understanding of the distinctiveness of different disciplines, the questions they ask, the methods adopted and the epistemic norms associated by academics and professionals of a disciplinary field. As such, they begin to develop learner agency, appreciating how 'science has some similarities and some differences with other ways of knowing' (Billingsley 2022) alongside recognizing the value of different disciplinary perspectives, how they interact and the benefit of multidisciplinary enquiry. Accordingly, the practical nature of the Discovery Bag workshops demonstrate how epistemic insight pedagogy offers a participatory space that removes barriers to learning, seeking to meet diverse learning needs and different contexts.

Adopting this approach enables students to think about what makes each discipline distinct within the context of a big question, such as 'Why did the Titanic sink?', facilitating opportunities for teachers to plan investigations that enable their students to 'think like a scientist' or 'think like a historian', either in the classroom or at home. Students are then empowered, stimulating their innate curiosity about the big questions they want to ask, which perhaps begin with their initial self-awareness of 'Who am I?'. To this end, the epistemic insight pedagogy advocates an inclusive learning environment where all students can exercise agency and their unique capacity for learning, made possible through the practical and agentic nature of the activities which offer clear signposting of disciplinary knowledge throughout all of the pedagogical tools and resources. This approach enables students to view themselves as independent critical thinkers who can collaborate with others about their learning of wider issues and challenges in our world today, for example, the impact of climate change.

A series of impact studies will highlight how a positive change to teaching and learning can occur in one classroom or across a whole school through an innovative school curriculum change, with the potential to significantly impact a school's future objectives and outcomes. Moreover, incorporating epistemic insight pedagogy into planning evidences a positive shift in pupils' engagement in learning, and one that *sparks* children's curiosity. By continuously signposting the distinctive nature of individual disciplines, children from the early stages of primary school can begin to navigate their curriculum with confidence and exhibit agency over their learning. It is anticipated that unpacking the Discovery Bag resource will continue to encourage interest in *Essential Experiences in Science* across wider educational institutions and communities, nationally and internationally.

Impact One: Co-creating pedagogy to support epistemic agency from teacher to student

Developing epistemic agency in younger students arguably begins with supporting trainee teachers and teaching practitioners to gain pedagogical awareness of how to identify the distinctiveness of disciplines and to find ways to cross those disciplinary boundaries. Teachers were invited to take part in a professional learning journey to initially explore science enquiry and multidisciplinary thinking which was underpinned by Epistemic Insight Initiative tools and resources located on Zenodo.org. The Zenodo repository facilitates engagement with our research through sharing of resources, insight and collaborations, thereby acknowledging the important role of trainee teachers and experienced educators in generating their pedagogical knowledge base. By promoting a co-created pedagogy, teachers as 'insiders' can be active in the research, test out and reflect upon teaching and learning in their classroom rather than having research 'done to them'. Hence, we engaged with primary teachers in co-creation of pedagogy within their classroom, supporting design and delivery of activities that stimulate the development of science knowledge and skills through exploration of big questions about the world around us and the nature of reality. The Discovery Bag activities provided exciting substantive content links to curriculum science, for example, air resistance and gravity. Furthermore, acknowledging 'working scientifically' through science vocabulary, such as 'observation', and taking account of 'disciplinary knowledge' described as being the knowledge of the practices of science, its methods, preferred questions and norms of thought (or what science values) (DfE 2013). Therefore, the resource helped reduce the burdens associated with planning practical science lessons, particularly for teachers where science is not their specialism, offering support to develop science 'expertise' identified by Ofsted (2021) as a means for students 'to *get better* at science'.

'The smallest of experiments can really engage a child', a key aspect of the Discovery Bag articulated by one teacher, who acknowledged how dropping a paper spinner, or counting how many water droplets can be added to a coin before it overflows, can capture epistemic curiosity. As such, the Discovery Bag activities presented opportunities for teachers to explore big questions confidently with their students through science and other disciplinary lenses including humanities, arts and technologies present within primary curricula. By embedding epistemic insight into their teaching practice and lesson planning, and by modelling appropriate disciplinary vocabulary, educators recognized how the resources afford children greater freedom to investigate, which suggests co-created knowledge is taking place in the classroom. Therefore, children have the opportunity to engage with how different disciplines understand and ask a question, investigate a question, to then know they have a good answer for the discipline they are working in. Subsequently, children become more confident when navigating their learning, supporting greater surety of what makes a discipline distinct and how different domains of knowledge can work together. Evident when children acted as an 'expert' in the classroom, articulating how to 'think like a . . . scientist, geographer, artist, mathematician' and so on in their lessons, demonstrating the value of multidisciplinary thinking. Consequently, the Discovery Bag interventions provide a research-based solution to compartmentalized learning, that is accessible and can be tailored to different contexts. Hence, collaboration with teaching practitioners enriches the resource to provide a more holistic learning experience that motivates epistemic curiosity and fosters agentic learning.

Impact Two: Epistemic insight breaking down barriers to learning

The epistemic insight pedagogy facilitates a shift towards a more equitable approach to teaching and learning, one that considers the learning experience of all learners. Thus, as advocated by Thomas and May (2010), we aim for an inclusive classroom that respects diversity and seeks to remove barriers to learning and enable every student to participate. Collaborating teachers who had been supported through professional development sessions subsequently applied the Epistemic Insight Initiative pedagogy in their classrooms. They report the inclusive nature of the activities which enable every student, whatever their learning stage, to begin to experience being epistemically insightful and hence development of their epistemic agency and their autonomous 'voice' as promoted by Efthymiou and Kington (2017).

A collaborating Year 6 primary school teacher attested to the inclusivity of the Discovery Bag investigations and how they were accessible to all students within their classroom. They explained how even those with greater SEN within a cohort can have their aspirations to be scientists encouraged even though they may have difficulties with the written tasks associated with their learning. As such, when participating in the hands-on *Essential Experiences in Science* activity – 'Why did the Titanic sink?', all students had the opportunity to fully participate in the learning activity by 'thinking like a scientist'.

All students during the investigation had the opportunity to predict what would happen in an experiment to sink a model Titanic. They tested a hypothesis, controlled variables, repeated the test and, importantly for Key Stage 2, undertook scientific observation. Being engaged in this practical activity and observing the outcomes helped one particular student to be [as noted by the teacher] *'the same as everybody else . . . that's the beauty of it'* (referring to the investigations). Furthermore, the teacher was delighted that all children in the class could access the Discovery Bag resources and activities to *'get so much out of it'*.

The investigation also offered an opportunity to respond to the big question through a different disciplinary lens, and the children were encouraged to 'think like historians'. The class took part in an impassioned debate about 'who was to blame' for the sinking of the Titanic. They gave testimony and rationale to elicit a conclusion about which character(s) on board could have been responsible for the disaster. For example, was it Captain Smith and was he speeding? Or the lookout Frederick Fleet and where were his binoculars, why did

FIGURE 2.2 *Thinking like a scientist ('Why did the Titanic sink?').*

he not see the iceberg? As historians, students were invited through a series of character cards (see Figure 2.3 for an example) to begin to consider the origin and any bias from the historical resources presented to them, and whether they should accept a particular account or artefact as the complete picture of the disaster. Therefore, they were beginning to be epistemic agents, acknowledging the value and distinctiveness of different disciplinary perspectives.

During the history investigation they relied on past accounts and records of the event to look back in time, whereas in the science investigation they physically took part and observed a 'hands-on' experiment to sink a model Titanic. In addition, teachers acknowledged how epistemic insight pedagogy supported other curriculum learning, for example in English language. By advancing their knowledge base through the Discovery Bag activities, students were then able to write a persuasive letter as a Titanic survivor, justifying why they were not

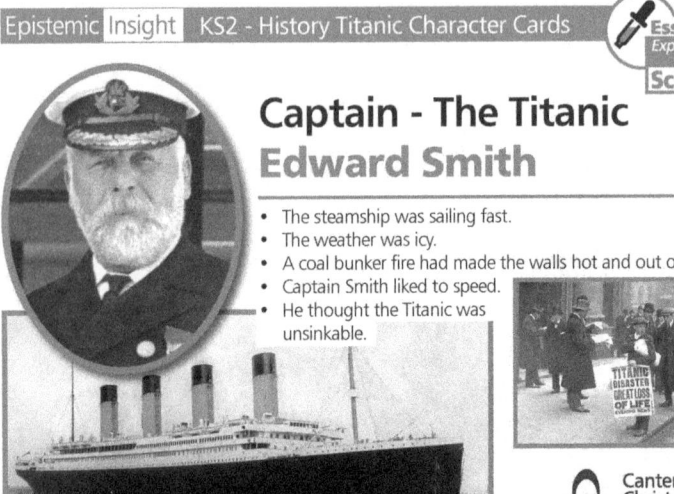

FIGURE 2.3 *Thinking like a historian ('Who sank the Titanic?').*

to blame for the disaster. Therefore, it was evident that children made gains in their epistemic agency, and were 'thinking like scholars' of distinct disciplines, offering them greater knowledge insight into their current learning and future career aspirations. As a result it is concievable that students, whatever their learning stage, can feel empowered to express – 'you know what, I want to be a scientist!'.

Impact Three: Embedding epistemic insight and big questions across a whole primary school curriculum

Our recent collaboration with a primary school helped teachers in all year groups through a series of professional development sessions to co-create and implement an innovative whole-school curriculum plan, focused on big questions. Teachers delivered the epistemic insight pedagogical approach, modelling 'thinking like a scholar', resourced by the Discovery Bag activities. Consistent with the project rationale, the initiative provided a research-based solution to compartmentalized learning and introduced children to a more holistic learning experience. As Bernstein (2000) identifies, students' epistemic curiosity is largely driven by their teacher and how they themselves perceive disciplinary boundaries, and as such teachers from Early Years to Year 6 were invested in developing their epistemic insight pedagogy. Introduced at the start of the academic year, this innovative curriculum has already revealed evidence of a significant impact on teaching methodology and a clear shift in children's epistemic agency.

In the 'Why is the sky blue?' investigation activity, the impact upon students' curiosity was evident. Each student is provided with a pair of simple diffraction glasses to investigate the light spectrum, to test scientific ideas and make clear observations of their natural world.

The students enjoyed experimenting with the diffraction glasses and demonstrated epistemic agency by testing out what they could see in different light conditions, articulating their findings when comparing observations of how the glasses reacted in the dark to how light refracted in bright conditions (Figure 2.3). One teacher described this opportunity as a 'golden moment with teaching', recognizing how students can find joy in their learning by investigating their own ideas, which they prove or disprove, while simultaneously improving their understanding of science. During the workshop, teachers were observed regularly using appropriate language to signpost relevant methods and norms of thought for different disciplines – for instance, observation in science or investigating people and events from the past in history. Implementing EI learning strategies encouraged development of student epistemic agency, realized when they applied key and distinct disciplinary vocabulary to their learning.

Furthermore, a Year 5 student revealed how Epistemic Insight Initiative tools had encouraged development of their epistemic agency. They explained the previous difficulties encountered when navigating their learning prior to being introduced to and having access in the classroom to the Discipline Wheel tool – '*I actually found it hard to find what type of lesson we were in.*' Hence, practical application of this pedagogical tool developed these younger students' understanding of the complexity of knowledge. They began to appreciate that their learning is not limited to one or two subjects as articulated by a student '*I thought there was only Maths, English,*

FIGURE 2.4 *Sparking primary students' interest in science.*

Science, and topic, but then there's more!' Therefore, students are empowered to better navigate their learning and realize that as a multidisciplinary thinker, there are many domains of knowledge open to them for interrogation.

From September 2022, the whole school has continued to embed *Investigating Big Questions with Epistemic Insight* into curriculum planning from Early Years to the end of Key Stage 2. Informal observations of lessons and feedback from teachers revealed how development of pistemic insight helps children to form links between disciplines and how teachers can model appropriate vocabulary and signpost distinct disciplinary lenses, helping their students to understand how to accomplish this more effectively. Implementing EI pedagogy in their classroom gave opportunity for those 'light bulb moments' (one teacher noted they strive for). Those moments when a child realizes something for the first time and then wants to find out more. The EI classroom provided a space for those moments to occur. One teacher stated *'Today was full of that . . . '* A video of the sessions and interviews are available to view on YouTube and included in the reference list (LASAR 2023).

Therefore, adopting a whole-school curriculum change began with teacher development of practical science and multidisciplinary enquiry skills, which in turn enabled primary students to view a big question through different disciplinary lenses and to begin to ask, 'what makes a "good" question for this particular discipline?' or 'what disciplinary lenses will help me to respond to a big question?'; thereby commencing their agentic learning journey. Consequently, every lesson delivered in the school now has a big question and children have the opportunity to model their teacher's vocabulary and focus on distinct disciplinary methods and norms of thought; whether they are thinking like scientists, mathematicians, artists or theologians. The implementation of epistemic insight in the school has become a central focus for learning walks to monitor progress and its continued momentum. As such, the school has embraced a multidisciplinary mindset where children have the opportunity to develop their epistemic agency.

Big question: Why does this matter?

'Future-ready students need to exercise agency, in their own education and throughout life' (OECD 2018: 4). In response to this assertion, LASAR's work provides a consistent framework where students gain the insight and skills to be wise and compassionate epistemic agents, who have 'learnt how to learn' (OECD 2019: 2) and as such are becoming 'good with knowledge'. The Discovery Bag investigations enabled teachers to facilitate gains in epistemic insight when exploring the nature of scientific knowledge and what it means to 'think like a scientist', before developing awareness of how science relates to other ways of knowing, that is, I can think like a scholar! In addition, epistemic agency advances throughout the EI framework as students progress through their school stages and an increasingly complex curriculum. As such, students develop a 'good' epistemological base to navigate their learning across different and distinct knowledge domains as an open-minded multidisciplinary enquirer.

Thus, through these positive impact illustrations, it is argued the epistemic insight pedagogical approach, when applied to primary schools, equips learners from the first phases of their education to be epistemic agents through a tried and tested framework that proactively engages children and kindles their curiosity whatever their educational stage of learning. Consequently, it is anticipated that our pedagogical approach alongside the Discovery Bag investigations can easily be adapted through co-creation with practitioners to fit a range of local and global contexts and will become accessible to the international arena.

'How do clouds stay up?' illustrates how the investigations could be applied to different contexts – helping primary students to explore the science of water droplets to identify how nature behaves through learning about the water cycle. The encounter with the nature of science will be similar in any geographical context; however, exploring science in the social context may differ across regions or cultures. Therefore, as prescribed by Cutler (2006), understanding the science behind global issues and challenges such as water scarcity or acid rain must recognize the local perspective. Hence, Epistemic insight pedagogy enables teachers to facilitate a transition in learning beyond science to consider local and global perspectives that look to other disciplinary domains for help. By applying the Discipline Wheel tool, children are encouraged to become multidisciplinary enquirers, affording opportunities for epistemic agency beyond 'thinking like a scientist' by considering the value of how a range of other different disciplines can respond to the big question. Thus, by expanding the investigation to consider issues of 'sustainability', for example, provides an opportunity to contemplate the global concern for future water resources, as well as recognizing concerns that are pertinent to a local community, such as the scarcity of water, water pollution or securing flood defences. Therefore, offering more children access to our practical science and big questions resources and activities reasoned to ignite their epistemic curiosity and to become 'good with knowledge'.

Therefore, Lasar's research offers interventions that take children on an epistemological journey, which expands their thinking beyond the limits of the initial learning content to consider other perspectives or domains of knowledge. Bernstein advocated that research has 'consequences for the basis and orientation of teaching and thus the knowledge base and motivations of the students' (2000: 63). Accordingly, our primary-age research project can demonstrate impact through the investigations to explore and cross these boundaries of knowledge (Billingsley et al. 2016) which facilitate development of a 'good' multidisciplinary enquirer, seeking to reduce gaps in learning. Consequently, Epistemic insight pedagogy can ignite students' curiosity and encourage their individual agency in learning, ascribed as a key component of the OECD learning compass which recognizes the importance both in the present and for the future of an equitable multidisciplinary education, where 'students have the ability and the will to positively influence their own lives and the world around them' (OECD 2019: 2).

Teacher notes and resources:

Noted in this chapter and available to view in the *Teacher notes and resources* chapter are the following investigation cards:

- Why do spinners spin?
- Why did the Titanic sink?
- Who sank the Titanic?
- Why is the sky blue?
- How do clouds stay up?

References

Bernstein, B. (2000). *Pedagogy, Symbolic Control, and Identity: Theory, Research, Critique*. Lanham, MD: Rowman & Littlefield.

Billingsley, B. (2022). 'The EI Curriculum Framework (Updated Version 2022)', 24 November. https://doi.org/10.5281/zenodo.7357633.

Billingsley, B. et al. (2016). 'How Students View the Boundaries Between Their Science and Religious Education Concerning the Origins of Life and the Universe', *Science Education*, 100(3): 459–82. https://doi.org/10.1002/sce.21213.

Billingsley, B. et al. (2018). 'A Framework for Teaching Epistemic Insight in Schools', *Research in Science Education*, 48: 1115–31. https://doi.org/10.1007/s11165-018-9788-6.

Billingsley, B. and LASAR. (2023). *The Epistemic Insight Glossary (Version 3)*. Zenodo. https://doi.org/10.5281/zenodo.7566007.

Cochran-Smith, M. and S. L. Lytle (1993). *Inside Outside: Teacher Research and Knowledge*. Columbia University: Teachers College.

Cutler, M. (2006). 'Science Across the World, Exploring Science Locally and Sharing Insights Globally', *Chemistry International-Newsmagazine for IUPAC*, 28(4): 8–11. https://doi.org/10.1515/ci.2006.28.4.8.

DfE (2013). *Science Programmes of Study: Key Stages 1 and 2*, 34. Department for Education, London. https://assets.publishing.service.gov.uk/media/5a806ebd40f0b62305b8b1fa/PRIMARY_national_curriculum_-_Science.pdf

Efthymiou, E. and A. Kington (2017). 'The Development of Inclusive Learning Relationships in Mainstream Settings: A Multimodal Perspective', *Cogent Education*, 4(1): 1304015, https://doi.org/10.1080/2331186X.2017.1304015.

LASAR (2023). *Investigating Big Questions with Epistemic Insight 'EI': A Day with Bromstone Primary School*. https://www.youtube.com/watch?v=JLiG-kHmxQk (accessed 4 March 2023).

OECD (2018). *OECD Future of Education and Skills 2030- OECD Future of Education and Skills 2030*. https://www.oecd.org/education/2030-project/ (accessed 12 December 2022).

OECD (2019). *Conceptual Learning Framework: Student Agency for 2030*. https://www.oecd.org/education/2030-project/teaching-and-learning/learning/student-agency/ (accessed 19 December 2022).

UNESCO (2020). *National Education Responses to Covid-19: Summary Report of UNESCO's Online Survey*. https://unesdoc.unesco.org/ark:/48223/pf0000373322. (accessed 5 March 2023).

UNESCO (2021). *UNESCO Recommendation on Open Science*. https://unesdoc.unesco.org/ark:/48223/pf0000379949.locale=en (accessed 6 March 2023).

Ofsted (2021). *Curriculum Research Reviews*. GOV.UK. https://www.gov.uk/government/collections/curriculum-research-reviews (accessed 10 December 2022).

Thomas, L. and H. May (2010). *Inclusive Learning and Teaching in Higher Education | Advance HE*. https://www.advance-he.ac.uk/knowledge-hub/inclusive-learning-and-teaching-higher-education (accessed 7 December 2022).

UNESCO (2019). *Broadening the Application of the Sustainability Science Approach*. https://en.unesco.org/sustainability-science/guidelines (accessed 29 March 2023).

3

Big Questions about Humanity's Place in the Cosmos and Epistemic Insight Pedagogy among University Trainee Teachers

Maureen Kanchebele Sinyangwe

Introduction

It is acknowledged that Initial Teacher Education is meant to prepare student teachers to effectively teach and enhance learners' learning (Sandholtz 2011). 'Practical competence in teaching' gained through practice (McIntyre 2003: 45) is needed too. Practically engaging student teachers in answering the big questions themselves is one way of preparing them for their future in helping learners to reflect on the big questions about humanity.

Initial Teacher Education institutions in Zambia generally offer trainee teachers compulsory education courses which relate to education theory in trying to explain practice. These courses generally include philosophy of education, educational psychology, sociology of education and special education and ethics in education among others. Such courses are generally designed to provide general knowledge and skills for teaching (Banja and Mulenga 2019). Trainee teachers being prepared for primary school teaching also generally take foundational course content such as in Mathematics, Literacy and Languages, Physical Education, Integrated Science, Social Studies and Home Economics, and from which they choose the one(s) they are to specialize in in their third and fourth year. This was probably because in the past teachers were expected to teach all subjects to one group of learners each year, a situation which has since changed from when the then Ministry of General Education (Zambia) introduced subject specialization (Ndhlovu et al. 2021) at primary school. It is expected that through these courses, they will further develop skills and knowledge relating to the content area of the teaching subject(s) they must choose to specialize in.

Subject specialization which had been a preserve for the secondary school (MOGE 2019) is now being practised in primary school. This has its own benefits. It is argued that with specialization, teachers would have an in-depth understanding and mastery of subject content, would be more competent to teach the subjects they specialize in and be more efficient (Kapfunde 2000; Ndhlovu et al. 2021). On the other hand, this leads to subject compartmentalization, which has potential to promote curriculum fragmentation (Moono et al. 2019; Ndhlovu et al. 2021). Billingsley (2017: 57) also argues that 'While immersing students in the questions, methods and norms of thought of a single discipline at a time is critically important, students also need frameworks and bridges to enable them to move successfully between their subject compartments'. When in third year, the students are supposed to add on what is generally considered as methodology courses and content which 'are pedagogical in nature' (Nalube 2014: 17) and aligned to their specialized or chosen teaching courses. These courses further contribute to the development of pedagogical content knowledge which was initiated in their first year of study and include techniques, strategies and procedures for teaching the content of the chosen subject of specialization. The opportunity to interconnect learning across subjects appears to be less robust under subject area specialization (Lumya 2022; Ndhlovu et al. 2021), but there is a need to explore ways of presenting and developing in such a way that they are seen to be interconnected. Using the epistemic insight pedagogy and asking the big questions could allow for this.

Epistemic insight and epistemic agency

Epistemic Insight (EI) is considered as 'knowledge about knowledge' (Billingsley 2017: 59). This involves appreciating the distinctiveness of an individual subject area where there is in-depth understanding of the types of questions, methods, approaches aligned with an individual subject area to inform knowledge. This also stretches to help identify how it is linked to other subject areas, hence accommodating a multidisciplinary approach in learning and solving of the problems of the world. The epistemic insight approach is important for teacher education, where there seems to be a focus on individual subject areas, as it allows for an interdisciplinary approach to the bodies of knowledge. EI can allow student teachers to consider how the individual subject area matches against other subject areas to solve problems from different perspectives and to deal with issues that are important and which learners are likely to be asking. The uniqueness of each subject area is explored as is the interconnectedness of the subject areas especially with relation to application of the knowledge to real-life situations. The Epistemic Insight (EI) Curriculum Framework presents a pedagogical and learning framework for development of epistemic insight (Billingsley 2022). Epistemic agency may be considered as involving learners taking personal and collective responsibility for acquiring and advancing knowledge (Scardamalia 2002; Erkunt 2010). While knowledge or reality may be looked at with different lenses, a shared understanding emerges because of the interaction among learners. It is argued that epistemic insight and agency should be developed and developed in context, but starting with the (trainee and serving) teachers.

Exploring the 'Big Questions' and their value

The university's timetable for primary trainee teachers is already packed with lessons in the different subject areas such as already mentioned above. The time for the mathematics lessons was used to pilot an exploration of the 'Big Questions' and their value. The lesson for the day was on the aims and value of teaching/learning mathematics as well as beliefs about mathematics teaching/learning which are subtopics for the main topic 'An introduction to Mathematics and Mathematics Education'. This opportunity was seized to pilot and ask the nine trainee teachers to individually write down their responses, talk about their responses (interviews) and then later as a group (FGD) talk about the big questions. Big questions are 'complex and invite enquiry through many disciplines . . . [they] seldom have simple agreed-upon answers' (Billingsley and LASAR 2023) and focused on humanity and humanity's place in the cosmos. They included: 'What does it mean to be alive?' And 'Why do we exist?'. Some students indicated that they initially saw this as '*off-topic*' and as '*off questions*'. One trainee teacher for instance stated: '*I was wondering why we had to start looking at things that are not mathematics.*' They, however, were able to admit how they got to see the interconnectedness to mathematics and appreciated the value in engaging in the exploration of the big questions. This was confirmed by a trainee teacher who indicated that '*I did not get it at first but . . . I found this lesson very interesting and learnt a lot more than I thought*' and another expressed the view that

> if lessons were taught like this . . . I would have seen sense in learning the subjects that I have learnt before and how that they are all important in dealing with issues of the world as there is not always one [correct] answer applying . . .

Another trainee asked '*when are we doing this again?*' '*as I would like to learn more on how you prepare for such lessons*'.

The trainee teachers' responses to the big questions pointed to an exploration through different disciplinary lenses, and their value. The responses included:

> '*God has a plan for us to be here even though I don't know exactly what that plan is for me . . . how does one even know?*'
>
> '*I think I know, but I don't know how to explain it . . . it would sound better in English, but I still don't know how to explain it not even in Bemba* [one of the main local languages in Zambia]'
>
> '*I actually don't know for sure why I am here on earth . . . maybe it is to help fill the space*'

'It was my parents' wish that I be born . . .'

' . . . such are questions I avoid . . . because they are hard and there [is] no way of knowing . . .'

Through the one-to-one interviews the trainee teachers had an opportunity to think through once again and exercise their freedom to speak out on the big questions asked. Through the focus group discussions they realized that there was more to the big questions than they thought, especially that they had opportunities to engage with how others responded to the questions with reference to different disciplines. *'That to me was a science or religious studies question and I would not at any point think of it otherwise'* stated one trainee teacher. *'some answers given initially did not making sense, but it is making sense to look at it that way, I am seeing connections and sense now . . . . And is an opportunity to convincingly now acknowledge that we are both right based on our different way of looking at things'* stated another trainee teacher. This demonstrated that the learning experience of all learners were considered and therefore diversity acknowledged and accommodated, and that the trainee teachers had openly started resonating with and appreciating multidisciplinary thinking. Views such as *'I wish I was aware of this way of thinking when writing my essays in social studies and education courses'* were raised and pointed to the value of epistemic insight pedagogy in enhancing learning and understanding of other courses being undertaken and its contribution to the improvement in reading, thinking and writing skills. *'I have realised I have freedom to question my ideas and confirm how true or not true they were. . . . I know better now'*, articulated one of the trainee teachers.

The student teachers had a chance to first address or respond to the big questions by writing down their thoughts on paper. Some also went ahead and shared other questions, covering a variety of topics they thought would be worth addressing too. These included: *'What is life?'*, *'How can one come to know why they are still alive and not dead?'*, *'Why don't people live for a long time like over 100 or 150?'*, *'What is free will?'*, *'Why do people have to die?'*, *'Is free will really free?'*, *'Why do we fall sick?'*, *'Why do we have to eat?'*, *'What is health?'*, and *'What food is the right food for health?'*. Whether the questions and or the questioning had a local perspective of things to them or not, this was an indication that students do indeed have and are curious about life questions and (could be) interested to ask given a platform and opportunity to. It further demonstrated that they could decide what they would want to learn. They can be active players in and agents in their own learning 'deciding what and how they will learn' (OECD 2019: 2). It can be argued that giving student teachers this opportunity to exercise independent thinking and to collaborate with others to discuss the big questions contributed to them being more thoughtful, open and engaged in thinking more about knowledge and knowledge production. The liberty to ask questions such as indicated above, whose answers were not definitely only fitting in the boundaries of mathematics or mathematical knowledge demonstrated that given opportunity, lessons in mathematics or other subjects for that matter may not necessarily have to be delivered in isolation of the other. It is concluded that this ignited students' curiosity and enabled students to realize that knowledge and reality can be explored using different lenses, a point key to moving away from 'Entrenched subject compartmentalisation' (Billingsley, Nassaji and Abedin 2017: 27) and its limits in knowledge production and acquisition discontinued.

If the student teachers uphold multi- and interdisciplinary ways of thinking, knowing and learning, then it would relatively be easier to model it and drive epistemic curiosity among the learners in the schools. Teachers having disciplinary boundaries or pursuing compartmentalized learning is likely to negatively affect children's epistemic curiosity (Bernstein 2000). Student teachers indicating that '*this has somehow changed my way of looking at issues of life and about learning in general.*' And another also mentioning that '*I have experienced to think through things deeper*' and '*who knows it can be more than this if we continued learning like this*' were suggesting a process of learning that was somewhat different from the way they were used to learning. It is a case of advancing the call for learning how to learn (OECD 2019; Fukunda, Lander and Pope 2022; MacMahon, Caroll and Osika 2022; Abu Khurma, AL Darayseh and Alramamneh 2022).

Looking forward

Teachers' behaviour and teaching practices (including teaching styles, methodologies, teacher feedback practices) have an impact on learners' motivation, behaviour and learning outcomes in different subject areas (Hein 2012; Leyton-Román et al. 2020; Gan and Liu 2021; Imron et al. 2020). To spark children's curiosity, teachers will have to demonstrate and facilitate it such as through multidisciplinary investigations. Epistemic Insight pedagogy has potential to spark learners' learning curiosity for the present and the future lives. If this is not ignited and nurtured in learners in schools, chances of embracing multi- and interdisciplinary education may be hampered. It is argued that developing epistemic insight and agency in young learners will have to start with the teachers and trainee teachers who themselves are the models and implementers of epistemic insight pedagogy for learning.

An opportunity was seized to pilot the exploration of the big questions among the trainee teachers. The value has been confirmed and the need for more opportunities for the demonstration of epistemic insight pedagogy and exposure to dealing with big questions as such expressed. It is suggested and concluded that if the trainee teachers are to benefit more from epistemic insight learning experiences and are to model epistemic insight to learners, then more ways of it being part of the initial teacher training be sought. For instance, epistemic insight (pedagogy) will have to be part of or integrated into their curriculum and subjects of specialization. This would allow for topics strategically integrated in the lessons in advance and more carefully planned lessons. In addition, epistemic insight (pedagogy) may have to reflect in their teaching and learning practices during teacher training and preparation including in the lesson planning process, peer teaching and right through their teaching practice. In addition to benefitting the trainee teachers as expressed above, integration of epistemic insight pedagogy may contribute to providing the needed foundation for STEM integration in the Zambian schools. Though still in its infancy stage in Zambia, STEM education is argued to be relevant in providing learners with the skills set, and opportunities, to be problem identifiers, problem solvers, innovators and inventors

(NSC 2018, 2019). There are several considerations to be made to integrate STEM in the schools successfully and for learners to ultimately benefit from STEM education. El-Deghaidy and Mansour (2015: 52) for instance suggest that for teachers to introduce STEM education in their schools they need to first have 'deep content knowledge, strong belief in innovative teaching strategies that has at its core student-centred teaching, interdisciplinary learning to building bridges across subjects.' This further gives the support for epistemic insight pedagogy implementation in the Zambian context from Initial Teacher Education and training level.

References

Abu Khurma, O., A. Al Darayseh, and Y. Alramamneh (2022). 'A Framework for Incorporating the "Learning How to Learn" Approach in Teaching STEM Education', *Education Sciences*, 13(1): 1.

Banja, M. K. and I. M. Mulenga (2019). 'Teacher Education at the University of Zambia and Teacher Quality with Specific Reference to English Language', *Makerere Journal of Higher Education*, 10(2): 171–90.

Bernstein, B. (2000). *Pedagogy, Symbolic Control, and Identity: Theory, Research, Critique*, Vol. 5. Rowman & Littlefield.Lanham, MD.

Billingsley, B. (2017). 'Teaching and Learning About Epistemic Insight', *School Science Review*, 98(365): 59–64.

Billingsley, B. (2022). 'The EI Curriculum Framework (Updated Version 2022)', The EI Curriculum Framework (Updated Version 2022) | Zenodo (accessed 24 April 2023).

Billingsley, B. and LASAR. (2023). *The Epistemic Insight Glossary (Version 3)*. Zenodo. https://doi.org/10.5281/zenodo.7566007.

Billingsley, B., M. Nassaji, and M. Abedin (2017). 'Entrenched Compartmentalisation and Students' Abilities and Levels of Interest in Science', *School Science Review*, 99(367): 26–31.

El-Deghaidy, H. and N. Mansour (2015). 'Science Teachers' Perceptions of STEM Education: Possibilities and Challenges', *International Journal of Learning and Teaching*, 1(1): 51–4.

Erkunt, H. (2010). 'Emergence of Epistemic Agency in College Level Educational Technology Course for Pre-Service Teachers Engaged in CSCL', *Turkish Online Journal of Educational Technology-TOJET*, 9(3): 38–51.

Fukuda, S. T., B. W. Lander, and C. J. Pope (2022). 'Formative Assessment for Learning How to Learn: Exploring University Student Learning Experiences', *RELC Journal*, 53(1): 118–33.

Gan, Z., Z. An, and F. Liu (2021). 'Teacher Feedback Practices, Student Feedback Motivation, and Feedback Behavior: How are They Associated with Learning Outcomes?', *Frontiers in Psychology*, 12: 697045.

Hein, V. (2012). 'The Effect of Teacher Behaviour on Students' Motivation and Learning Outcomes: A Review', *Acta Kinesiologiae Universitatis Tartuensis*, 18: 9–19.

Imron, A., B. B. Wiyono, S. Hadi, I. Gunawan, A. Abbas, B. R. Saputra, and D. B. Perdana (2020). 'Teacher Professional Development to Increase Teacher Commitment in the era of the ASEAN Economic Community', in *2nd Early Childhood and Primary Childhood Education (ECPE 2020)*, November, 339–43. Atlantis Press.

Kapfunde, C. L. (2000). *Introduction to Educational Management: Module PGDE 305*. Harare: Zimbabwe Open University.

Leyton-Román, M., J. J. L. González-Vélez, M. Batista, and R. Jiménez-Castuera (2020). 'Predictive Model for a Motivation and Discipline in Physical Education Students Based on Teaching–Learning Styles', *Sustainability*, 13(1): 187.

Lumya, B. (2022). *Teacher Specialisation and Pupil Performance in Selected Primary Schools of Kaputa District: Exploring the Benefits, Challenges and Implications*. Doctoral dissertation, The University of Zambia.

MacMahon, S. J., A. Carroll, A. Osika, and A. Howell (2022). 'Learning how to Learn – Implementing Self-Regulated Learning Evidence into Practice in Higher Education: Illustrations from Diverse Disciplines', *Review of Education*, 10(1): e3339.

McIntyre, D. (2003). 'Theory, Theorizing and Reflection in Initial Teacher Education', in *Conceptualising Reflection in Teacher Development*, 45–58. London: Routledge.

MOGE (2019). *Specialisation of Teaching at the Primary Subsector*. Lusaka: Circular to Provincial Education Officers dated 5 April 2019.

Moono, M., G. M. Mwinsa, B. Mwanabayeke, E. Sikota, C. Mwiinga, M. Sinkala, C. Mubanga, and W. Chakanyika (2019). 'The Implementation of Subject Specialisation in Primary Schools: Analysis of its Benefits and Challenges', *International Journal of Multidisciplinary Research and Development*, 6(11): 64–72.

Nalube, P. P. (2014). *Student-Teachers Learning Mathematics for Teaching: Learner Thinking and Sense Making in Algebra* (Doctoral dissertation, University of the Witwatersrand, Faculty of Humanities, School of Education).

Ndhlovu, Z. B., B. Nkhata, F. M. Chipindi, B. Kalinde, C. Kaluba, E. Malama, and H. Chipande (2021). 'Subject Specialisation in Primary

School: A Theoretical Review and Implications for Policy and Practice in Zambia', *Journal of Curriculum and Teaching*, 10(4): 13–24.

NSC (2018). *Concept Note on Technical Schools*. Lusaka, Zambia.

NSC (2019). Available online: Directorate of National Science Centre (nsc.gov.zm) (accessed 21 April 2023).

OECD (2019) *Conceptual Learning Framework: Student Agency for 2030*. Available online: Student_Agency_for_2030_concept_note.pdf (oecd.org) (accessed 20 April 2023).

Sandholtz, J. H. (2011). 'Preservice Teachers' Conceptions of Effective and Ineffective Teaching Practices', *Teacher Education Quarterly*, 38(3): 27–47.

Scardamalia, M. (2002). 'Collective Cognitive Responsibility for the Advancement of Knowledge', in B. Smith (ed.), *Liberal Education in a Knowledge Society*, 97: 67–98.

4

Big Questions – And Their Value in Extra-Curricular Activities That Teach Epistemic Insight

Laura Hackett

Introduction

Can we bring dinosaurs back? Is there life on Mars? Why do we exist? Why can't we live more than 100 years? These are examples of real 'Big Questions' about human personhood and the nature of reality, asked by students as young as eight years old. Data we have collected indicates that many students are interested in asking these 'Big Questions' and want to think about how science can work together with other disciplines to explore these topics. This chapter will look at how we have been able to harness this interest in 'Big Questions' to explore 'knowledge about knowledge' with students.

The following pages outline my work with a group of upper primary school students in an extra-curricular 'science and Big Questions' club, providing details for teachers or other club leaders to replicate.

Being a qualified primary school teacher, this is an area I feel very drawn to – I love working with young people and seeing their excitement when new learning 'clicks' into place for them. When working as a teacher, I often found it a shame to have to re-direct class discussion that went off on a tangent, no matter how interesting or engaged the children may have been, because it was 'off-topic' from the intended scheme of work for that day. The sessions on science and big questions provided a unique space where these types of discussion were, at last, 'on-topic'. The freedom to wonder aloud (without needing to provide the 'right' answer) seemed to be almost a relief from the ordinary means of schooling. This chapter demonstrates the impact of these session plans on students' knowledge and understanding of epistemic insight, enabling them to recognize the distinctiveness of science as a discipline, and introduce them to different ways of knowing.

Interest in 'Big Questions'

Data from over 4,000 primary and secondary students surveyed by the LASAR Centre shows that 70 per cent of students agree, to a greater or lesser extent, that they like thinking about big questions about human personhood and the nature of reality. Students have an appetite for this type of thinking – and big questions are ideally suited as an approach that is inclusive and able to widen the pipeline from school to university study, and undergraduate to postgraduate study. They are a powerful motivator for students to gain insights into the nature, application and communication of knowledge – what we, in our research, call epistemic insight. Epistemic insight is focused on big questions about human personhood and the nature of reality, that seldom have simple, agreed-upon answers, and where science and religion both have something to say.

A 'Big Question' that many young students find appealing is: 'Can a robot be like a human?' On the one hand, it can be explored through the lens of science by making observations such as 'Does the robot move?' or 'Can it sense its environment?', 'Can it respond to stimuli?' and 'Does it require energy?'

We can also explore the question through the lens of religion – 'Can a robot experience emotion?', 'Can it appreciate beauty?', 'Can it form a relationship with another human?' or 'Does it have its own set of beliefs?'

Thinking about a big question in this way cannot be contained to just one subject in school or university, since there are multiple disciplines helping us to look at the question – not only science and religious education but drawing upon perspectives from other subject disciplines like history, geography, arts and psychology. Other big questions like 'What does it mean to be me?' do not require prior knowledge and appeal to the universality of asking 'Who are we?' and 'What is our purpose?' (if any).

While students demonstrated (from survey and interview responses) an interest and desire to think and talk about topics such as these, big questions remain an underused opportunity to develop epistemic insight and 'knowledge about knowledge' among students. One major barrier to their use in schools, and at home, is time for their discussion. School timetables are already packed with lessons, with topics planned out weeks and months in advance. Since they rarely have quick or simple answers, ample time would need to be set aside to enable students to delve deeper into exploring a range of possible explanations. The National Curriculum limits the amount of time that teachers can provide to investigating big questions because they are not currently part of the required learning. In the words of a secondary school teacher who was interviewed about her experiences when attempting to introduce big questions into her lessons: '*It's very difficult, when you've got a curriculum set up, to input new things*.'

Similarly, a case study that we conducted involving eight parents of primary-aged children found that all parents cited busyness or a lack of time as a barrier to discussing big questions with their children. Parents found difficulty '*carving out time where we can get some peace and quiet to do it*' and described '*not getting the chance*'. One parent elaborated: '*with our current lifestyle of busyness and after school club and work and everything, I think we'd struggle to fit them in.*' This gave us an idea – we hypothesized that an after-school club had the potential to be the ideal space for facilitating discussions about big questions with interested students – children are already at school and parents can benefit from the additional childcare free of charge, which adds another incentive. Extra-curricular clubs provide the added benefit of being more relaxed in their content than lesson time, as there is freedom from the limitations of the curriculum.

Creating activity resources

We created epistemic insight activity resources for use among primary- and lower-secondary-aged students, to provide an opportunity to explore big questions about human personhood and the nature of reality. We called these resources 'Discovery Bags' and within each bag was a series of investigations which focused on questions such as: 'Why is the sky blue?', 'How do we make sense of the weather?', 'What does it mean to be alive?' and 'Why do we need water?' Students could then explore an investigation card containing prompts for discussion, using both scientific and religious viewpoints, as well as perspectives from other subject disciplines. The bag also contained a piece of science equipment and instructions on how to conduct a simple investigation, such as an anemometer (wind-measuring device) for exploring how we make sense of the weather, a pipette for exploring the uses of water, a kit to make a 'bristlebot' (a simple robot constructed from a battery, motor and the bristle end of a toothbrush) to explore whether they could make a robot that was truly alive and a pair of diffraction glasses for exploring the colours contained in visible light.

Discovery Bags were first tested with a handful of local parents and children to ascertain the usefulness of the materials, the clarity of the instructions and the interest of the children in these activities. The initial prototype was simply an old pillowcase containing a laminated investigation card, a worksheet and an anemometer. The anemometers turned out to be more trouble than they were worth – after having painstakingly fixed each one with super-glue to stop the handle from falling off, we were alerted to the fact that they were not sensitive enough to pick up any wind less than a mild gale, and that the families had resorted to other means to make them work, the most efficacious method: a hairdryer. However, the act of using such an unusual piece of equipment was a success – parents and children enjoyed coming together to attempt the experiment and discuss the investigation card.

In response to feedback, we subsequently developed a parent information guide to be used alongside the investigation cards – the breadth of knowledge required to have a meaningful discussion about these topics is vast and we wanted to be inclusive of parents with all types of educational backgrounds.

The parent guide condensed subject-specific information from a range of disciplinary viewpoints such as providing prompts for discussion. For instance, in the bag themed around colours, it had questions like: 'How did people in the past use colour to express their identities, e.g. purple/red clothes worn by royalty' (history), 'How do different colours evoke different moods, e.g. red linked to anger, yellow happiness' (psychology) and 'How do religions use colour in different ceremonies?, e.g. Holi' (religious education). The guide also gave a more detailed explanation of the scientific phenomena experienced through the experiments (such as how prisms work) and introduced students to other concepts that bridge science and religion (such as the 'Goldilocks zone') when thinking about how our planet is perfect for life – not 'too hot' or 'too cold' but 'just right' for water to exist as a liquid.

The student worksheets underwent a series of changes after being tested by the families, to become simpler in their approach. While the original worksheets attempted to invoke discussion about the big question by writing down their thoughts on paper, the parental guide was intended to get discussions going more naturally through a conversation between parent/carer and child. Therefore, the worksheets were updated to promote the use of scientific language and inquiry – asking students to predict what they will observe and their actual observations. We also included a space to write down any multidisciplinary questions arising from the big question. The design focused on encouraging students to implement the terms 'observation' and 'discipline' in their answers. At the end of the session, students were prompted to share anything that surprised or challenged them, as a space for plenary and reflection on the day's activity. This question was particularly interesting for us as researchers, to gain insight into the strengths (and weaknesses) of the sessions, and to glean information on any shifts in young people's thinking after engaging with our resources.

Once we were happy with the content of the Discovery Bags, a local primary school was approached and offered the opportunity to run a free after-school club to pilot the resources for their Key Stage 2 students (aged seven to eleven). The school is situated in an area of high deprivation, with higher-than-average numbers of children receiving free school meals and SEN support (special educational needs) compared to the national average across mainstream primary schools in England. Thirty-one1 children in KS2, from Year 4, 5 and 6, signed up for the club, which ran for four sessions of one hour each week. The sessions were led by a member of the LASAR research team (a qualified primary school teacher) and supported by the school's science coordinator. Below is an example of how a typical club session ran.

Example session: Why do we have rainbow colours?

Each session began with a scientific focus, by asking the students to think of as many questions as they could about the topic (in this instance, about rainbows). Students would typically suggest scientific questions like: 'Where do rainbows come from?', 'What are rainbows made of?', 'What causes a double rainbow?' and 'Why do some rainbows stand out more than others?' They were interested to learn that these questions (including different types of 'why' questions) could be answered by science through observation of the natural world, and that most of these types of questions could be answered by the end of the session.

Next, the students took part in a science experiment using a piece of intriguing scientific equipment. For the topic of colours, the activity involved using a pair of diffraction glasses to observe different objects. Each student was given a piece of red card and a torch, as well as a pair of diffraction glasses. Students were then invited to predict what they would observe when using the glasses to look in turn at the red card and the torch light (without staring directly into the beam). Diffraction glasses work by splitting up the colours contained in visible light so that each can be individually observed. When students look at the red card, all colours are absorbed apart from the colour red, which is reflected back into the eye and so the card appears red. But when they look at the light from the torch, containing all colours, the eye can see what looks like multiple rainbow beams dancing around the torch light. Naturally, students are fascinated by this, and enjoy taking the glasses off and on to observe the effects. Once the excitement dies down after a few minutes, the scientific explanation of what rainbows are made of can be given (that a raindrop acts as a prism to split up the colours contained in visible light into a spectrum of rainbow colours, similar to the diffraction glasses).

Building on what students learn from the experiment, the session leader facilitates a discussion about a big question from a multidisciplinary perspective. This big question was discussed using the Discipline Wheel – a tool developed by LASAR to help students identify the ways in which other disciplines can help to address a real-world problem. In this example, the deeper big question about human personhood and the nature of reality that we explored was: 'What is the significance of a rainbow?' Interestingly, we found that students struggled to move past the scientific ideas of how rainbows were formed (i.e. through sunlight and raindrops). This is where the sessions benefitted from the support of a research team member, as students were supported to see how other paradigms from the Discipline Wheel can also interpret a rainbow. For instance, religious education has much to say about rainbows – from the biblical symbolism of God's faithfulness to Noah, to Hinduism in which the rainbow is known as 'Indra's bow' (Indra being the god of thunder, lightning and rain); to ancient Greek mythology in which Iris, goddess of the rainbow, was thought to connect earth with the gods.

Impact on students' knowledge about knowledge

The breadth of questions arising from primary-aged students' minds is fascinating and demonstrates not only an interest in exploring a range of disciplines but also that young children have the capacity to grow and develop this area of knowledge. It is incredible to see students working within the Epistemic Insight Framework (Billingsley et al. 2018) in such a short space of time and being able to identify the similarities and differences that science has with other ways of knowing. It is also exciting to be able to challenge students' assumptions about science having all the answers – while science cannot answer a big question alone, it informs our thinking about them in conjunction with other disciplines. This was demonstrated in students' ability to suggest ways of thinking about a topic from a perspective *other than* science. In the session described above, students were introduced to the rainbow not only as a scientific phenomenon but a cultural symbol. We discussed how, in the national lockdown, households and businesses had displayed images of rainbows in their windows as an act of solidarity with the NHS. Turning to the discipline of geography, students were amazed to explore the significance of rainbow colours in the world around them, that colours keep us safe – in the case of red and green traffic lights to help direct the flow of cars, and in the animal kingdom as camouflage against predators or as warnings not to approach certain creatures with coloured markings that could be poisonous or deadly. By the end of the club session, students were able to generate questions for other subject disciplines such as: 'How did the colours get their names?', 'What would happen if we didn't have colours?', 'Why are bubbles so pretty?' and 'Who decided that red means hot and blue means cold?'

Feedback from the science coordinator at the pilot school was overwhelmingly positive about the after-school club:

> *It's been a really lovely thing for them to do. . . . When you have a small club like that, you can have conversations – you're teaching but you're listening to the children at the same time, so there's a lot of discussion backwards and forwards – whereas when you do it in class it's very much the teacher putting ideas forward.*

If we look at students' qualitative responses from post-surveys after participating in the club, we can see students thinking in more epistemically insightful ways and thinking more deeply about big questions, drawing upon a range of disciplines to explore a variety of topics. Many gave examples of thoughtful questions about human personhood and the nature of reality, developing the ideas they had been thinking about in the club – for instance, no longer asking 'Where do rainbows come from?' but asking, 'Where does rain come from?', 'Why is water blue?', 'Why are living leaves green?' and 'Why do we have different coloured eyes?' We also saw a shift in students' understanding of the term 'discipline' and of the nature of science. Before the intervention activities, most students did not know the meaning of the word 'discipline', while those who did could not separate it from the idea of being disciplined (e.g. 'A discipline is a punishment, like: "you need discipline"'). After the session, approximately half of the students surveyed demonstrated a shift in their understanding (e.g. 'A discipline is' . . . maths, English, the arts, science and geography).

In the words of one primary student who said they had 'lots' of big questions: 'What else is out there?', 'Will we ever answer this fully?'. The absence of simple, easy answers to life's big questions can be challenging for students, as they move from enjoying thinking about these topics by themselves, to engaging with a range of different big questions that they may have never thought about before, perhaps even leading to more questions than answers. It is this element of challenge that we believe motivates students to think about and enjoy these topics. Our evidence shows this is an area of great interest that is greatly underused at present for developing deeper multidisciplinary thinking. Time and space to explore big questions about human personhood and the nature of reality needs to be provided within the curriculum for both primary and secondary students.

Investigating big questions as part of the school day

A typical school timetable currently focuses on learning about one discipline at a time. In science lessons, students are usually given a question or experiment that is planned by the teacher and are guided to reach the correct answer, or replicate the predetermined experiment outcomes, by the end of the lesson. This is by no means a criticism of the teacher – the limitations and pressures of an outcomes-driven school system leave little time for deviating from the lesson plan into the realm of big questions. However, it means that students are unlikely to be encouraged to think of their own questions that would be good for science to answer, much less to bring in elements of history in a science lesson, or science in a religious education lesson. This leads to a lack of understanding of the distinctiveness of each discipline, and how disciplines might work together to think about shared topics or questions. The result is that children miss out on the process of thinking more deeply about the preferred questions, methods and norms of thought of that discipline, and don't experience how working with a given disciplinary lens shapes and limits the answer that you get.

The extra-curricular club outlined in this chapter continued to have an impact on the students at the pilot school after the project was over. In consultation with the science coordinator, more epistemic insight resources were provided to the school, covering a variety of topics including air resistance and gravity ('What makes a good parachute?') and water tension ('Why do we need water?'). These sessions became part of the school's science planning and were used to bring epistemic insight into the science classroom. We hope to gradually move away from a model of 'entrenched subject compartmentalisation' (Billingsley 2017) where content from disciplines like science, English and history is separated with clear subject boundaries and lessons delivered in isolation from one another. Instead, we advocate moving towards a more multidisciplinary approach of classrooms with permeable walls (Billingsley and Ramos Arias 2017) in which students can ask a question in a science lesson that bridges religion, or a scientific question in a religious education lesson. Research-engaged practitioners, such ITE students at Canterbury Christ Church University, have begun to demonstrate that this is possible – by using a Shakespeare play in English literature to incorporate discussions on morality, religion and history (Robinson 2020); by using teaching about the Black Death in history to teach about the Covid-19 pandemic in science (Stockham 2020); and by using the visual timetable of a Reception class to explore the big question 'How do we keep safe and healthy?' (Goddard 2020).

Teacher notes and resources:
Noted in this chapter and available to view in the *Teacher notes and resources* section in the final chapter, you can find examples of the D Wheel and some of the investigation cards discussed.

References

Billingsley, B. (2017). 'Teaching and Learning About Epistemic Insight', *School Science Review*, 98(365): 59–64.

Billingsley, B. and A. Ramos Arias (2017). 'Epistemic Insight and Classrooms with Permeable Walls', *School Science Review*, 99(367): 44–53. ISSN 0036-6811.

Billingsley, B., M. Nassaji, S. Fraser, and F. Lawson (2018). 'A Framework for Teaching Epistemic Insight in Schools', *Research in Science Education*, 48: 1115–31.

Goddard, K. (2020). 'Exploring Reception Children's Epistemic Insight (EI): A Small-Scale Case Study', *The Epistemic Insight Digest*, Autumn(1): 7–21.

Robinson, B. (2020). 'How Using the Epistemic Insight Discipline Wheel to Answer a Big Question ("How Do We Determine Mortality?") Can Develop My Skills as a Teacher?', *The Epistemic Insight Digest*, Autumn(1): 66–72.

Stockham, C. (2020). 'Can the Application of the "Discipline Wheel" Model Enrich Students' Understanding of Epistemic Insight when Studying the Black Death?', *The Epistemic Insight Digest*, Autumn(1): 40–8.

PART III

What Is the Epistemic Insight Future of Knowledge Initiative?

The **Future of Knowledge Initiative** builds upon the foundation of the Epistemic Insight Initiative and expands its scope and focus areas to add the broader landscape of higher education, generative artificial intelligence (GenAI) and scientific research.

The arrival of GenAI adds a new urgency to our research agenda because now we have entered an age where conversational AIs can help us to see across knowledge boundaries and bring together knowledge from different disciplines and fields of research. But this new agency comes with a risk. If students mash together different types of knowledge, without insight into their different natures, it will be like a high-rise building that contains building materials, but without a plan to say where anything goes. 'The Future of Knowledge' is a work in progress to produce templates, reasons and case studies to foster current and new dimensions of epistemic insight that will help students, scholars and educators to thrive.

Puzzles we explore:

- Reimagining libraries: Can libraries transcend their physical walls to become vibrant hubs for learning in the digital age? What roles can AI, librarians and libraries play together to give knowledge creators and workers the skills they will need?

- Multidisciplinary learning: We are painting a future in which students at every level are agentic in their learning. Is it reasonable to propose that teachers/tutors can encourage curiosity, creativity and critical thinking while delivering a curriculum of knowledge and knowledge about knowledge that is planned and deliberate?

- Sustainability: Where, if at all, does a global theme like sustainability fit into this education and science research and innovation strategy? Is there a sense in which it can be said to lead it?

Key ideas

1. **Interdisciplinarity:** This is a central theme, emphasizing collaborations across disciplines to tackle complex questions and spark innovative solutions. The initiative will continue to explore specific methods and frameworks for fostering interdisciplinary collaboration in research and education. In this part we highlight co-creation as a strategy that actively brings different specialisms together – across disciplines, across professions and/or across phases of education.

2. **The future of libraries and information curation:** One of the chapters in this book sets the scene for our interest in reimagining libraries in the digital age. The Future of Knowledge Initiative will continue to explore ways that AI and other technologies can be leveraged to create more personalized, dynamic and accessible learning environments. It will also discuss questions about the role of human librarians and curators by explaining the pivotal importance of human agency in an age of increasingly intelligent machines.

3. **Lifelong learning, lifelong curiosity:** The position we bring into the Future of Knowledge Initiative is that in schools, universities, science and beyond, education is about cultivating curiosity, open-mindedness and a thirst for exploration that helps to make us who we are.

Statement of support

I am greatly encouraged by the new Epistemic Insight Initiative on the Future of Knowledge and I look forward to being able to contribute further. I believe strongly that, at this stage in the twenty-first century, this interdisciplinary approach which takes a rigorous look at the nature of knowledge is more vital than ever for philosophical, educational, political, ethical and theological reasons in the light of the loss of confidence in any concept of common truth, the fragmentation of knowledge and all the attendant dangers which follow. Looking at the nature of knowledge and trying to develop a much more interdisciplinary practice are very sound and durable approaches that have a real ability to make deep and important contributions, not just to education, but to many of the major issues which we face in the twenty-first century. These issues, which include AI and climate change, need people who are able to think widely and deeply if we are to find good ways forward. The potential fruitfulness of the kind of approach Epistemic insight embodies is enormous and can play its part in good engagement with other related initiatives around the world.

The Right Reverend Dr Richard Cheetham,
Co-Director of Equipping Christian Leadership in
an Age of Science and Commissioner with the
Anglican Communion Science Commission

5

Future Libraries' AI Focusing on Motivations to Learn

A Technologist's View

Ted Selker with additional creative input and expert knowledge from Berry Billingsley

Introduction

Epistemic insight focuses on not just serving up topics to remember but contextualizing educational experiences around domains to look at problems. Here's how I explain it and relate to it:

I sadly can't easily remember facts without relating to the concepts that make them useful. For me to care, I find myself needing to see how the facts matter for understanding and solving problems in the world. Some learners stubbornly ask broad questions of teachers that might seem like they are derailing a teaching unit and the curriculum it is part of. It can be difficult for a teacher, as school curricula is often built from taxonomizing things to learn for a march towards mastery in each context. Some topics are important, as we need alphabets to learn to read and cartesian coordinates to graph. Immersed in the topic of the moment, the learning of some facts becomes key.

As a child, I saw spelling as a convention that I didn't need to learn. But not knowing how to spell continues to be a problem because of its support of language and communication. People don't remember topics in isolation but in the context of what the knowledge can be used to do. But there is often a siloing of knowledge into classes and tests in disparate domains without explaining the conceptual connections. Seeing the big picture helps put them together. Furthering the ideas needs context approach to learning; the 'Epistemic Insight' movement was developed to help contextualize ways of thinking about knowledge. It starts by considering problems from multiple perspectives or domains. These domains are science, geography, history, theology, languages, literature, the arts, philosophy, engineering and maths. Each domain helps people see a question from a different perspective.

Indeed, such a base lets us communicate better with other people. It becomes a social construct, which after all is what communication is. Reasons for learning include both meaning and learning to be part of a knowledge culture.

Library transformed

A library is a place that catalogues all of knowledge and has librarians that might help us learn where it is and how to use it.

Why go to a library?

We go to libraries with our hunger for learning information and understanding. Our learning can be our effort to get knowledge for knowledge's sake. Our learning can be to get good at crossword puzzles. Our learning can be to answer other questions for ourselves and others too. Our learning might be a respite, reading about others or fantasy worlds to take us away from the reality of our lives and troubles. Our learning might also be to try to learn to create understandings that we can use to solve new problems, in possibly creative ways. These examples of reasons to learn require different frames of reference and ways of thinking.

How do we engage with a library?

'What are you trying to do?', the reference librarian would ask me to decide what kinds of reference information to suggest. The way I construct search queries has developed. I can include search terms to guide what kind of information results the search engine gives me. The World Wide Web is the library of all things that people have put online.

A library has materials that are written for various readers. Some introduce a topic for children, some are for people with lots of other knowledge, and others for people that are experts. The step changes of search and now GenAI are bringing library activities to everyone all day long everywhere. GenAI accesses materials that have been put on the web as a library. It fields complex constrained questions the way a librarian might.

GenAI also responds with stories tuned to any way we describe how we like to absorb information. We might ask for it to respond with a long or concise answer, a list, a poem, in old English or maybe in Bengali . . .

GenAI's packing of the knowledge includes connecting stories between islands of things we have asked about. When being told to speak in Australian or Indian English, the GenAI system adjusts. GenAI, like people, coalesces ideas into more approachable stories. As any library search, exploration with the future library always starts by framing a problem, but now uses a combination of using Gen AI and also web content in generating and testing results. Ways of finding and refining our understanding of the world's knowledge are on our desk computer and mobile phone. They respond to questions, find information and present it to us at a level and in the language we can understand. They are primed to remember the interaction as they respond to critical evaluation statements and follow-up questions.

Library-like knowledge exploration happens everywhere

Library work has never just been done in libraries. While the new libraries might include quiet places with supportive librarians when we need help deepening or broadening our exploration, the new future library allows us to explore and learn wherever we take our smartphone.

Early scientists carried instruments to learn about things wherever they went. We do the same with our phones that can sense noise, light, level, heart rate, distance, altitude and more. It lets me illuminate, calculate, magnify, reflect as a mirror, convert units, tune to a note and more. When I am on a plane, for example, I can measure the altitude and noise level of the cabin with a phone app. We still have to ask the questions to learn; I can use these direct measurements as seen in the screengrab from my phone to drive GenAI or web queries.

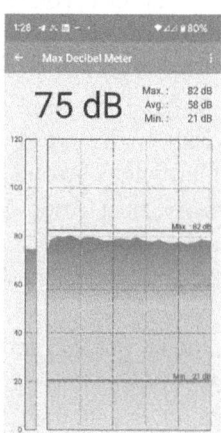

In 2010, I was visiting NYC and within a block of where I wanted to be. I didn't think to check with my phone and asked a couple, 'Do you know where this street is?' One of the couple pulled out a smartphone to ask it to show us on a map. Their partner and I were impressed with their ability to consult the world's knowledge for local guidance. The smooth and productive communication of ideas works when we have a grounding.

I wouldn't have been able to appreciate the smartphone's map had I not been taught how to read a map. The Discipline Wheel could be used with an app to guide us in a physical library to 'TA' the place where books on technology can be found. More likely an 'Epistemic Insight' app will be guiding us to various online library resources. In such cases, epistemic insight is here to remind us that we must learn across the domains to utilize knowledge. The new library can help orient and focus our knowledge exploration more easily and quicker than ever before.

We are just developing our use of these new tools and new knowledge resources. Search impacts how and what we do to learn and find things. We can be sad or nostalgic for the books on a big table in the library: the way we organized them with tabs, bookmarks, notes and references. Writing a multi-referenced piece, we would use the copier to take some of those references home or fill large backpacks with what we could check out. These multi-week excursions can now be done and documented in minutes with search engines.

Learning to use libraries

Libraries are always daunting; Why is it so quiet, large and vacant here? Where do I start? How do I use the card catalogue? The future online library might be everywhere, but it too needs introduction. We have to know how to ask questions, develop parts of ideas, winnow the direction, do follow-up searches and collect the information before writing. Our learning can help us know where to look (domains), how to relate things together (contextualizing domain knowledge), recognize what knowledge does and doesn't fit together (analysing relationships of knowledge across domains). Then there is the long arduous documenting all of this story with support for our analysis. And then along came generative AI (GenAI) to make assembling knowledge much more accessible.

Learning with GenAI

GenAI allows us to start with questions, name the domains that might be relevant, name the relationships that are being evaluated and the goal of the result. We can present these things explicitly to get results in any form we like. It seems to skip the arduous documentation phase, but maybe it doesn't. First, we need a teacher to help us formulate questions and the librarian to help us know how to find what we are looking for. Then we need the teacher again to help us learn how to analyse the responses. We then need the librarian again to help us know what and why to look up supporting things, possibly aided by the Epistemic Insight Initiative's Discipline Wheel tool, helping us ask the question from different perspectives.

Let's take the example of having GenAI consider the question of cow dung.

Prompt

Please make a concise list of ways to look at cow dung relative to each of science, geography, history, theology, languages, literature, the arts, philosophy, engineering and maths.

ChatGPT

Certainly, here's a concise list of ways to look at cow dung relative to different fields:

1. Science: Analysing its chemical composition and microbial content.

2. Geography: Examining its geographical distribution and impact on land use.

3. History: Tracing its historical use in agriculture and cultural significance.

4. Theology: Understanding its role in religious rituals and symbolism.

5. Languages: Studying linguistic expressions and idioms related to cow dung.

6. Literature: Analysing its portrayal in literature and folklore.

7. The arts: Exploring its use in traditional art and performance art.

8. Philosophy: Discussing ethical and metaphorical aspects.
9. Engineering: Utilizing it for biogas production and waste management.
10. Maths: Applying statistics and modelling for agricultural and environmental purposes.

The above GenAI response is impressive but is it what we really wanted? At this point we might think we are done but it's time to make the result our own. We can use the list to prompt our writing, or we can ask it to expand the responses. The domains above are not sacrosanct. We might also follow up by asking about dung economics, dung as a way to learn about cow health, its use as fertilizer, its use as fuel, a building material, its impact on the environment and so on.

Below we follow up by asking about the philosophical issue of the metaphorical aspects alluded to above.

Prompt

Please make a concise list of ways to look at the metaphorical aspects of cow dung.

ChatGPT

Here are some concise metaphorical aspects of cow dung:

1. Growth and potential.
2. Humility and simplicity.
3. Transformation and renewal.
4. Natural resource utilization.
5. Life's challenges leading to growth.
6. Purity and purification.
7. Cultural and traditional values.
8. Utilitarianism and practicality.

We ask, consider and incorporate things that are appropriate into our knowledge and our work product.

I had a Research Assistant (RA) whose classmate turned in a result of something written by GenAI and got kicked out of class. My RA started from such a process but then looked up facts, put things in their own words, considered how the writing should fit the assignment better and continued to ask more questions. They got an A+.

There are so many new ways to use GenAI. For example, as a tutor, we can ask GenAI questions in every direction without embarrassment until we are satisfied. We prompt it with what knowledge and assumptions to start with, what style and viewpoint and length of response we want it to produce. We might want it to include images, video, graphs. All this is easy for GenAI. It can create its answer in almost any media form.

Asking GenAI to write about technology of a future library

Prompt

Make a 150-word statement about how generative AI and web content to be used to create the future library would help people learn from different domain perspectives. Describe how it could help in learning, research, preparing presentations, personal growth and entertainment explaining how human librarians and teachers might help guide people to use the library.

ChatGPT response

In the envisioned future library empowered by generative AI and web content, the role of human librarians and teachers would be indispensable in guiding individuals to make optimal use of this advanced resource.

Librarians would curate and oversee the AI-generated content, ensuring its accuracy and relevance, while teachers would collaborate with them to align educational materials with curricular needs. They would collectively provide personalized guidance, teaching users how to navigate the library effectively, critically evaluate AI-generated information and enhance digital literacy skills.

Furthermore, human educators would fine-tune personalization algorithms to match individual learning preferences and goals. They'd offer ongoing support, answering questions, providing feedback and helping users maximize the utility of AI tools for tasks like research, presentations and data analysis.

Importantly, these experts would address ethical and privacy considerations, ensuring responsible AI use and adherence to ethical standards. In sum, human librarians and teachers would bridge the gap between users and AI, offering valuable insights, support and ethical guidance to ensure the future library becomes a powerful and responsible resource for learning and research.

In the above discussion, telling GenAI the goals of my query fills in knowledge and structure to help explain the topic. As in this chapter, its description of librarians requires development. The librarians of the future library will work at a higher and more interesting level. In this case, I hope my chapter is better than the above GenAI piece and brings in more perspectives, but I only gave it 150 words to work with. Even with this constraint and not much direction, GenAI produced an interesting answer.

A library is only as good as its books

We must take care with GenAI to know what it should and shouldn't be expected to explain well. We enable fantasy when we misremember what others said, but it's more delicate now with GenAI also responding in this way. The lazy lawyer that didn't check and let GenAI help them imagine a precedent that didn't exist lost his case. The scientist might hope someone wrote a justifying piece for an article and find GenAI making a story about such an article it has been encouraged to imagine. It is becoming more important than ever to check one's sources to establish truth. The new generative library requires us to focus on improving our critical, analytical and question-asking habits. The library needs people as well as online oracles to form solutions.

By reading things that have been written, GenAI learns what typically happens; it does not learn about the unusual 'black swans'. But we also want to explore topics that haven't been popular, are only partially known or are rare. We go to the library to learn about what we don't know. We must remind ourselves to expect today's GenAI to respond with aggregated commonly available vernacular information, not the incisive special case. We need guidance to learn how to find the unusual.

Librarians and library user have new and worthy roles

With future libraries on the web and GenAI, we have tools that can explain things smoothly and productively wherever we are.

Do we not need a teacher or librarian to guide us? We need them more than ever; the last few years social media has shown that we can get so deeply siloed that we might learn little from new facts. The power of GenAI can be squandered, as any tool can. We need nudges to use it, guidance to know how to work with it and analysis to interpret its knowledge to know when to look for other places to evaluate its responses. And GenAI itself relies on many subsystems with strategies beyond Large Language Models (LLMs) that organize all the written material it can, and as human-guided reinforcement learning that helps understand prompts and present results. As well as using new technologies to help us explore, libraries offer a calm context, and librarians offer structure to help us concentrate on knowledge.

We teachers and librarians rely on books and online resources because we don't remember everything. We certainly don't have the ability as LLMs do to remember what hundreds of millions of people have said about a topic. The storyteller of old celebrated books they could refer to and get more stories from. So, we will do better by using the new generative library to get more and better material for learners.

Learning to learn is what we are doing in classes, in libraries and in life. Life isn't about memorizing answers, it is an open book test in which we need to know how to find answers. As we have better tools for finding and organizing knowledge, the framing value of librarians becomes more important. With these new tools, people can produce things never before possible. They can assemble things across domains with grace. They can see and present countervailing facts instantly. The librarian is free to help formulate big questions, consider analysis, teach people to question what they see, consider broader contexts and create magnificent well-referenced solutions.

Conclusion and summary

This chapter positions new library technologies in terms of their power and the opportunity they give us for learning. It also focuses on how the learning stance and style we bring to questions impacts what and how we learn. The idea here is that web content and generative AI give parents, teachers and librarians new tools to create and test curricular and content ideas as they have never been able to be tested before.

These new tools allow a curious person to ask the same question from every perspective they can imagine. The Epistemic Insight Initiative Discipline Wheel can be a powerful guide for perspectives to ask such questions. The results that GenAI can provide are well-formed responses tailored to the requested style and language. A result of an articulate response is that it is easier to understand and learn from. The results of studying will not be the ability to write something up but the ability to compare different ways of thinking and answering questions. When a writeup is needed, the GenAI user has to know how to find reliable sources, and check the stories GenAI has presented to develop the point of view they are hoping to develop and share.

Recommendations

Be the mentor helping people use the tools that are available everywhere. As William Gibson said, 'The future is already here it's just not evenly distributed'. The future of libraries doesn't involve spending hundreds of millions of dollars on books and buildings. I recently watched in awe as a group of Bengali tourists in a rainforest resort were laughing their heads off at a ChatGPT response. It seems they had asked it to present something as the most famous Bengali poet would; one of them was singing the Bengali answer.

Be the mentor that encourages people to ask questions. Understanding is comparing alternative ideas, not having one idea. Asking big questions has always been the hard part.

Be the mentor that encourages people to find the problems with each of the solutions they are considering. The future library lets us ask what is wrong with an idea as easily as what is compelling about it.

Be the mentor that encourages people to see and combine knowledge that comes to bear on a question. We can enjoy the diversity of solutions and also how they combine from science, geography, history, theology, languages, literature, the arts, philosophy, engineering and maths.

6

Research Co-Creation and the Development of Epistemically Insightful Curricula

Finley I. Lawson, Mandy Dhaliwal, Michelle Lawson and Henry Coates

Introduction and context

Drawing on a four-year process of co-creating research-engaged curricula opportunities in primary and secondary schools in England, this chapter examines the processes, pedagogy and tools that enable the development and implementation of epistemically insightful learning experiences within formal school settings. The processes and interventions being discussed have been implemented in English primary (age five to eleven) and secondary (eleven to eighteen) school settings but have global applicability as they are designed to work within curriculum and assessment constraints. Furthermore, it explores the potential tensions between finding an approach to curriculum design that best fits the needs and experiences of individual schools and implementing the findings of generalized evidence-based educational research undertaken within a university context. We discuss the process and impact of establishing a research-led co-creation partnership designed to transform curriculum practice and policy while maintaining teachers' agency within a whole-school approach to curriculum transformation. Drawing on our findings we argue that the 'best practice' for researcher–participant relationship is one where the research actively involves the participants, as a community, rather than the research being 'done on' them. This is evidenced by the high return rate of student surveys and the fact that within three years one of the schools has moved from previously being 'research-engaged' as participants to being a research-led school where staff training and development takes place through inter-departmental research communities.

Moreover, we describe and discuss the practices that enabled participating teachers to develop their epistemic agency so that they were co-creators of research within a whole-school approach. This included the co-design of interventions and lessons, shared evaluation of the programme success, and the co-development of template resources that could be adapted by individual teachers. Existing practitioner literature highlights the benefits of research engagement in individual schools and the importance of access to mentoring and research expertise (Sharp et al. 2006) alongside similar guidance for the role the researcher should take in offering a 'guiding light' (Sanders et al. 2006). However, this places research engagement within the framework of school improvement plans over a sustained ethos. A decade later Nelson and Sharples (2017) highlight that evidence-informed practice is often divided between desk-based 'research' by teachers as separate from 'academic research' conducted by 'universities or professional research organisations' (Nelson and Sharples 2017), a model which emphasizes the teachers' role as a consumer rather than creator of rigorous research (echoed in Dimmock 2016). Indeed, McAleavy goes as far as to say, even where teachers and schools do have 'research leads' they are 'in uncharted waters without a compass. There is no blueprint for the work of the Research Lead and the coordination of research activities in schools is not necessarily straightforward' (McAleavy 2015). The process is still relatively under-discussed, although Godfrey (2016) has provided a valuable framework for developing a co-creation model (although he focuses on the creation of a research ecosystem within a school, led by the senior team). The co-creation partnerships discussed here have been developed by collaborating with school senior leaders who handed control to teaching staff, by collaborating with classroom teachers with the approval of senior leaders, and as part of whole-school curriculum re-design where the whole school collaborated at a strategic level and classroom teachers developed stage-appropriate implementation. Although each approach comes with its own opportunities and challenges, it highlights how co-creation can produce diverse implementation of the same pedagogy and shared research aims.

Since 2019 we have been making use of a design-based implementation approach (DBIR) to co-creating educational research. As a cross-institutional team of teachers, researchers and school senior leaders, we have grappled with where and how to provide opportunities for students to become 'epistemically insightful' (equipped with an understanding of the nature of knowledge within disciplines and across disciplinary boundaries). Previous research by the centre discovered that there are pressures within schools that dampen students' expressed curiosity in questions about the nature of reality and human personhood and limit the development of their epistemic insight into how science, religion and the wider humanities relate. Thus, the Epistemic Insight Initiative was developed to understand the kinds of interventions, tools and pedagogies that would address the current challenges posed by a compartmentalized curriculum. The challenge we faced was how we could transform whole-school curriculum practice without removing teacher agency and ensure that the intervention(s) met the needs and experiences of each school community, without becoming so contextualized that the findings and approaches couldn't be generalized to have wider applicability (and ultimately impact).

As universities, part of our role is to produce (and facilitate the production of) knowledge. As the REF puts it, we should be *'illustrating the benefits research delivers beyond academia, including how it brings tangible changes to aspects of society and life, and the public value it delivers'* (HEFCE, 2022 'REF Key facts'). Yet, within educational research, there is a perceived disjunct between the research undertaken by universities (or professional research organizations) and the research used and undertaken by teachers and practitioners in schools and other educational settings. This is highlighted in practitioner-focused literature where evidence-informed practice is often divided between desk-based 'research' by teachers as separate from 'academic research' conducted by universities or research organizations, a model which emphasizes the teachers' role as a consumer rather than creator of research (Nelson and Sharples, 2017). This divide can also border on a dismissal of teachers' ability to engage with academic research by insisting, for example, that we shouldn't 'expect teachers to learn to read research' and our role as researchers should be to create 'teacher-friendly research' with the implication that this is somehow 'less than' academic research (Miller, Drill and Behrstock 2010). Beyond a call to consider broader dissemination avenues for our research, why is this divide important?

Our answer is impact. Not solely, or even primarily, in terms of a 'REF-able' impact, but because we know that education research has the power to transform students' experiences of learning and thus broaden their aspirations for higher education. While there is a wealth of literature on the importance of research engagement within Initial Teacher Education and professional development (e.g. see Hagger and McIntyre 2000; Murray et al. 2009; Hine 2013), how to ensure that the ecosystem reciprocal is still relatively under-discussed? Finally, educational research is about improving the opportunities and outcomes for those in education. For this to happen, the change/intervention must continue to be implemented outside an individual project, and often within the constraints of existing curricula and assessment frameworks. This means that teachers and educators need to not be seen as a resource for 'local expertise' but as a crucial part of the research ecosystem.

The establishment and development of a co-creation relationship across a diverse group of primary and secondary schools has taken approximately three years and has been led by both teachers and senior leaders. The lynchpin with these relationships has been a shared recognition of the challenges identified within the previous research and an interest in examining how students can be better equipped to navigate disciplinary and curricula boundaries. This shared goal means that the school and research centre aims are aligned and therefore the core data collected can be standardized across the schools, but with the addition of contextualized questions that address the specific questions of each school. These local questions alongside school-level data for the core questions are shared with the school to support their practice and development plans. As a research centre, we analyse the data from across the partner schools, with the advantage that, as the research addresses shared concerns, teacher engagement with the research is high. This ensures a 95 per cent plus response rate across multiple data collection points for each cohort. Teachers and school leaders receive training on the philosophical framework underpinning the research and the learning tools but work in collaboration with the centre to develop lessons and curricula that meet the aims of the research. As researchers, we act in more of a quality assurance role during the intervention development, which means that the teachers are at the forefront of shaping the intervention for their students and within their institutional constraints. This close collaboration means that we address two of the key features required in building research in schools: (a) 'a willingness to embed the research activity into existing school systems' and (b) 'access to sources of expertise and advice' (Sanders et al. 2006). In one school, this saw the movement from ten teachers being involved in the initial curriculum design (plus delivery by seven members of the senior team) to, in the second year, the entire professional development programme being restructured around research-engaged Professional Learning Communities, where staff undertook their own action-research projects; now in its third year all staff including support staff are in mixed research teams as part of their professional development.

Sharp et al. (2006) identify a range of benefits to schools in being research engaged, including teacher retention, raised standards and school development. But the biggest impact we have noticed, shared by our partner schools, has been the combined impacts on teacher development/practice and their epistemic agency to investigate the educational questions that matter to them, empowered by an ethos that acknowledges that not every intervention will succeed. Eighty per cent of participating teachers in one school agreed that it has improved their understanding of disciplinary methods of their own discipline in relation to one they don't teach. Across the schools, teachers have changed practice within their teaching and been empowered to better signpost students to links with other subjects. As researchers, we have seen our work embedded in ways and places that we could not have envisioned, and also saw a genuine interest from schools to engage in research that required the time and expertise of sometimes the whole staff body (particularly when working with primary school partners). It is this kind of impact with whole year groups, even whole schools taking part in research-engaged curriculum interventions and redevelopment that would not be possible were we using a 'traditional' research model that excluded co-creation. The power of co-creation is that these 'interventions', if they can still be called that, will continue far beyond the directly funded projects that started them because those involved have ownership of what is taking place.

Instead of focusing on the contextual and theoretical framework that has shaped the development of these practices in schools, which is addressed elsewhere in this book, the main focus of the chapter is a discussion of the shape such curricula have taken across a group of very different school settings. This includes the innovative places and spaces that teachers and leaders have found to provide opportunities for students to become 'epistemically insightful' whether this is in creating dedicated curriculum time, making use of extra-curricular and homework spaces in the existing timetable, or adopting shared language throughout the school. This responds to research that emphasizes that students should be equipped and eager to work with different types of knowledge within and across their curriculum subjects.

Before continuing, it is worth a brief note on terminology to identify how co-created research differs from simple 'research-informed' practice, in these contexts. Jones and Netolickey make use of the definition of Barends, Rousseau and Briner (2014: 2) of evidence-based practice in their research summary for the Chartered College of Teaching (2023), which defines evidenced-based practice as 'based on a combination of critical thinking and the best available evidence'. As highlighted above, the focus of research/evidence-engaged practice emphasizes the role of teachers as users of research – for example in Facilitating Research-Informed Educational Practice for Inclusion. Brown et al. (2022) identifies five key steps or aspects of research use in education:

1) accessing academic research;

2) being able to comprehend academic research;

3) being able to critically engage with research evidence . . .

4) relating research evidence to existing knowledge and understanding; and, where relevant

5) . . . embarking on new courses of action or developing new practices.

While such discussions can be helpful to understand how research is used by teachers and practitioners, such an approach continues to fail to engage with Taylor's comment that practitioner experience should shape research. In a blog for Cambridge University Press, Taylor argues that '[i]f we are to meet the needs of learners . . . then research in education and other related disciplines should inform pedagogical practice' (Taylor 2018). However, she goes further to identify what we argue lies at the heart of the importance of co-created research and that is, 'the reverse is equally true; the wisdom and experience of practitioners should shape the work of researchers'.

This is where co-creation, and a DBIR methodology, comes into play to recognize the agency and expertise of teachers and practitioners. Penuel and Fishman describe DBIR as

> [An] approach to relating research and practice that is collaborative, iterative, and grounded in systematic inquiry. DBIR builds the capacity of systems to engage in continuous improvement, so that we can accomplish the transformation of teaching and learning we seek. (Penuel and Fishman 2014a)

In this space, the key to co-creation is the recognition of a 'joint focus' or challenge that is shared by researchers and teachers alike and that the design process for testing (and/or developing) the intervention 'include[s] the professional development and other supports needed to implement curricula and programs with integrity' (Penuel and Fishman 2014b). This approach has benefits to both parts of the research ecosystem and sets the framework for the relationship between university-based researchers and practitioner-researchers to be a reciprocal one, whereby what happens in the classroom (and/or the processes that lead up to delivery) informs the programme design. Furthermore, both theory of change and implementation and/or pedagogical theory shape the intervention but also develop from it. This means that different responses are developed in relation to the context rather than assuming that a 'one-size-fits-all' approach can or will work. The flexibility in implementation means that not only does co-creation lead to the development of capacity for change *beyond* the funded interaction, but it also supports researchers to understand common approaches/languages that work across settings. This evidence base can then be used to inform further testing of the attitudinal or attainment impacts of specific aspects of the shared programme through, for example, randomized control trials or difference-in-difference methodologies. In this manner, the co-created research then feeds back into the research development, yet with the inclusion of capacity-building and training activities within the research implementation means that school communities are equipped with the processes and skills that allow them to embed effective practices beyond the life of the original project. Co-creation over schools as 'just' participants ensures that the schools' input is not viewed only as a means to an end for a particular project, but that the partnership allows the community to achieve and build on the shared goals that brought them to the project in the first place.

The remainder of this chapter will briefly outline two case studies of co-created research within secondary schools (age eleven to eighteen) in England, before identifying key lessons learnt, before highlighting some key recommendations for those looking to adopt a similar co-creation approach to educational research.

Case Study 1 – A selective girls' secondary school (with mixed sixth form)

With an increasing emphasis on the importance of curriculum intent by Ofsted and the OECD for students to be equipped in understanding knowledge formation within and across disciplines, there is an apparent tension between external assessments focused on isolated disciplinary knowledge and the expected learning experience in the classroom.

In this case study, 10 teachers, 2 researchers and 7 senior leaders grapple with where and how to provide opportunities for 180 secondary school students to become 'epistemically insightful' – in response to research that emphasizes that students should be equipped and eager to work with different types of knowledge within and across subjects. Teachers worked collaboratively with researchers to organize the design and delivery of trial lessons and assessments to support students' negotiation of discipline/subject boundaries. The HEI team provided surveys for teachers to administer. Examining the process of research co-creation highlighted multi-department and cross-career stage opportunities for professional development alongside the research generation.

The key feature of this case study was that the staff involved in the development and delivery of the programme came from a breadth of departments and career stages. While the decision to be involved in the research project came from the senior leadership team, it was a small group of teachers who co-designed the programme which has then been taught by senior leaders.

In the first year the lessons were delivered during the first three terms (September–February) within an existing space of the year 7 (age 11) curriculum during their first year at secondary school. Teachers designed the initial programme following group CPD where the research aims and curriculum opportunities were shared with them and were supported by the research team to develop an overarching big question for the programme that fit into the school's ethos and values. The research team then provided iterative design and development support within the creation of the curriculum to ensure that each section of the programme supported students to compare and contrast two disciplinary approaches to each sub-question. In collaboration with the school, the learning review 'exit slips' at the end of each section contained repeat measures from the baseline survey allowing teachers to assess impact on key learning objectives as the programme progressed.

Following the collaboration between the school and researchers in the first year and the impact on teachers' perceptions of their agency to investigate curriculum delivery, the second year saw the school re-shape their teacher development programme to reflect a research-led framework. Teachers (and from the third year support staff) work in cross-departmental/inter-hierarchical groups to undertake close-to-practice research and write up their findings for (initially) internal publication (see Figure 6.1). This led to staff undertaking their own research across a range of educational issues, including the further development of the initial research programme. This included collaborating with the researchers to design and deliver an extra-curricular 'elective' programme on social justice grounded in epistemic insight pedagogy, running the 'year 7' programme as an 'elective' for post-16 students (to understand the impact of the developing students' disciplinary knowledge on this pre-university group), and most recently developing a homework strategy for year 8 (twelve-year-olds) to consolidate students' understanding of

FIGURE 6.1 *Research ecosystem development.*

disciplinary approaches to knowledge (epistemic insight) as they move through the school.

Reflections and lessons learnt

This case study, by necessity, provides only a brief overview of extensive work undertaken through co-creation of research with teachers and leaders; however, in this instance co-creation allowed us to move from a planned model of a stand-alone 2-week intervention with a small group (15–30) of students, to working with a whole year group (150–80) in each academic year, in addition to learning from the teachers' own research projects. Furthermore, it enabled the pedagogy (and 'intervention') to become embedded within and contribute to the expression of the school's ethos and values for staff and students. Co-creation allowed us to understand that what appeared to be 'easy' disciplinary interactions on paper, were more complex for students in this age group due to the order of the wider-curriculum delivery. For example, understanding the similarities between the textual analysis methods used in English literature and history was difficult for students who didn't yet have a firm grounding in these concepts in the move from primary to secondary education; however, they were able to contrast how making use of historical and geographical evidence could lead to different approaches to managing peoples' responses to natural disasters. In this sense students were better able to grasp the impact of differences in disciplinary methods over how disciplinary norms of thought (values) may shape different answers despite similar methods of investigation.

This school provided a unique setting because the senior team commitment to the research programme ensured that students and teachers valued its delivery and shared an understanding of its place within the school's ethos. Alongside this, the crucial engagement of teachers in the creation of the programme and the opportunity for them to see its development within the school supported the development of teacher agency, with teacher-led research projects feeding back into the design of future research projects and opportunities. This combination of active teacher and leader engagement meant that the programme and related projects are continuing to be developed and delivered beyond the funded programme.

Case Study 2 – A coastal mixed comprehensive school

In this case study we discuss a teacher-led project to redevelop and increase the perceived relevance of an interdisciplinary curriculum space for year 9 (age thirteen) students in a school that is in an area of significant disadvantage where the community has traditionally low progression rates of higher education despite the academic ability to attend. The placement of this programme within the year prior to GCSE's (external assessment) subject choices meant that it played a very different role in students' educational journey to the year 7 programme discussed above.

In line with the above programme, the whole year group (approximately 120 students) took part in the programme, with the aim of improving students' understanding of the relationship(s) between their curriculum subjects and engagement with their wider learning. The programme worked across modern foreign languages (in this instance French) and the humanities. Whereas in Case Study 1, the programme was delivered to supplement the national curriculum requirements (compulsory curriculum content for English state schools), here the school was using the programme to cover the national curriculum content. This introduced a new challenge of creating curriculum and content from scratch that both delivered the required content and supported students in understanding the nature of knowledge formation within these different disciplines (something which, at the time of writing, isn't explicitly addressed within the national curriculum). In addition to having different curriculum needs, the development of the programme beyond the first two terms (the programme ran for six terms) and the design had to take place on an iterative and responsive basis due to a greater level of uncertainty around the pace of content delivery. Finally, whereas the 'assessment' for the Case Study 1 school was only required in relation to a final research project produced by the students, here a new challenge to both researchers and teachers arose in the school management requiring regular assessment points. This meant that a key aspect of theory and delivery output in this setting related to establishing how to assess students' understanding and application of the nature and communication of knowledge in a range of formats.

The co-creation of the research programme within this setting occurred at an individual level. While the data collection tools (excluding a few adjustments to reflect school-level differences – e.g. timing of research projects/content-specific questions) and student 'scale' of engagement (both programmes worked with a full year group) were consistent across both settings, Case Study 2 reflected the development of theory and practice at the 'micro' rather than the 'macro' level – what does this look like for individual teachers working to address disciplinary boundaries within their classroom? The unique setting of a pre-existing interdisciplinary curriculum space was both an incredible strength, in that the students and teachers were already tackling learning in a novel way, and also a challenge as the exemplary work done by the classroom teachers to build students' understanding of disciplinary methods and norms of thought was not being picked up through either shared language or practice outside the boundaries of the classroom.

While the wider-ranging study 1 provided detail on the strategic processes that support the embedding of epistemic insight pedagogy and practice, the narrower focus in study 2 provided an opportunity to home in on the individual learning activities and core language that were needed to support students to engage with a new way of learning beyond their existing experience of a compartmentalized curriculum. This led to teachers, researchers and students taking part in activities such as those in Figure 6.2, to provide explicit teaching on the nature of disciplinary methods to develop students' understanding of how different disciplines can arrive at different answers to the same question due to the information provided by the discipline's methods. This built on the initial findings from the first year with Case Study 1 around students' comprehension of how disciplines arrive at knowledge.

This comprehension of disciplinary methods came to the fore in what was originally designed as an interim assessment, where students approached the issue of the importance of Uluru through

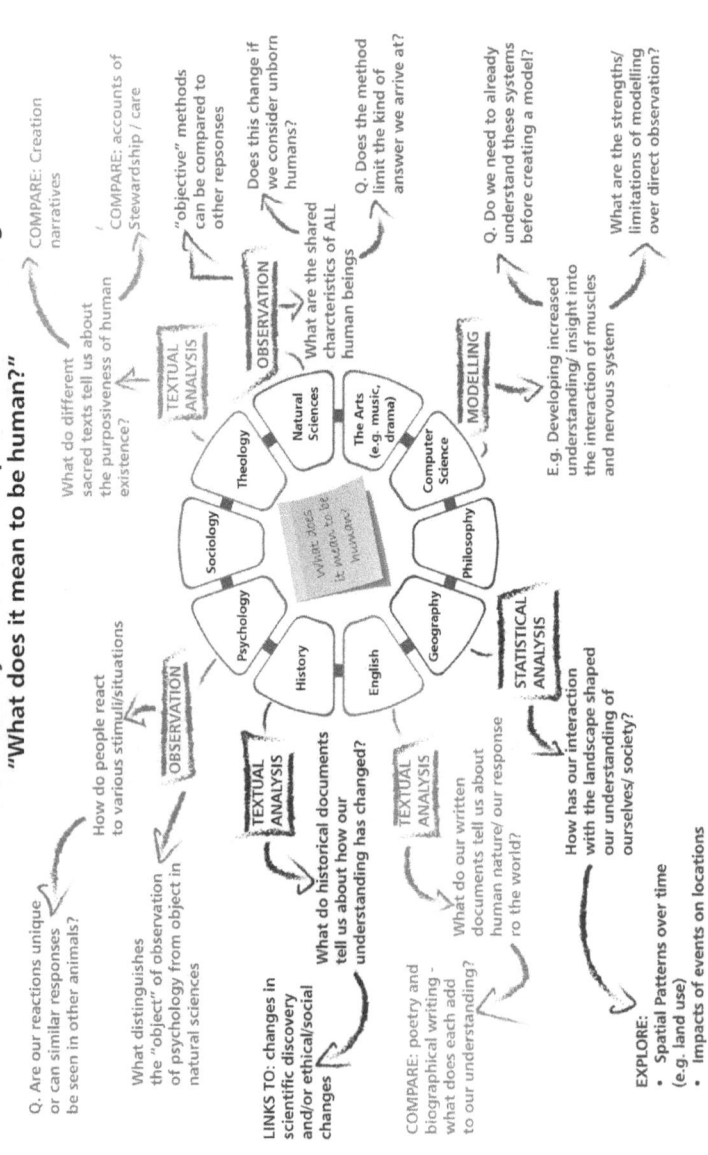

FIGURE 6.2 *Development of students' understanding of disciplinary methods to tackle a shared question.*

their chosen disciplinary lens. Students investigated the significance of Uluru through supported independent research projects that explored questions such as 'Is it "just a rock" and only of geological interest?', 'What are the minerals in the rock?', 'What do paintings on the rock's caves tell us about its religious significance?', 'How has Uluru been portrayed in art?' and so on. These investigations allowed teachers and students to examine 'content' questions around the composition of and watershed from Uluru (for example), but also wider questions around colonialism, how disciplinary values may lead to conflicting priorities on tackling big questions in society.

Reflections and lessons learnt

As found in this case study, co-creation requires a different commitment from the participating staff that isn't required from those acting solely as research participants, and that is a level of openness and flexibility to respond to the theory and design changes that emerge from the implementation of the programme. This requires willingness from teachers to adapt the delivery of the agreed curriculum to respond to the evidence of which pedagogies and/or activities work to support the development of students' understanding. Where activity is teacher- rather than management-led, this also requires the support of leadership colleagues to enable teachers to develop innovative practice.

In this context the intervention to develop students' understanding of the nature of knowledge was particularly timely due to supporting their understanding of disciplines prior to their GCSE choices and enabling them to appreciate the contributions made by different disciplines to answer complex questions. Students were supported to frame and research their own multidisciplinary questions by developing a curriculum that started with narrow or tightly defined questions that could be addressed by one or two disciplines to broader questions that required multiple disciplines to arrive at a full answer. This was undertaken by moving from teacher-led enquiries to student-initiated research projects, through careful modelling and scaffolding. This modelling also required teachers to develop their own knowledge and confidence in the interaction of disciplines in addressing the issues being discussed, this occurred through collaboration with the researchers but also, more crucially, through collaboration with teachers in other departments to learn from their expertise. This highlights a key feature of epistemic pedagogy that enables its delivery by teachers working in isolation and teams working in collaboration – it doesn't require individuals to become experts with the curriculum content of disciplines outside their own, but rather to have an increased understanding, through collaboration, of the nature of knowledge formation in other disciplines.

Shared conclusions and recommendations

Both case studies highlight the powerful role that co-creation can have on the development of educational research, particularly in understanding how changes to pedagogical or curriculum practice can be delivered within different educational settings. Co-creation of research provides teachers and leaders with greater ownership of the research project, as they are actively involved in its development rather than having the research 'done to' them. This ownership of the research supports the rate at which practices are embedded within the learning setting due to connected shared goals that unite the aims of teachers-as-researchers and the research team.

The next steps within a co-creation partnership are to understand how HE partners can use our position to amplify the voices of practitioners as valuable partners and contributors to the educational research landscape. The piece that we are keen to continue to develop our understanding of is how to 'close the loop' and support teachers to share their research-engaged practice into teacher education directly (through knowledge exchange opportunities with students on QTS programmes) and with educational researchers. In placing practitioner research within the 'research landscape' we truly recognize its value within the research ecosystem and can share how generalized interventions/findings can be implemented in practice, in schools (or other settings), daily, which is surely the impact we want our research to have. If the role of higher education is to produce knowledge, we must ensure that our practice includes acting as a knowledge broker, supporting and enabling the production of knowledge by the communities it serves and feeding that back into the wider research environment.

To conclude, we highlight the impact that co-created curricula innovation can have on both students and staff, including the rate at which staff and students develop their confidence in addressing questions from multidisciplinary perspectives and deepening understanding of the relationship and links between different curriculum areas. We provide suggestions for next steps for colleagues who wish to implement such practice within their teaching or schools, based on our findings to date and feedback from teachers and leaders involved in the project, and suggest some areas of future development, particularly in relation to the interaction between practitioner research and teacher education programmes.

References

Barends, E., D. M. Rousseau, and R. B. Briner (2014). 'Evidence-based Management: The Basic Principles', *CGIAR GENDER Impact Platform*. In: *In Search of Evidence: Empirical findings and professional perspectives on evidence-based management*. VU University Press, Amsterdam, 203–220.

Brown, C., S. MacGregor, J. Flood, and J. Malin (2022). 'Facilitating Research-Informed Educational Practice for Inclusion. Survey Findings From 147 Teachers and School Leaders in England', *Frontiers in Education* 7. Online only: https://doi.org/10.3389/feduc.2022

Dimmock, C. (2016). 'Conceptualising the Research–Practice–Professional Development Nexus: Mobilising Schools as "Research-Engaged" Professional Learning Communities', *Professional Development in Education*, 42: 36–53. https://doi.org/10.1080/19415257.2014.963884.

Godfrey, D. (2016). 'Leadership of Schools as Research-Led Organisations in the English Educational Environment: Cultivating a Research-Engaged School Culture', *Educational Management Administration & Leadership*, 44: 301–21. https://doi.org/10.1177/1741143213508294.

Hagger, H. and D. Mcintyre (2000). 'What Can Research Tell us About Teacher Education?', *Oxford Review of Education*, 26: 483–94. https://doi.org/10.1080/713688546.

HEFCE, H.F.C. of E. (2022). *REF 2021* [WWW Document]. Higher Education Funding Council for England. https://www.ref.ac.uk/ (accessed 29 March 2023).

Hine, G. S. C. (2013). 'The Importance of Action Research in Teacher Education Programs', *Issues in Educational Research*, 23: 151–63. https://doi.org/10.3316/aeipt.197941.

Jones, G. and D. Netolicky (2023). 'Research-informed Practice: A Framework', *The Chartered College of Teaching*. https://my.chartered.college/research-hub/research-informed-practice-a-framework/ (accessed 4 May 2023).

McAleavy, T. (2015). 'Teaching as a Research-Engaged Profession: Problems and Possibilities', *Education Development Trust*. Reading, UK.

Miller, S. R., K. Drill, and E. Behrstock (2010). 'Meeting Teachers Halfway: Making Educational Research Relevant to Teachers', *Phi Delta Kappan*, 91: 31–4. https://doi.org/10.1177/003172171009100706.

Murray, J., A. Campbell, I. Hextall, M. Hulme, M. Jones, P. Mahony, I. Menter, R. Procter, and K. Wall (2009). 'Research and Teacher Education in the UK: Building Capacity', *Teaching and Teacher Education, Teaching Learning and Development in the UK*, 25: 944–50. https://doi.org/10.1016/j.tate.2009.01.011.

Nelson, J. and J. M. Sharples (2017). 'How Research-Engaged are You?', *Impact: Journal of the Chartered College of Teaching*. Online only: How research-engaged are you? (chartered.college)

Penuel, W. R. and B. J. Fishman (2014a). *DBIR Introduction* [WWW Document]. Design-based Implementation Research. https://learndbir.org/ (accessed 4 June 2023).

Penuel, W. R. and B. J. Fishman (2014b). *DBIR- Organising the Design Process* [WWW Document]. Design-Based Implementation Research. http://learndbir.org/principles/organizing-the-design-process (accessed 4 June 2023).

Sanders, D., C. Sharp, A. Eames, and K. Tomlinson (2006). *Supporting Research-Engaged Schools: A Researcher's Role*. https://www.academia.edu/415234/SANDERS_D_SHARP_C_EAMES_A_and_TOMLINSON_K_2006_Supporting_Research_Engaged_Schools_A_Researcher_s_Role_Slough_NFER (accessed 4 June 2023).

Sharp, C., A. Eames, D. Sanders, and T. Kathryn (2006). *Leading a Research Engaged School*. Nottingham: National College for School Leadership.

Taylor, K. (2018). *What Do We Mean by Research Informed Practice in Education?* Central Evaluation and Monitoring. https://www.cem.org/blog/what-do-we-mean-by-research-informed-practice-in-education (accessed 4 May 2023).

7

How Can We Educate Future Generations to Effectively Respond to Global Challenges and Live Sustainably?

Developing Agentic Learners through an Epistemically Insightful Curriculum

Agnieszka J. Gordon and Sherralyn Simpson

Introduction

As acknowledged by Nelson Mandela, education is the most powerful agent for change (Perkins 2022) with impacts for the economy and society. Then how curriculum interacts with a constantly shifting global arena is arguably relevant to teaching and learning. . . .

There is increasing dialogue taking place internationally about 'global citizenship' promoted by United Nations (UN 2021) and described as a call to action for individual and collective social responsibility. As such, there is growing momentum to listen to and represent the voices of all people and communities worldwide in the conversation, sharing decisions and actions responsibly concerning social, environmental and economic sustainability (Oxfam 2023). Therefore, there is growing interest in moving the conversation into the classroom from policy makers, educators and students alike. Engaging with sustainability issues and challenges in the classroom will arguably better prepare students to become aware of the wider world and understand their role in it. This is echoed in the Global Education 2030 Agenda, and Sustainability Goal 4 (SDG4), which embeds the notion of global citizenship, acknowledging the fundamental role of equitable education provision (UNESCO 2016) to develop learners' knowledge and skills, supporting the sustainability of our global community (UN 2021). Equally, the international influence on education policy by the OECD (Organisation for Economic Co-operation and Development) emphasizes the integration of global themes within curriculum design, such as sustainability, health, well-being and cultural identity (2018).

However, there is limited time and space within the curriculum to explore sustainability, as ' . . . it isn't an inspection must!' (Dunlop and Rushton 2023). As such, it is often confined to theory or content-based learning in the science lab or in a geography lesson, for example. Likewise, sustainability is mainly limited to key scientific concepts of climate change, or the study of weather as prescribed by the national curriculum (DfE 2021). If, as it is proposed, education is key in enabling students to respond to social and environmental challenges, then those big questions and real-world problems require space in the classroom to be contemplated. For example, questions which confront the impact of fossil fuel energy usage, climate change, plastic pollution or sustainable energy production are all current and emotive, with not one simple answer. Recognizing the complexity of sustainability and related challenges reveals how there is no easy solution and acknowledges the power of connecting knowledge and expertise from across a variety of disciplinary domains. Perhaps moving away from a restrictive siloed approach to teaching and learning offers an opportunity for students to access distinctive disciplinary approaches when responding to complex real-world problems such as food sustainability and environmental challenges. Adopting the Epistemic Insight Initiative pedagogical approach (Billingsley et al. 2018) can help develop educators' capacities to confidently address and respond to these complex issues through our pre-designed interdisciplinary workshops. Delivery of our workshop investigations facilitates natural opportunities for students to express their curiosity and link knowledge across boundaries, encouraging critical 'future-ready' (OECD 2018) thinkers within all classrooms, no matter what the subject boundary.

Those experiencing the Epistemic Insight Initiative pedagogy begin to explore the nature of distinct disciplinary domains: how they work, their norms of thought, what methods they use and what questions they ask. Thus, helping to enrich understanding of global issues from different disciplinary lenses and finding value in multiple perspectives, worldviews or contexts. The pedagogy offers support to learners to 'think like a scientist' or 'think like a sociologist' or an economist and so on, drawing on distinct knowledge from different disciplinary perspectives when addressing the multidisciplinary nature of real-world problems and as such fostering development of epistemic insight or 'knowledge about knowledge' (Billingsley and Hazeldine 2020). This approach aligns with the OECD Compass 2030 principles to promote student agency by taking responsibility for one's own learning (OECD 2019). Therefore, this chapter identifies how the pedagogy fits into the current educational landscape, aiming to transform education by exploring how knowledge works within and across disciplines. As such, it will present practical teaching and pedagogical strategies and tools for the classroom that support teachers to help their students to confidently address sometimes difficult or complex global issues and sustainability challenges through epistemic insight tools and pedagogy.

The first workshop focuses on ways to produce sustainable energy using wind power and can be adapted for delivery to primary-age students up to older age groups, such as students starting their higher education studies at university foundation level. Scientists have identified how the earth's natural 'greenhouse effect' historically kept the temperature stabilized (average of 15 degrees centigrade), however human interference largely through burning fossil fuels has disturbed the balance, significantly increasing carbon dioxide levels, causing our planet's temperature to rise. The search for and utility of renewable energy sources is therefore a pressing issue for the world and as such arguably considered an important issue to include in curricula. The UN asserts 'the science is clear: to avoid the worst impacts of climate change, emissions need to be reduced by almost half by 2030 and reach net-zero by 2050' (United Nations 2023). Consequently, the workshop offers opportunity to explore alternative energy and its transition as central to sustainability through a science lens by exploring how scientific views and the field of engineering perceive the challenges of wind power as a renewable energy source. Students discover that boundaries within the investigation can be expanded beyond 'the science' to include socioeconomic considerations, for example public health concerns from noise levels, environmental impacts of wind farms, and for instance land use or the effects on wildlife habitats. Hence reflecting on how other disciplines can interact with the question of wind power generation, to form a much fuller picture. This widening of perspectives aligns to an increasing diversity of analysis taking place across the world by 'multiple disciplines' including the social sciences to evaluate and mitigate climate change, as reported by the Intergovernmental Panel on Climate Change (IPCC 2022).

The second workshop is targeted at students aged sixteen to eighteen years. It first focuses on the issue of overfishing and how it can negatively impact sustainability of fish stocks, thus affecting more than 820 million people worldwide, who depend on fishing for employment and nutrition (FAO 2023). This is indeed a complex problem which must take account of a sustainability divide between developed and developing countries (FAO 2018) and therefore the workshop presents an accessible investigation which has the option to delve deeper into marine life declines by considering the impact of pollution on our oceans. Titled 'Sustainability and the Sea', we initially explore overfishing and then pollution as questions for science, before considering how a critical and multidisciplinary approach can contribute to a deeper and pertinent response to the decline in marine life. The discussion may also consider theological perspectives such as stewardship or 'looking after the earth'. Hence not only seeking knowledge from different disciplinary domains and expertise but also asking questions such as who is responsible? Who are those responsible, responsible to? And why are they responsible?

Workshop 1: How to produce sustainable energy using wind power – exploring real-world problems through epistemic insight pedagogy

It has become increasingly clear that our society needs to move to sustainable energy sources and reduce our reliance on fossil fuels (Holechek et al. 2022) There are many naturally occurring power sources that we can investigate, for example, solar power, wave and tidal energy and, very importantly for the UK, wind power. Although the number of wind farms around the UK has increased hugely in recent years, they can be controversial and certainly do not represent a perfect solution to the problem.

The workshop objectives

The workshop aims to explore a big question related to engineering and sustainability by examining the scientific and engineering challenges in capturing wind power, but also understanding the broader contexts that need to be considered to ensure that this technology is used in a sustainable, efficient and socially acceptable way. The practical exercise of building a model wind turbine is used at the primary level to help the students implement some of the scientific and engineering principles they have learnt. By explaining and drawing how and where they would build a wind turbine in the real world, students make use of knowledge drawn across a variety of disciplines.

The workshop makes science relevant and practical (ASPIRES 2022) and helps students understand the nature of science by showing them how science works and collaborates with other disciplines to solve problems. The workshop gives children an opportunity to learn how to connect knowledge across disciplines and develop skills to work as a team to solve problems.

Learning outcomes

By the end of the workshop, students will

- understand terms: epistemic insight, discipline and appreciate similarities and differences between disciplines;
- understand how a variety of disciplines can enrich and answer a big question or a problem;
- appreciate how science informs all aspects of our lives;
- increase awareness of science's strengths and limitations;

In this workshop, students consider ways that science and other disciplines inform our response to the workshop question but cannot fully answer it within one discipline. They design and test their own 'wind turbines' and draw on other disciplines to explain how they would use this technology in real-life contexts.

The workshop has been designed for primary-stage students and subsequently adapted and successfully delivered to the university foundation-level engineering students (Gordon, Simpson and Hassanin 2022). The workshop can easily be adapted for all the school stages and within Initial Teacher Education (ITE) to develop teacher trainees' epistemic insight pedagogy and tools. Adaptation can be made to relevant content of the specific curricula; for example the Discipline Wheel can contain chemistry, biology and physics instead of science, or engineering disciplines can be added to enrich when working with engineering students.

During the workshop, students examine the question 'What is the best way to get power from the wind?' using the Discipline Wheel to help them explore the question through a variety of disciplines.

We start from explaining who a scholar is (someone who undertakes an academic study of a complex topic) and encourage the students to become a scholar for a day and help us explore the workshop question. At this stage, it is good to explain the term big question to students. We explain that big questions are complex questions, requiring several disciplines to find a comprehensive answer and see a big picture. A useful tool for this part is a picture of a big elephant (Schmaltz 2003; Masi 2021) based on John Godfrey Saxe's famous fable 'The Blind Men and the Elephant' (Saxe 1963) in which six blind men attempt, and ultimately fail, to describe an elephant to each other's satisfaction. They cannot describe the elephant fully as they can only see them through a small magnifying glass and therefore are unable to see an elephant (Figure 7.1). This is a particularly useful metaphor to encourage students to see why a bigger picture and a multidisciplinary approach are often needed to solve complex problems.

We subsequently divide students into groups to work on the workshop question using the Discipline Wheel (see an example of the Discipline Wheel in the Glossary) which presents a range of disciplines to help (LASAR 2019a). This gives students an interactive means of exploring a question and role-play through 'thinking like a

FIGURE 7.1 *The blind men and the elephant.*

historian', 'thinking like an engineer' and 'thinking like a geographer'. At this stage, we also explain the term 'discipline' and relate disciplines to school subjects, indicating that not all disciplines are reflected in school curricula. In addition, we discuss similarities, differences and limitations of disciplines. We explain how different disciplines approach problems in different ways and how important it is to know that they also have limitations. This is particularly important for science – we explain how knowledge in science evolves and that what is 'true' at a given point can become 'not true anymore' as we get more knowledge and understanding.

The facilitator (teacher or tutor) then asks a question: Which disciplines on the Discipline Wheel can help us answer our big question today, promoting group discussion regarding relevant disciplines?

Two objectives from the Epistemic Insight Framework form the foundation of the workshop (Billingsley et al. 2018; Billingsley 2022). The first objective explores 'the nature of science in real-world contexts and multidisciplinary arenas' and the second objective considers 'ways of knowing and how they interact'. Students begin by considering a series of smaller questions related to science and engineering exploring wind turbine characteristics such as shape of the base and turbine, materials, properties and functionality. The facilitation and helping with questions such as 'how do we decide where to build?', 'what is the best shape of the turbine/base?' and 'can we build in beautiful places/next to someone's house?' should lead to the conclusion that science and engineering do not provide enough disciplinary knowledge to answer the posed question fully. It is good to ask the students what disciplines would be useful to enrich the answer to the big question explored in this workshop. Geography, history and disciplines exploring social aspects (psychology, ethics, sociology) are good choices here. For example, history might say that learning from past mistakes can improve wind turbine design or teach engineers not to build in certain places. Science will help to decide on the shape and materials for a turbine and establish the strongest base shape. Geography will be useful to explore the terrain structure, landscape or wind strengths. It would be useful to explore the global wind atlas with the students.

The workshop has a hands on activity for students to design and build their own wind turbines using simple materials, which are then tested. Figure 7.2 presents wind turbines built and tested by Year 5 students.

Materials used for building the wind turbine:

- Pinwheel template
- Various types of tape, for example marking tape, insulating tape, cellar tape
- Lolly sticks
- Long sticks or straws
- Newspaper for rolling (optional)
- Cardboard (optional)
- Split pins
- Plastic bases/corks
- String
- Plasticine (optional)
- Hairdryer (for testing a wind turbine)

FIGURE 7.2 *Example wind turbines.*

Give your students a choice of materials and let them build wind turbines of their design in teams. This activity is all about creativity, scientific skills and teamworking skills, and as such students do not rely on teacher instructions. The idea is for students to produce the design for a wind turbine based on their earlier learning, construct it and test it as a team. You can make it a competition. Let them test their creations using a hairdryer. Is it sturdy and stable enough? Does the shape and size of a base make a difference and how? Who will make their turbine to spin first? Whose turbine is faster? Spins longer? Which design is sturdier? Ask them to compare and reflect on all the aspects of their design and how it can be improved based on comparisons/their design experience. Which turbine withstands strongest wind and why? Get your students to note, analyse and compare their observations.

The workshop design helps students to appreciate big questions in general and the factors that influence the development and implementation of wind energy. They will consider how geography, ecological and ethical concerns can impact the location, size and design of wind farms. They will also consider how science and engineering contribute to the design of wind turbines, think about their properties, materials and efficiency. The activity also teaches students about the nature of a range of disciplines and how a multidisciplinary approach to big questions and a complex problem offer a complementary solution to them to get a fuller answer.

They learn that different disciplines have different preferred questions, methods and norms of thought. Science gathers evidence through scientific inquiry; predicting, testing and observing while other disciplines such as ethics and politics seek to take into account people's feelings, points of views and beliefs. Geography is about people and places and gathers evidence through maps and observations.

Workshop 2: Sustainability and the Sea: Applying epistemic insight pedagogy. What is causing the decline in marine populations and how do we solve it?

The Epistemic Insight workshop titled 'Sustainability and the Séa' is an example of how multidisciplinary thinking can be developed in the

Key Stage 5 classroom. The investigation examines how a range of disciplinary perspectives and different questions asked by different disciplines help to inform why there is a decline of marine life in our oceans. Although regarded as a real-world problem, international dialogue suggests there are opportunities to halt the decline through positive action (UN. Org 2022). Consequently, development of epistemic insight will help to educate students to respond to this global challenge perceptively.

Objectives

The workshop explores this real-world problem by employing the Epistemic Insight Framework (Billingsley 2022) to examine 'The nature of science in real-world contexts and multidisciplinary arenas'. In a role-play activity, students form a *Marine Life Challenge Committee* to support thoughtful discussion, individual critical thinking and collective decision making. The first task determines questions that are amenable to science through implementation of a pedagogical tool known as the Bubble Tool (see Figure 7.3). Asking for example, 'What are the reproductive behaviours of different species of fish?'

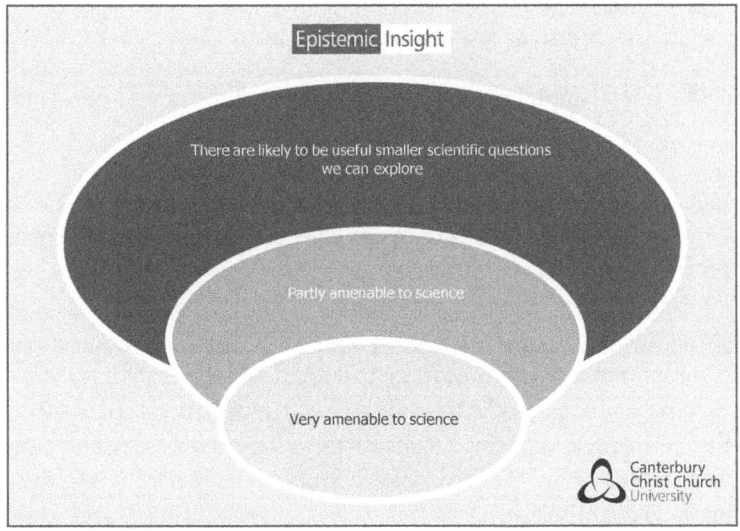

FIGURE 7.3 *The Bubble Tool.*

is very amenable to science investigation. By establishing a good question for science, students gain greater awareness of the nature of science and can more confidently explore how science informs our thinking and contributes to solving the decline in marine life. Secondly, questions less amenable to science, such as, 'How does a reduction in certain species of fish in a region, impact fisherman's livelihoods?', offer opportunity to consider other disciplinary perspectives in addition to science, accessing other relevant domains of knowledge and expertise. Therefore, the complexity of marine decline is exposed, and epistemic insight offers teaching strategies and tools which challenge students' perception of scientific enquiry, develop their multidisciplinary thinking and encourage student agency; defined by OECD (2019) as 'the capacity to set a goal, reflect and act responsibly to effect change'.

Learning outcomes

By the end of the workshop, students will be able to

- identify what makes a question a science question,
- explain how science contributes to solving the problem of marine decline, but may have limitations, and
- demonstrate how different disciplines address the real-world problem of marine decline.

Activity 1: At the start of the session, students are presented with stimulus background material to provide some suggested context to the problem, focusing on the decline in marine life in our oceans. For example, key statistics that identify a near 50 per cent decline of some species of sea creatures between 1970 and 2012 (Blakemore 2015) and a recent intergovernmental report found one-third of marine mammals are currently threatened with extinction (IPBES 2019), may be helpful. In addition, overfishing is described as 'draining the ocean's vitality' by the American ecologist Carl Safina (1997) who sums up the problem:

If you're overfishing at the top of the food chain, and acidifying the ocean at the bottom, you're creating a squeeze that could conceivably collapse the whole system (Hawthorne, 2018).

Students are invited to think about which disciplines can help solve marine decline. The background material raises many questions and comments about marine decline from students who (in small groups of four to six) list their questions before sorting them into questions for science to answer and questions for other disciplinary domains to investigate. To assist their thinking here, the teacher introduces the Bubble Tool to the whole class. This epistemic insight pedagogical tool can provide a clear illustration of both individual and collective reasoning when confronted with how amenable a question is to science. Each of their questions is allocated to one of the 'bubbles', determining if the question is very amenable or partly amenable to science or requires a more multidisciplinary response which may include smaller scientific questions. The nature of science is then deliberated as a whole-class discussion, prompting cognisance of what makes a good question for science, and how science responds to the question through specific methods and norms of thought. To give an example, science can investigate the natural world when observing the behaviours or habitats of different fish species to learn about marine decline. Student understanding can be formatively assessed through the Bubble Tool activity where students identify what makes a question a science question.

Activity 2: Students form a 'Marine Life Challenge Committee' in small groups and respond to the big question – What is causing the decline in marine populations and how do we solve it? There are two marine decline issues for exploration within the workshop, and groups either work on either issue 1 or 2. These issues provide an interesting opportunity for research discovery for students, alongside time to individually reflect on their own perspectives while learning from others collectively.

1. First, how can we address the impact of overfishing that depletes fish stocks beyond sustainable recovery resulting in species extinction?

2. Second, how are the oceans coming under stress from various sources of pollution and how can these challenges be adequately addressed?

Each group focuses on one of the issues above, initially exploring it as scientists by internet and desk research of questions pertinent to the issue, which can be asked by different fields of natural science, for example, 'What are the annual catch limits in a region?' and 'What are the levels of fish stocks in the North Sea?' This task will reveal that science has a lot to say about sustainability and ways to manage or resolve marine decline, but it does also have limitations. At this point students will be starting to consider other questions that science cannot answer and other ways of knowing, such as, 'Can we blame overfishing on overpopulation?' and 'What are the economic consequences of marine pollution?' Critical discussion and application of the Bubble Tool (LASAR Centre, 2019b) will highlight other disciplinary questions. Each group as a 'committee' will then create and present a statement to share with another 'committee' to recognize and explain how science contributes to solving the problem of marine decline and why it may have limitations. This activity can be formatively assessed through peer review/feedback, and by observing their presentations in conjunction with the Epistemic Insight Framework – version 2 (Billingsley 2022), where students will clearly identify and articulate methods and norms of thought for science, and begin to contrast with other disciplinary perspectives.

Activity 3 offers an interdisciplinary approach, where students are encouraged to be agentic learners and to think critically about how different domains of knowledge may be able to come together to create a synthesized resolution to marine decline. Supported through the Epistemic Insight 'Discipline Wheel', this pedagogical tool facilitates multidisciplinary thinking by exploring a range of different knowledge perspectives. The question or problem, for example: 'How to resolve overfishing or pollution?' is placed in the centre of the wheel. Each student in a group is allocated a distinct disciplinary specialism i.e Economics, Geography etc (a segment on the Discipline Wheel). Students demonstrate agency by considering how their individual disciplinary perspective addresses the issues of overfishing or pollution, with the aim to find solutions.

For example, the historian might consider how human behaviour has affected marine populations over the last century, whereas a socioeconomic standpoint may focus on how overfishing might be the cause of lost employment for those working in the fishing industry. Hence, gaining insight into the conundrum of sustainability and how science or other disciplinary approaches might investigate it. Moreover, students may begin to explore more philosophical or spiritual perspectives, advocated by Gus Speth as a 'new consciousness' (2023) who points out how the challenges of sustainability go beyond science's capabilities by highlighting humanity's flaws in terms of greed, selfishness and apathy (see Figure 7.4), and who promotes a multidisciplinary consciousness as a way forward.

Applying the Discipline Wheel facilitates critical thinking about big questions from a range of disciplinary perspectives including science, thus breaking down those 'subject' boundaries (Billingsley and Hazeldine 2020) which arguably are prevalent throughout the

> "I used to think the top global environmental problems were biodiversity loss, ecosystem collapse and climate change. I thought with 30 years of good science we could address those problems, but I was wrong.
>
> The top environmental problems are selfishness, greed and apathy - and to deal with these we need a spiritual and cultural transformation and we scientists don't know how to do that."
>
> Gus Speth

FIGURE 7.4 *Gus Speth's quote.*

timetable, underpinned by the current National Curriculum (DfE 2013). In their 'Committee' groups, students bring together their disciplinary specialisms to present a collective 'multidisciplinary' response to another group, which addresses their big question about overfishing or ocean pollution. This activity is a useful summative assessment of students' application and synthesis of different disciplinary perspectives, demonstrating student agency. By taking ownership of their learning, students critically evaluate the value of interconnecting distinct specialisms in response to the real-world problem of marine decline. Therefore, the presentations support students' understanding of sustainability issues through the process of 'teaching' their peers in an epistemically insightful way.

Conclusion and reflections

Applying innovative epistemic insight pedagogy to explore global issues through the multidisciplinary exploration of big questions enables students to become epistemic agents who can think critically about the nature, application and communication of knowledge. Hence, the workshops support students' collaborative thinking to develop links across a range of disciplinary specialisms, facilitating unrealized synthesis of distinct knowledge domains to achieve greater insight when addressing real-world challenges. A knowledge application that is coordinated and coherent, described as interdisciplinarity by Choi and Pak (2006).

Billingsley (2020) suggests that students can be helped to gain a richer and deeper understanding of the nature of science by discussing how science interacts and compares with a range of other disciplines, therefore acknowledging how real-world questions, opportunities and challenges such as producing sustainable energy or finding effective ways to stop marine decline may require multidisciplinary thinking. In addition, epistemic insight helps students appreciate the importance of exploring science-related problems not only through a variety of STEM disciplines but complements and enhances the solution through the inclusion of social sciences and humanities perspectives. Therefore, these epistemic insight-focused workshops offer practical teaching and learning benefits. Firstly, collaborative teaching opportunities with colleagues from differing specialisms become possible through practical science lessons and multidisciplinary discussions of contemporary topics. Secondly, students can become agentic learners who can think about, analyse and discover links between different knowledge domains, providing insight into future careers or fields of research, particularly how the actions driven by specific perspectives may impact current world problems.

Across the globe, the integration of collective fields of knowledge and expertise is being promoted as a means of achieving a more substantial impact when faced with real-world problems. If this connectivity is already being promoted in the real world then education must offer a more joined-up and holistic approach to learning, described by Albert Einstein in 1937 as 'Branches from the Same Tree' (2006). Thus connecting disciplines and forms of enquiry by integrating humanities and arts with science, engineering and medicine (National Academies of Sciences, Engineering, and Medicine, 2018). Using the phrase coined by Aristotle, 'The whole is greater than the sum of the parts', fits well with how education must respond to global challenges by moving away from the siloed approach prevalent in many education systems, transforming teaching and learning to be more 'future-ready'.

References

ASPIRES Research. (2022). *ASPIRES 3 Project Spotlight 2: 'Make it More Relevant and Practical': Young People's Vision for School Science in England.* London: IOE, UCL's Faculty of Education and Society. https://www.ucl.ac.uk/ioe/departments-and-centres /departments/education-practice-and-society/aspires-research/ additional-reports-and-resources (accessed 1 February 2023).

Billingsley, B. (2020). 'Science, Engineering and Big Questions', *School Science Review*, 101(376): 16–18. https://www.ase.org.uk/system /files/SSR_March_2020_016-018_Billingsley_theme_editorial.pdf (accessed 6 February 2023).

Billingsley, B. (2022). *The EI Curriculum Framework (Updated Version 2022) (Version 2)*. Zenodo. https://doi.org/10.5281/zenodo.7357633.

Billingsley, B. and L. Hazeldine (2020). 'Shattering the Subject Silos: Learning About Big Questions and Epistemic Insights', *Impact: Journal of the Chartered College of Teaching*, Summer (9).

Billingsley, B., M. Nassaji, S. Fraser, and F. Lawson (2018). 'A Framework for Teaching Epistemic Insight in Schools', *Research in Science Education*, 48(6): 1115–31. https://doi.org/10.1007/s11165-018-9788-6 (accessed 3 February 2023).

Blakemore, E. (2015). *Some Ocean Populations Declined by Nearly 50 Percent between 1970 and 2012*. Smithsonian Institution. https://www.smithsonianmag.com/smart-news/ocean-populations-declined-nearly-50-percent-between-1970-and-2012-180956660/ (accessed 1 February 2023).

Choi, B. C. K. and A. W. P. Pak (2006). *Multidisciplinarity, Interdisciplinarity and Transdisciplinarity in Health Research, Services, Education and Policy: 1. Definitions, Objectives, and Evidence of Effectiveness*. https://pubmed.ncbi.nlm.nih.gov/17330451/#:~:text=Results%3A%20Multidisciplinarity%20draws%20on%20knowledge,a%20coordinated%20and%20coherent%20whole (accessed 27 March 2023).

DfE (2013). *National Curriculum*. https://www.gov.uk/government/collections/national-curriculum (accessed 26 January 2023).

DfE (2021). 'COP 26: Everything you Need to Know About the Department's Quest to Put Climate Change at the Heart of Education', *Education Hub. Gov.uk*, 9 November. https://educationhub.blog.gov.uk/2021/11/09/cop-26-everything-you-need-to-know-about-the-departments-quest-to-put-climate-change-at-the-heart-of-education/ (accessed 6 February 2023).

Dunlop, L. and E. Rushton (2023). 'The Education for Sustainability Teachers and Students Really Want', *Schools Week*, 31 January. https://schoolsweek.co.uk/the-education-for-sustainability-teachers-and-students-really-want/ (accessed 31 January 2023).

Einstein, A. (2006). *The Einstein Reader*. New York: Citadel Press.

FAO (2018). *The State of the World Fisheries and Aquaculture: Meeting the Sustainable Development Goals*. Rome. Licence: CC BY-NC-SA 3.0 IGO. https://www.fao.org/3/i9540en/I9540EN.pdf (accessed 31 January 2023).

FAO (2023). *Fisheries and Aquaculture*. Food and Agriculture Organisation of the United Nations. https://www.fao.org/rural-employment/agricultural-sub-sectors/fisheries-and-aquaculture/en/ (accessed 31 January 2023).

Gordon, A., S. Simpson, and H. Hassanin (2022). 'Interdisciplinary Engineering Education a Need for the 21st Century. How Teaching Epistemic Insight Can Motivate and Empower Engineering Students to Make Wise and Compassionate Decisions in Real-World Contexts', *The Epistemic Insight Digest*, Autumn (5): 6–16. Zenodo. https://doi.org/10.5281/zenodo.7099429.

Holechek, J. L. et al. (2022). 'A Global Assessment: Can Renewable Energy Replace Fossil Fuels by 2050?', *Sustainability*, 14(8): 4792. https://doi.org/10.3390/su14084792 (accessed 6 February 2023).

IPBES. (2019). *Global Assessment Report on Biodiversity and Ecosystem Services of the Intergovernmental Science-Policy Platform on Biodiversity and Ecosystem Services (Version 1)*. Zenodo. https://doi.org/10.5281/zenodo.6417333.

IPCC (2022). *Climate Change 2022: Mitigation of Climate Change, IPCC Sixth Assessment Report*. https://www.ipcc.ch/report/ar6/wg3/ (accessed 6 February 2023).

LASAR Centre (Learning about Science and Religion). (2019a). *Epistemic Insight Discipline Wheel*. Zenodo. https://doi.org/10.5281/zenodo.5220854.

LASAR Centre (Learning about Science and Religion). (2019b). *Epistemic Insight Bubble Tool*. Zenodo. https://doi.org/10.5281/zenodo.5221113.

LASAR Centre (Learning about Science and Religion). (2023). *Epistemic Insight Framework- Primary and Secondary*. Zenodo. https://doi.org/10.5281/zenodo.7585233.

Masi, N. (2021). 'This Book has Culturally Diverse Characters: Isn't That Enough?', https://usspittingfacts.blogspot.com/2021/03/this-book-has-culturally-diverse.html (accessed 7 February 2023).

National Academies of Sciences, Engineering, and Medicine. (2018). *The Integration of the Humanities and Arts with Sciences, Engineering, and Medicine in Higher Education: Branches from the Same Tree*. Washington, DC: The National Academies Press. https://doi.org/10.17226/24988.

OECD (2018). *OECD Future of Education and Skills 2030- OECD Future of Education and Skills 2030*. https://www.oecd.org/education/2030-project/ (accessed 12 December 2022).

OECD (2019) *Learning Compass 2030- Organisation for Economic Co-operation and Development*. https://www.oecd.org/education/2030-project/teaching-and-learning/learning/learning-compass-2030/ (accessed 14 December 2022).

Oxfam (2023). *What is Global Citizenship?* https://www.oxfam.org.uk/education/who-we-are/what-is-global-citizenship/ (accessed 31 January 2023).

Perkins, K. (2022). '"Education is the Most Powerful Weapon Which You Can Use to Change the World" (Mandela)', in E. Tarry (ed.), *Challenges in Early Years and Primary Education: Employing Critical Thinking Skills During Turbulent Times*, 1st edn. Abingdon, Oxon: Routledge. https://www.routledge.com/Challenges-in-Early-Years

-and-Primary-Education-Employing-critical-thinking/Tarry/p/book
/9781032139852 (accessed 14 December 2022).
Safina, C. (1997). *Song for the Blue Ocean: Encounters Along the World's Coasts and Beneath the Seas*. New York: Henry Holt and Company.
Saxe, J. G. (1963). *The Blind Men and the Elephant*. New York: McGraw-Hill.
Schmaltz, D. (2003). *The Blind Men and the Elephant, Mastering Project Work*. Berrett-Koehler Publishers, Inc. ISBN 1-57675-253-4.
Speth, G. (2023). *A New Consciousness and the Eight-fold Way Towards Sustainability*. [Podcast]. https://anchor.fm/earth-charter/episodes/Gus-Speth--A-New-Consciousness-and-the-Eight-fold-Way-towards-Sustainability-eosn9o/a-a4b66th (accessed 7 February 2023).
UNESCO (2016). *Sustainable Development Goal 4 and its Targets*. UNESCO. https://en.unesco.org/education2030-sdg4/targets (accessed 14 December 2022).
United Nations (2021). *Global Citizenship*. United Nations. https://www.un.org/en/academic-impact/global-citizenship (accessed 14 December 2022).
United Nations (2023). *Renewable Energy – Powering a Safer Future*. United Nations. https://www.un.org/en/climatechange/raising-ambition/renewable-energy (accessed 1 February 2023).

PART IV

The Future of Knowledge and Higher Education

Higher Education is a pivotal time for students to develop their capacities to contribute to human flourishing in their life and work. The multidisciplinary environment of universities represents an unprecedented opportunity for building the epistemic insight needed for this.

It is well established that creativity, thinking critically and problem-solving are some of the most 'in-demand' skills – both for the jobs market and in projects that aim to increase human flourishing. These skills call for expertise and skills in multidisciplinary reasoning. Students and society will benefit if graduates are ready to question, work with and apply different types of knowledge. However, creative dialogue across disciplinary perspectives can be hindered by course and subject silos. 'Knowledge Labs' are spaces for encouraging dialogues between disciplines that don't often come together – like Dance and Computer Science. These spaces mean that students can gain insight into how disciplines work, learn about another discipline and reflect anew about their own discipline – seen in a new perspective. Students then work together on a collaborative project with the aim of producing products that can make the world a better place. And with the parallel aim of becoming wise and compassionate epistemic agents, better equipped to co-create holistic solutions to global and local opportunities and challenges. We are seeking funding to develop 'knowledge labs' in ten partner higher education institutions across five nations. Alongside guidebooks, website, scholarly papers and books, this proposed project will produce a portfolio of short videos by students published and shared online. Encouragement to participate will be provided through competitions and virtual spaces to join up with others and share ideas and expertise.

Meanwhile models of what this future might look like are being developed at Canterbury Christ Church University, picking up on the opportunities and challenges created by the arrival of GenAI.

Puzzles we explore:

- How can universities encourage collaboration across departmental divisions and provide a more joined-up experience that includes options like interdisciplinary courses, collaborative research projects and faculty development programmes designed to promote cross-pollination of ideas and perspectives.

Key ideas

1. **Epistemic insight in higher education:** Building upon the groundwork laid by the Epistemic Insight Initiative in schools, the Future of Knowledge project seeks to adapt and advance these strategies to work in higher education settings.

2. **Promoting co-creation and collaboration:** By bringing together researchers, tutors and students, this strand of the Future of Knowledge Initiative seeks opportunities and co-creates strategies to cultivate critical thinking, metacognition and an awareness of diverse perspectives across departments that have previously worked in silos.

3. **Goals and objectives**: Over time this strand of research aims to produce frameworks and practical tools that universities can share to help many more knowledge creators and workers to become wise and compassionate epistemic agents.

Statement of support

For the last six years, research and development into epistemically insightful approaches to education has produced an impressive impact in teacher education, schools and schools outreach in England. By opening classrooms to 'Big Questions', the rewards have included a new enthusiasm for learning together with creative and critical thinking about how to respond to society's most pressing questions and issues. As a result of this research, we are now seeing encouraging signs of a sea-change in how schools help students to get to grips with the multidisciplinary nature of knowledge. It is exciting therefore to see that in this proposed new initiative, the international reach and depth of the research will be increased. I am persuaded that if universities can capture the power and potential of epistemically insightful learning, tomorrow's graduates will be ready to make their mark in our collective journey towards mutual flourishing.

Rama Thirunamachandran, Professor, Vice-Chancellor and Principal, Canterbury Christ Church University, UK

8

Dancing with the Digital

An 'EI' Workshop Designed to Bridge Disciplines and Spark Students' Epistemic Creativity

Lee Hazeldine, Karl Bentley, Angela Pickard and Allan Callaghan

Introduction: The importance of cross-disciplinary education

The education system in some countries, including England, encourages students to choose between the sciences and the arts. One of the risks with specialization is if students only experience a narrow set of problems and become poorly equipped to work with problems that call for multidisciplinary approaches. Thinking and working across disciplines is perceived as an important competency in which to tackle the seismic challenges of digital/technological disruption and socio-political change within the twenty-first century

(Advance-HE 2022). Such competency is perceived as part of a wider trend in which we are moving from an 'age of enlightenment', with its discrete silos of thought, to an 'age of entanglement' (Oxman 2016) in which knowledge moves beyond boundaries and becomes entangled in new ways when faced with rapidly changing contexts and intersections within the world.

What is needed then is an education system that can accommodate students' disciplinary preferences while also equipping students with a good level of interdisciplinary understanding. These goals correspond with wider educational ambitions articulated by the OECD, where 'future-ready [citizens] will need both broad and specialised knowledge' (OECD 2018: 4) in which to think effectively across disciplinary boundaries within an increasingly changing and interconnected world.

With these thoughts in mind, researchers with the Epistemic Insight Initiative sought an opportunity to create an encounter for students from two specialist disciplines that are on opposite sides of the science–arts divide. This chapter describes the first workshop for the research which was delivered as an enrichment session for students on the BA (Hons) Dance Education and BSc (Hons) Computer Science courses at Canterbury Christ Church University.

Epistemic insight (EI) means 'knowledge about knowledge' and particularly, knowledge about disciplines and how they interact (Billingsley et al. 2018). The primary aim for the session was for students to learn about their own and each other's questions and perspectives on the world.

The aims of the research were to discover the following:

- What are students' attitudes to a cross-disciplinary workshop, designed to encourage experimentation with interdisciplinary approaches?

- What, if anything, do students learn about their own and each other's disciplines?

- To what extent can a collaboration across courses stimulate creative responses, allowing greater ideas and possibilities to flourish?

Why mix opposite disciplines?

Dance and Computer Science were deemed as appropriate disciplines for this intervention as an epistemic understanding of both the arts and sciences is increasingly recognized as vital for producing citizens that are open-minded to the potential of 'what if' when addressing changing issues and contexts within society (Leroux and Bernadska 2014). The transdisciplinary importance of both the arts and science for addressing contemporary challenges is manifest in the acronym STEAM: Science, Technology, Engineering, Arts and Maths. STEAM education has been linked to 'increased innovation' (Colucci-Gray et al. 2017: 28), and economic activity, which includes a mix of arts and science, has been recognized as performing better than those that do not (NESTA 2016). Tutors from both courses also participated in the workshop. The role of the tutors was to encourage and provoke critical discussion about the epistemic domains of their own discipline and their potential application to given questions, contexts and topics during the event. Two members of the EI team also participated to facilitate opportunities for interdisciplinary collaboration.

Workshop Part 1: The initial encounter

The setting for the workshop was a dance studio, providing students with a space to explore their own physical and scholarly contexts as both human persons and epistemic agents within particular disciplines – this first step was designed to encourage students' epistemic curiosity – how do students think about a problem as a dancer, and how do students think about it as a computer scientist? The workshop activities were designed to stimulate critical and creative dialogue about the role of human embodied agency in contemporary environments. Both dance and computer science consider ways multi-sensory environments can be interpreted through embodied experience – dance uses the physical, cognitive and sensory body to choreograph movements; computer science considers both input and output procedural responses to human actions.

The students were first asked to consider the space of a dance studio and think of ways in which their own discipline might interact with a human embodied experience within the space. To stimulate ideas, the tutors modelled possible ways in which their discipline might interact with bodies within the environment. The ways in which dance might react to the space through physical, cognitive and sensory responses were demonstrated and discussed; the ways computer science might react to the body in space through sensor technology and coding procedural responses were modelled and explored, primarily through the use of Arduino and Raspberry Pi interfaces (see Figure 8.1).

In the next section of the workshop, the tutors employed an EI strategy of posing a bridging question – which is a question that is pedagogically designed to bring the two disciplines together. Bridging Questions provide a fertile space for discussion about the similarities and differences between the disciplines, an objective in the Epistemic Insight Curriculum Framework (see an example within the Glossary in the final chapter).

In this case, the question was chosen because of its potential to provoke debate and, if needed, disrupt students' tendencies to view reality only through the lens provided by their own discipline. To this

FIGURE 8.1 *Sensor technology made available in the workshop.*

FIGURE 8.2 *Dancing robot example.*

end, the participants were asked: *Can a computer algorithm produce dance?*

To stimulate discussion, the students were shown a tangible video example (Boston Dynamics 2022) similar to the example shown in Figure 8.2.

The dancing robots in the video generate an uncanny effect in the viewer and provocatively disrupt typical disciplinary boundaries, suggesting a merging and blurring in which each discipline affects the other. The students were first asked to consider the question from the point of view of their own discipline; this required a critical consideration of the methods, processes and ways of thinking appropriate to the discipline and how these might address the question. After doing this, the students discussed their responses with students from the different discipline – with the aim of developing students' appreciation and insight into the differences and similarities between dance and computer science.

Findings and discussion from Part 1, the initial encounter

Students' responses to the bridging question highlighted the differences in mindsets experienced by students and tutors coming from separate disciplinary viewpoints. The Computer Science students believed that an algorithm could produce dance to the extent that it is understood as a procedural response with predetermined routines and patterns within a structure. Using the robot within the video as an example, the students described a mindset in which they perceived measured procedures and functions to be executed during specific timings that corresponded with the music. However, the Computer Science students conceded that neither computers nor the robot could think about their bodies in the ways humans can.

In contrast to a Computer Science mindset, the dance students asserted that there was 'much more to the moving body than the movements you see'; the dancer was always making cognitive decisions and embodied responses that were concerned with the qualitative 'meanings and expressions of the movements' – both groups of students agreed that computer algorithms used to produce the dancing robots could mimic these responses, but could not create the meanings and expressions sensed through the quality of human experience. The dance students also asserted that the computer algorithms could not experience the important aspect of empathy that is integral to a living embodied being – they highlighted how both dancers and their audiences could appreciate and admire the 'body's capacity for gesture and the beauty of muscle movements' in ways the robots never could; this appreciation extended to an empathy and admiration for the imagined efforts and training the bodies must have experienced to transcend typical bodily expectations in pursuit of aesthetic ideals. The dance students also felt that computer algorithm technology could not make decisions for improvisation that the embodied person makes within the flow of particular dancing contexts.

Both groups of students felt that the opportunity to enter into dialogue allowed them to develop insights and an appreciation of the potential and limitations within the methods and ways of understanding associated with each discipline. The Computer Science tutors and students highlighted how their own epistemic concerns generated a completely different and contrasting mindset while watching the video; during the viewing, they were 'trying to work out how the engineers did that? What procedures and functions within the code could have been used to create the dancing effect performed by the robot'.

Workshop Part 2: New ideas and creative works

Having considered different methods of understanding (the EITHER/OR associated with different disciplinary lenses in relation to a question) the students were then given a collaborative space to critically explore how two disciplines might converge (the AND that generates new potentials and possibilities of knowing at the point of intersection). In interdisciplinary groups, the students were asked to consider how the potential of the two disciplines might interact to produce an effective intervention. The challenge of exploring a space in new ways through the convergence of two disciplines provided an opportunity for students to build upon their epistemic curiosity and become epistemically creative agents. According to Battaly (2018: 176), epistemically creative people are 'motivated by curiosity to seek out and take on inquiries that engage their epistemic agency in ways that tend to generate something new'. Epistemic creativity often occurs when 'we cannot make sense of phenomena, anomalies, explanatory gaps, or the object of our inquiries' (2018: 170). As such, this activity provided the students with an opportunity to reflect on their understanding of ways of knowing connected with different disciplines and how these disciplines might interact to produce new insights and possibilities within particular contexts, the result of which cannot be given in advance – as such, the task provides a conduit in which modes of reflection, application and creativity corresponding to each discipline might interact to generate new realizations, resulting in increasingly complex and creative models of understanding.

Findings and discussion from Part 2: New ideas and creative works

Once given the project brief, students began to generate ideas about how the disciplines of Dance and Computer Science might creatively interact within the space of the Dance Studio – an environment explicitly designed for human movement. One idea was to include pressure sensors throughout the space to react to the amount of energy and effort given by dancers throughout a performance; another iteration of this concept was to judge where the pressure was in the room with regard to the audience and then make sounds and images respond to that area. Another idea was to use AR (augmented reality) and virtual reality glasses to position images, sound and text depending on where the dancers were moving – this was anticipated to enhance the meaning and expression of the dancers' movements.

During this collaborative activity, students worked together in an interdisciplinary group (see Figure 8.3). It was noted that students were inclined to seek strands of common interest to both disciplines: one example was the notions of movement and pressure, another example was the concept of rhythm and time. However, a reflection on these similarities soon revealed differences as the interpretation of these concepts tended to follow different trajectories depending on which course a student was aligned with. For example, when considering the concept of movement and pressure, whereas the computer scientists viewed pressure as a measurable quantifiable factor to execute procedural inputs and outputs, the dancers perceived

FIGURE 8.3 *Students participating in a discussion.*

pressure in terms of more refined expressive and symbolic gestures – one dance student stated that pressure for them was to 'walk, whip, flow, meander; it wasn't just understood in terms of [quantifiable] power'. This tendency to interpret these different strands through particular disciplinary lenses was also apparent in the tutor's dialogue with students too – although not exclusive, each tutor focused on their own epistemic lexicon; computer scientists focused on how the body could be negotiated with quantitative inputs, while the dance specialists highlighted the body's relation with qualitative outputs.

As the students articulated their approach to ideas, another theme became apparent, and this was the notion of style. One of the dance students highlighted how ballet leaned more towards the strict generalizable and repeatable routines they associated with science; however, other styles, such as Jazz and contemporary dance, were considered more free-form and improvised. This provoked a debate about where style can be found in Computer Science, with both the tutor and students declaring that there were definite styles to be found in the code programming conducted by unique individuals – as a tutor stated:

> There are definitely unique styles. When I look at a particular colleague's code, I know who has written it, I can see the human work behind the decision making, it is not crudely off some assembly line; for each content creator, there is some unique flair.

The debate therefore drew attention to a shared concern across disciplines for creativity, as a unique productive act. Although the creativity which occurs within each discipline might have a different epistemic focus, there was a consensus that how the given methods and knowledge were used, depended on the unique position of each individual's actions and relations to a given context, both within and beyond their own disciplinary boundaries; such contexts might radically alter the decisions, choices and strategies harnessed depending on the desired objectives/affect hoping to be achieved. Creativity was therefore perceived as an attribute of both disciplines and not exclusive to either, albeit that creativity in the areas of science and engineering tended towards the perception of and productive potential within the technology, whereas creativity within the art of dance leant towards the perception of and productive potential within culture (Oxman 2016).

Conclusion

Our research questions are as follows:

- RQ1: What are students' attitudes to a cross-disciplinary workshop that is designed to encourage experiments with interdisciplinary approaches?
- RQ2: What, if anything, do students learn about their own and each other's disciplines?
- RQ3: To what extent can a collaboration across courses stimulate creative responses, allowing greater ideas and possibilities to flourish?

In response to RQ1, we found that in the early stages of the workshop, students tended to stay with students in their own discipline and were reliant on their tutors to lead the discussion. However, students quickly warmed to working with peers from an 'opposite' discipline once they saw the examples that tutors presented of what the collaboration might produce. The strategy of introducing a contentious and provocative big question successfully aroused students' curiosity, disrupted habits of thinking and drew their attention to their different disciplinary assumptions and expectations.

In response to RQ2, we saw evidence of students building new insights into their own and each other's disciplinary perspectives. For example, as there was a recognition of a leaning towards qualitative and unique expressive relations in art in contrast to the generalized, measurable, quantifiable and repeatable within science. At the end of the session, students were asked what they considered to be the benefits and limitations within the intervention. Students stated that they enjoyed the session and that the opportunity to engage in interdisciplinary ways provided insights that would never have been considered in a regular singular disciplinary setting. As a dance student stated, a discussion 'provided the space to identify differences and similarities that we would have never thought about; interacting with others made us think how things can be combined and how so much could be done'.

In response to RQ3, we saw some evidence of students producing new creative works during the workshop. In the plenary, one of the dance students commented that the dialogue and interaction provoked new creative 'ways of thinking and possibilities within their own work that enhanced their practice'. As a Computer Science student pointed out, the intervention drew attention to the fact that there were 'lot more possible interactions between the two [disciplines] than you would initially think'. The key limitation identified by students was that there was not enough time and opportunity to fully explore the tools, forms, strategies and processes in any concrete practical way – this was a recommendation for future interventions, providing students the opportunity to bring to fruition their combined, interdisciplinary ideas.

References

Advance-he.ac.uk (2022). *Advance HE Strategy 2021–2024 | Advance HE*. https://www.advance-he.ac.uk/about-us/advance-he-strategy-2021–2024 (accessed 14 April 2022).
Battaly, H. (ed.) (2018). *The Routledge Handbook of Virtue Epistemology*. London: Routledge.
Billingsley, B. and S. Fraser (2018). 'Towards an Understanding of Epistemic Insight: The Nature of Science in Real World Contexts and a Multidisciplinary Arena', [Editorial]. *Research in Science Education*, 48: 1107–13 https://doi.org/10.1007/s11165-018-9776-x.
Billingsley, B and A. Litchfield (in Press). *Alchemy with Disciplines, School Science Review Boston Dynamics* (2022). https://www.youtube.com/watch?v=fn3KWM1kuAw&t=64s (accessed 28 April 2022).
Billingsley, B., M. Nassaji, S. Fraser, and F. Lawson (2018). 'A Framework for Epistemic Insight', *Research in Science Education*, 48(6): 1115–31.
Colucci-Gray, L. B., C. Cooke, R. Davies, D. Gray, and J. Trowsdale (2017). *Reviewing the Potential and Challenges of Developing STEAM Education Through Creative Pedagogies for 21st Learning: How Can School Curricula be Broadened Towards a More Responsive, Dynamic, and Inclusive Form of Education?* London: BERA.

Leroux, K. and A. Bernadska (2014). 'Impact of the Arts on Individual Contributions to US Civil Society', *Journal of Civil Society*, 10(2): 144–64.

NESTA (2016). *The Fusion Effect: The Economic Returns to Combining Arts and Science Skills*. https://media.nesta.org.uk/documents/the_fusion_effect_v6.pdf (accessed 15 April 2022).

OECD (2018). *The Future of Education and Skills: Education 2030*. Paris: Organisation for Economic Co-operation and Development.

Oxman, N. (2016). 'Age of Entanglement', *Journal of Design and Science*. https://doi.org/10.21428/7e0583ad.

9

The Nature-Knowledge-Values Framework – A Pedagogical Tool for Teaching NOS in Tertiary Education

Klaus Colanero and Kai Ming Kiang

Introduction

As university lecturers fostering scientific literacy in undergraduate students since more than ten years, we find the call to focus on *epistemic insights* (Billingsley 2017) particularly in line with our aims.

Science education at the tertiary level is usually included in science, engineering or medical curricula, while students of other disciplines are generally not required to engage with science education after secondary school. It may appear that, in the eyes of the public, university science education is only for specialist training and is unnecessary for students in non-science curricula. Such a situation, however, is in contrast with global science-related issues that we increasingly experience in recent years, from climate change to the Covid-19 pandemics, from food security to eating disorders, for example. More fundamentally, 'the citizen who is advised by a doctor about treatment options for themselves or a sick relative can only make an informed decision if they understand some basic science'. 'The citizen needs to have a basic understanding of science' (Taber 2017a).

It can be argued that, in a modern society, most people have been equipped with basic scientific knowledge after completing their secondary school studies. However, whether they agree with what they have learnt from their science classes in school is questionable (Miller, Scott and Okamoto 2006). Uncomfortably, one of the biggest challenges for science education today indirectly arises from the much-increased importance given to embracing diversity. In modern society, embracing diversity, be it of gender, race, political views or culture, is upheld as a civilized and desirable value. Besides its intrinsic value, embracing diversity may also contribute to mitigating conflicts, advocating communication across different groups of people and increasing mutual understanding (Pieterse and Noah 2007; Richardson and Gallagher 2011). However, when it comes to empirical and logical truth, modern science seemingly leaves little or no room for diversity. This, in turn, attracts strong controversies. For example, in New Zealand, the inclusion of Maori's traditional knowledge into a science curriculum has recently stimulated a heated debate (Gilson 2021). Similarly, the status of traditional Chinese 'science' too has been a controversial issue in Hong Kong and other places with Chinese cultural heritage (Kiang and Szeto 2021). So, are there universal truths or is science just a part of Western culture which contains the bias of Western supremacy? As such, is it not too naïve to assume that humans can really be objective in the pursuit of truth? These are just some of the typical questions raised against science outside of the science classroom.

To truly address these questions, it would seem appropriate to allow all students to understand more about the nature of science (NOS). Indeed, John Dewey (1916) already argued that familiarity with the scientific method, instead of scientific knowledge, is more important for non-science students at the tertiary level. However, how to teach NOS is a matter of continuous debate. In the past decades, in many countries, science educators have usually adopted the so-called consensus view in their secondary classrooms, assuming that there is an implicit consensus on the nature of science (NOS) and its teaching (McComas 2020; Erduran and Dagher 2014). In such curricula, students are taught that there are certain core elements of science, such as the empirical, theory-laden and tentative nature of scientific knowledge. And such core elements are supposed to make the greater validity of modern science self-evident. The consensus view provides a practical approach to NOS instruction for K–12, by hiding the complexity of NOS from students, and by providing a synthesis of what philosophers, historians and sociologists say about the meaning of NOS.

However, the consensus view has also received some major criticism as summarized in Hodson (2014) and McComas (2020). Its pedagogical effectiveness might be extremely limited in practice, because teaching a list of NOS elements without introducing other approaches to the study of nature, such as classical philosophical questions and ideas and traditional views of nature, may reduce the understanding of the rationale behind those NOS elements and may even result in an attitude of rejection towards science for those who are already sceptical. For such students, the learning about science becomes just a list to be memorized for obtaining good grades without incentive to internalize and integrate it with their personal beliefs and worldviews. Some scholars, such as Clough (2007), have suggested that the focus should be shifted from teaching the 'tenets of NOS' towards asking important and reflective questions about NOS. Introducing NOS as questions (Clough 2020), rather than answers, could turn out to be more meaningful and effective for students. It is also suggested that science be taught together with its history and philosophy for a more comprehensive understanding of the interactions between science and culture (Matthews 2015).

The suggestions made above are even more important for tertiary students who are more mature and have been exposed to all kinds of conflicting ideas. Instead of denying their doubts or confusion on science, it would be more constructive to give them the opportunity to challenge the perceived authority of science and guide them to critically compare science with other ways of understanding nature, such as the ways often adopted in different religions and different indigenous knowledge. This, from the point of view of teaching NOS, could be analogous to taking a 'vaccine' (Kiang and Szeto 2021), allowing students' minds to identify by themselves the strengths and limitations of modern science by placing it in front of the challenges that society presents. Moreover, in order for students to truly integrate science as a way of their own thinking, instead of just as facts to be studied and memorized, we think that science education should be designed in such a way that it enters in 'dialogue' with their specific culture, religion or other beliefs.

Billingsley (2017) suggested using big questions as the means to nurture K–12 school students' epistemic insight. The advantage of discussing big questions is that it naturally allows science and other ways of knowing to start off on equal ground. It easily bridges disciplinary gaps between science and other disciplinary knowledge, such as religions and cultures. For students at the tertiary level, we suggest that a deliberate and explicit reflection on the big Questions can be discussed along three more fundamental issues: (1) the fundamental beliefs about nature – the ontology issues, (2) the way of knowing – the epistemic issues, and (3) the values one upholds – the axiological issues. These three issues are indeed hidden underneath all scientific activities (Taber 2017b). We think that such a Nature-Knowledge-Values (NKV) framework is particularly suitable as a pedagogical tool at the tertiary level.

The Nature-Knowledge-Values framework

The NKV framework is intended mainly as a heuristic pedagogical tool that arises in the context of a core curriculum general education programme at the tertiary level: the General Education Foundation Programme of the Chinese University of Hong Kong, and in particular the course 'In Dialogue with Nature'. As a compulsory course for all undergraduates, roughly 4,000 students each year must take such a course, which is taught by at least 14 different lecturers in each semester (GEF, CUHK 2021). Being two of the course lecturers in the past ten years, we observed that the science-related classics-reading approach, the seminar-style discussions and the reflective essays writing, all contributed to implicitly lead both teachers and students to reflect on our values, on our notion of knowledge and on our beliefs about the nature of things (Colanero 2015; Kiang and Colanero 2020). However,

THE NATURE-KNOWLEDGE-VALUES FRAMEWORK

besides such implicit pedagogies to stimulate students' reflection, we thought pedagogically useful to try and make such a reflection more explicit both in our lesson preparation and in our teaching by proposing a more structured approach, the NKV framework.

We shall provide more details of the course in the next section when we present how the NKV framework can be used. Here, we should first clarify what the terms 'nature', 'knowledge' and 'values' refer to in the context of our framework.

- 'Nature' refers to all the things that exist and events that occur, that is, things and facts that are real (or at least some believe to be real), independently on whether we like them or not and independently on whether and how much we are aware of them. For example, atoms, God, aliens, black holes, gravitational force, ghosts, Platonic forms, the Chi (in traditional Chinese science) and so on. It should be noted that simply referring to the concept of reality, by itself, does not require taking an ontological position, but it stimulates teachers and students to explicitly reflect on our own existence and on what is actually there beyond what we can perceive and know.

- 'Knowledge' refers to our understanding of nature, that is, it refers to our representation of nature and to our endeavours to learn about nature, about what exists and how it exists: how do we know? For example, the atomic theory, meditation, Newton's laws of motion, the induction method, the experimental method, the symbolic correlations (in traditional Chinese science) and so on. The discussion of what ideas can be counted as knowledge and what not as knowledge, for example, beliefs, stimulates teachers and students to explicitly reflect on the methods of obtaining knowledge, and reflect on the limitations of human perceptions and cognitions. It also stimulates us to assess the consistency, internally and externally, of our representation of nature.

- 'Values' refers to anything that a person considers important. This does not strictly need to be based on reality, but it depends on how we *want* reality to be and how we don't want it to be. The types of values can be very broad, certainly including fundamental values such as honesty, love, happiness and justice, but also derived, or secondary, values such as medicines, money, energy sources, communication tools, traditions. Reflection on these values allows us to evaluate our priorities, personal goals or visions of the entire society. It also stimulates us to identify problems by comparing the difference between what we want reality to be and what it currently is.

In addition to reflecting on these three aspects individually, we find that, in our teaching practice, considering the six possible directional relationships between them (Nature → Knowledge, Knowledge → Nature, Nature → Values, Values → Nature, Values → Knowledge, Knowledge → Values) aids the teacher in formulating insightful questions and in showing how the various epistemic issues originate within the human experience. For example, it directs us to look into how our views on nature affect our knowledge. In this way we are led to examine the abilities and limitations of the human mind and human senses and the differences between physical and metaphysical theories. Also, it leads us to examine how our beliefs and knowledge about nature affect our values and vice versa. This helps us to introduce and structure the important discussion on the cultural and societal issues of science education such as *human aspect, cultural embeddedness, institutional aspect* and *rhetorical nature of science* (Taber 2017a).

The NKV framework consists of the three aspects, as well as all the possible relationships between them as mentioned above (see Figure 9.1). Such a framework is intended as a heuristic pedagogical tool whose usefulness lies in stimulating teachers and students to reflect on complex issues with a more structured approach. This may help students to reflect explicitly, and perhaps with greater sense of personal engagement, on their own prior knowledge and beliefs, or in general, their own worldview already constructed before taking this course.

The NKV framework that we are proposing is in line with some of the existing pedagogical approaches to NOS education. For example,

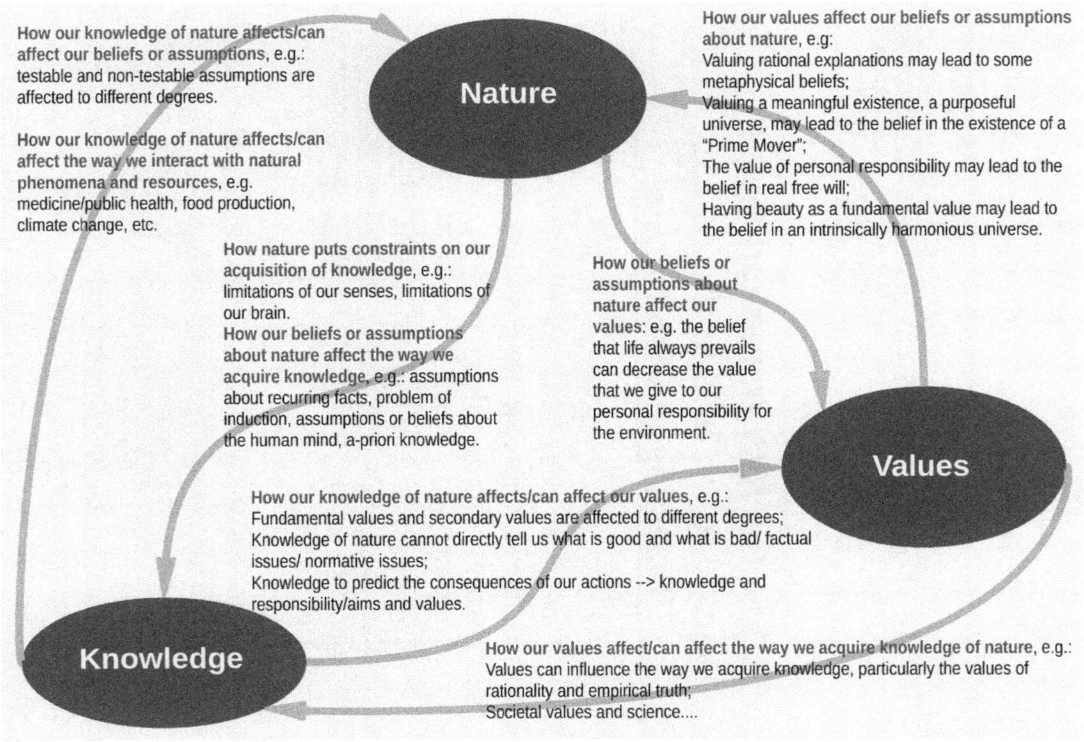

FIGURE 9.1 *Diagram illustrating the Nature-Knowledge-Values thinking framework (Klaus Colanero).*

it echoes the call for teaching the *knowledge about knowledge* (Billingsley 2017, McPhail 2020). It also echoes with the call for NOS education to be approached more comprehensively and contextually (Clough 2017, Allchin 2017, Osborne 2017, Hodson and Wong 2017). A pedagogical idea behind this framework is also to lead students to discover the complexity of science issues by themselves, so as to appreciate and understand the various aspects of the nature of science (McComas 2020; Taber 2017a; Clough 2017).

In the next section, we shall provide actual examples of how we use the NKV framework in the course 'In Dialogue with Nature'.

How the NKV framework helps us to teach NOS in the course 'In Dialogue with Nature'

The course 'In Dialogue with Nature' requires students and teachers to reflect on the human endeavour to understand and deal with nature through the reading and discussion of excerpts from classics of natural philosophy and science. The classics' excerpts that students read include texts by Plato, Aristotle, Euclid, Galileo, Newton, Darwin and Poincaré, as well as influential modern time scientists including James Watson, Eric Kandel and Rachel Carson. The excerpts also include texts that introduce traditional Chinese science, written by ancient Chinese 'scientist' Shen Kua and by two modern sinologists, Joseph Needham and Nathan Sivin. The pedagogical effectiveness of using classics has been reported (Kiang, Ng and Cheung 2015; Kiang, Cheung and Ng 2018; Kiang and Colanero 2020).

By presenting theories, arguments, questions, doubts produced by other human beings throughout history, the excerpts provide both a non-artificial context for NOS concepts and issues and a very wide range of opportunities to raise NOS-related discussion questions (Kiang and Colanero 2020). It should be noted that, while the course is based on classics reading, studying the classics is not the main aim of the course. Instead, we see reading, discussing and reflecting about the issues present in such classics as a medium for NOS education, which helps students to compare their scientific knowledge with their prior knowledge and beliefs or, more generally, worldviews, and then to try and integrate them if possible. Such an approach (Chan, Szeto and Wong 2012), compared to a specific science education course on either content knowledge or purely NOS theories, leads students to reflect on human knowledge of nature more in general, instead of immediately and directly focusing on what we nowadays call science.

Though such a course design is clearly conducive to develop teaching and learning activities that may lead to epistemic insights, it is nevertheless an institutional general education mandatory course with official Intended Learning Outcomes (ILOs) that are related, but not explicitly aimed, to a specific NOS education. In this context, we find the NKV framework helpful to (1) identify the specific content knowledge of the Intended Learning Outcomes, particularly in its relation to NOS, and to (2) formulate discussion questions more fine-tuned to achieve those ILOs.

Using the NKV framework to identify a specific content knowledge for the course's Intended Learning Outcomes

The Intended Learning Outcomes (ILOs) of the course are *to be able to*

1. *comprehend and discuss selected texts related to science, technology and nature*;
2. *identify the essential characteristics of how human beings view Nature*;
3. *formulate informed personal views on the societal implications of scientific explorations*;
4. *relate the developments in natural sciences highlighted in the course to contemporary human conditions*; and
5. *evaluate the scopes of application, achievements and limitations of highlighted scientific methods.*

Such broad intended learning outcomes are perfectly reasonable from an institutional perspective, particularly when the main intention is to stimulate and widen students' reasoning. In our teaching practice, however, we would like to probe students' achievement of those outcomes at a finer level, to better fine-tune teaching strategies. To this end we need to identify at least some subcomponents of those ILOs. We do so by analysing them from the point of view of the three aspects and six relationships of the NKV framework. Aside from the first ILO, which depends on the achievement of the other four and on the development of reading, writing and oral skills, our analysis for the remaining four ILOs is as follows:

- ILO no.2: *To be able to identify the essential characteristics of how human beings view Nature.*

    The corresponding NKV content knowledge is as follows:

    – Nature: The fundamental beliefs or assumptions about nature of different individuals and cultures, about the regularity of natural phenomena, whether natural phenomena follow fundamental laws; *primitive*, magical or mythological views of nature; assumptions or beliefs about the reality, physical and metaphysical; about the nature of the human being, particularly the human mind.

- ILO no.3: *To be able to formulate informed personal views on the societal implications of scientific explorations.*

    The corresponding NKV content knowledge is as follows:

    – Knowledge ↔ values: How our knowledge of nature affects/can affect our values; the concept of derived values (the means to achieve something); the non-direct relationship between factual knowledge and normative issues; scientific knowledge and responsible choices.

    – Knowledge ↔ nature: How our knowledge of nature affects/can affect our beliefs or assumptions; different implications of testable and non-testable assumptions; how our knowledge of nature affects/can affect the way we interact with natural phenomena and resources.

- ILO no.4: *To be able to relate the developments in natural sciences highlighted in the course to contemporary human conditions.*

    The corresponding NKV content knowledge is as follows:

    - Knowledge ↔ values: How new scientific discoveries and new technologies safeguard or threaten human values; how changing values affect the importance we give to scientific knowledge and how it directs technological developments.
    - Knowledge ↔ beliefs: How new scientific discoveries and new technologies safeguard or threaten existing beliefs about nature; how existing beliefs about nature make people more or less receptive of scientific developments.

- ILO no.5: *To be able to evaluate the scopes of application, achievements and limitations of highlighted scientific methods.*

    The corresponding NKV content knowledge is as follows:

    - Knowledge ↔ nature: How nature puts constraints on our acquisition of knowledge, for example, limitations of our senses, limitations of our brain and so on. How our beliefs or assumptions about nature affect the way we acquire knowledge, for example, assumptions about recurring facts and the problem of induction, assumptions or beliefs about the human mind.
    - Knowledge ↔ values: As before with particular focus on the famous 'is-ought problem', that is, factual knowledge cannot directly imply what should be done/what is good.

In this way we obtain a set of more detailed issues around which to design our course's discussion sessions.

It is essential to note that the content knowledge that emerges from the analysis of the ILOs through the NKV framework is not a static set of notions, but a specific set of possible relationships between human knowledge and other aspects of human life, that is, knowledge of how knowledge develops and influences.

Using the NKV framework to formulate discussion questions fine-tuned for the course's ILOs

In the implementation of such a general education course, the NKV framework helps us and our students to become more aware of important epistemic facts. First, that when we assess merits and weaknesses of a theory or of an approach to the study of nature, we necessarily refer to a set of values, either personal or shared by a group. Second, that, again necessarily, our rational arguments on the reliability of various forms of knowledge stand on the basis of some assumptions or beliefs about nature. These, though not irrational, should be made explicit and examined. Third, that both how we produce and how we use knowledge is not and cannot be unaffected by the values of the individual and of the community.

The resulting discussions, carried out iteratively throughout the whole course, allow students to realize not only the limitations of empirical knowledge and why scientists make use of a large set of theoretical tools, including inductive reasoning and notions of mathematical simplicity, but, at the same time, to also realize the social value of empirically testable hypotheses. When teachers or students find it convenient, they may use terms such as 'ancient Greek science', 'traditional Chinese science', 'Platonic or Aristotelian science', 'empirical science' and 'experimental science' (or experimental philosophy, as Newton would say). Certainly, the concept of 'modern science' must be thoroughly analysed and discussed, but the NKV framework leads to reflect naturally, non-arbitrarily, on the distinction between the epistemic approach of modern science and its specific theories, between its foundational values and the historical cultural context in which modern science emerged. Such an analytical reflection can be carried out with reference to the other types of science mentioned above.

Below we provide examples of specific discussion questions that we use in our seminar-style lessons, formulated with the help of the NKV framework. Referring to the possible interactions between Nature, Knowledge and Values facilitates our task of deciding what and how we should ask students, with the aim of directing their reflection towards essential aspects of NOS.

In the specific context of our classics-based course, we relate our discussion questions to specific passages from our text collection, but we could also relate them to any other relevant modern material such as scientific articles, essays or current issues.

In the following list we show (1) the aim of an in-class discussion, (2) a specific discussion question, (3) a brief description, from the point of view of the NKV framework, of the typical discussion that occurs in our classes and (4) the aspects of NOS that are involved, as taken from Taber (2017a):

- Aim: To realize how certain facts of nature affect what and how we can know (Nature → Knowledge).

    Question: *'If we could observe as many living organisms as we like (but still a finite number) with perfectly accurate instruments, do you think it would be possible to identify with certainty the features common to all living organisms?'*

    Discussion: We make use of Plato's and Aristotle's considerations with regard to the pursuit of *true knowledge* to reflect on the limitations of empirical observation (a fact of nature) and of the induction process (a knowledge acquisition process). Regarding such a question, students, in small groups, usually quickly understand the *problem of induction* and acquire greater awareness of the roots of the temporary nature of scientific knowledge.

    Aspects of NOS: *Nature of scientific knowledge, limits of science.*

- Aim: To understand that our choice of methodology to study nature affects what we believe to be the reality and how confident we are in our beliefs (Knowledge → Nature).

    Question: *'Why did the ancient Greeks believe that the celestial region is perfect? Why do we trust our current scientific understanding of the world (such as Newton's laws or evolutionary theory)?'*

    Discussion: The introduction of Newton and Darwin's findings allows students to reflect on why we trust our current scientific understanding and why ancient Greeks believed in theirs – it involves a change of methodology in obtaining knowledge. Teachers and students reflect on the separation between physical and metaphysical questions by the pioneers of modern science and on their quantitative and experimental methods in studying nature. Also, students gradually realize that modern science knowledge, while limited to physical phenomena, can make certain metaphysical beliefs more reasonable than others.

Aspects of NOS: *Nature of scientific knowledge, limits of science.*

- Aim: To reflect on how our values affect our beliefs or assumptions about nature (Values → Nature).

Question: *'Why would both the ancient Greek and ancient Chinese philosophers assume that things cannot come out of nothing or disappear into nothing?'*

Discussion: Teachers can guide students to realize that the fundamental reason for the assumption mentioned in the question is that those philosophers valued a rational account of nature, which can provide predictability, in contrast to *magical* or *primitive* views of nature, which trade rationality and predictability for more flexible and ad-hoc explanations.

Aspects of NOS: *Nature of scientific knowledge, human aspect of science, cultural embeddedness of science.*

- Aim: To reflect on how our beliefs or assumptions about nature can affect our values (Nature → Values).

Question: *'Do you think that evolution by natural selection improves the species?'*

Discussion: Students realize that the belief that there is a finality in the evolutionary process may, for example, lead people to give more value to competition or to be less concerned about human effects on the environment. At the same time, through teacher-led discussions, they acquire greater awareness that such a belief, like other metaphysical

THE NATURE-KNOWLEDGE-VALUES FRAMEWORK

assumptions, are not obvious and are not implied by our scientific knowledge.

Aspects of NOS: *Human aspect of science, cultural embeddedness of science.*

- Aim: To realize that scientific theories do not emerge from a completely value-free process or environment (Value → Knowledge).

Question: '*How do Poincaré's arguments on the role of beauty and usefulness in scientific research fit with the modern science requirement of objectivity and testability?*'

Discussion: Most students highlight the fact that personal interests and preferences may provide a strong motivation for engaging in specific scientific investigations. On the other hand, they usually need the teacher's guidance in realizing that, at the same time, such a bias does not compromise the non-subjectivity of scientific knowledge.

Aspects of NOS: *Logic and creativity in science, nature of scientific knowledge, nature of scientific method, human aspect of science, cultural embeddedness of science.*

- Aim: How scientific knowledge can (and perhaps should?) orient our choices and actions at the service of our values (Knowledge → Value)?

Question: '*Do you think that scientific knowledge has anything to do with a responsible way of living in society?*'

Discussion: This question, particularly with the help of an excerpt from Rachel Carson's *Silent Spring*, allows to look at another aspect of the relationships between knowledge of nature and human values. Can a responsible person neglect scientific knowledge when making decisions about nature? Is there a moral duty for everyone to have sufficient knowledge about nature, so that we can correctly predict the consequences of our actions, that might affect ourselves as well as the society, and act according to our values?

Aspects of NOS: *Human aspect of science, institutional aspect of science, rhetorical nature of science.*

Scope and limitations of the NKV framework in our teaching practice

Though we found the NKV framework very helpful in our teaching, we realized that contrary to what we might have hoped, it does not automatically increase students' epistemic insight in all areas. In fact, from students' arguments during in-class discussions and in written assignments, we can clearly observe that, throughout the course, their awareness of epistemic problems grows and widens, but they continue to struggle with some important specific issues. One of the authors ran a series of 'surveys for learning' as a preliminary investigation designed around the NKV content knowledge of the ILOs (Colanero 2022). The main aim of the surveys was testing coherence of students' answers. From such surveys, we have found three specific and fundamental NOS issues for which students appear to struggle more in forming non-self-contradictory views:

- the distinction between the concepts of reality and physical phenomena.
- the difference between reasonable inductive inference and logical deduction.
- the relationship between factual knowledge and normative issues (particularly the fact that, though scientific knowledge can and should inform our choices, it does not directly indicate what we should do).

Further work is in progress both to support the preliminary findings and to test the effectiveness of more specific teaching interventions.

Conclusion

The strategy described above allows teachers and students to not only identify the fundamental epistemic or, more generally, philosophical problems related to science, but also to understand how they originate within the human experience. This provides a conceptual contextualization of science education, particularly of the various NOS aspects proposed in the science education literature (McComas 2020; Taber 2017a; Clough 2017). Taber's insightful discussion on science, beliefs and values (Taber 2017c) can emerge naturally and in an organically connected way from the NKV framework. It should be clear that the NKV framework does not aim to reduce the complexity of science and science education. Rather, it can be said that it brings the complexity to light by requiring teachers and students to look explicitly and deliberately at all the possible interactions between our beliefs or assumptions about nature, our knowledge and our values, and by consequently discovering the origin of the various aspects of NOS.

We do not see the NKV framework as an alternative to the existing NOS teaching approaches, but as a framework which can be used in synergy with them. Besides providing a natural contextualization for NOS teaching, it may also contribute to addressing some concerns regarding the use of lists of NOS aspects in teaching (Kampourakis 2016, Erduran, Kaya and Dagher 2018, Romero-Maltrana and Duarte 2022).

References

Allchin, D. (2017). 'Beyond the Consensus View: Whole Science', *Canadian Journal of Science, Mathematics and Technology Education*, 17: 18–26. https://doi.org/10.1080/14926156.2016.1271921.

Berkovitz, J. (2017). 'Some Reflections on "Going Beyond the Consensus View" of the Nature of Science in K–12 Science Education', *Canadian Journal of Science, Mathematics and Technology Education*, 17: 37–45. https://doi.org/10.1080/14926156.2016.1271927.

Billingsley, B. (2017). 'Teaching and Learning About Epistemic Insight', *School Science Review,* 365: 98, 59–64.

Chan, C. W., W. M. Szeto, and W. H. Wong (2012). *In Dialogue with Nature*, 2nd edn. Office of University General Education, the Chinese University of Hong Kong. Hong Kong.

Clough, M. P. (2007). 'Teaching the Nature of Science to Secondary and Post-secondary Students: Questions Rather than Tenets', *The Pantaneto Forum*, 25(1): 31–40.

Clough, M. P. (2017). 'History and Nature of Science in Science Education', in K. S. Taber and B. Akpan (eds), *Science Education*, 39–51. Sense Publishers: Rotterdam.

Clough, M. P. (2020). 'Framing and Teaching Nature of Science as Questions', in W. McComas (ed.), *Nature of Science in Science Instruction: Rationales and Strategies*, 271–82. Springer International Publishing.

Colanero, K. (2015). 'Two Dialogues for a Foundation Beyond the Two Cultures Dichotomy', in *General Education International Conference 2015 – Foundations of General Education,* 12–13 June. The Chinese University of Hong Kong. https://www.oge.cuhk.edu.hk/oge_media/uge/conf2015/theme3_Colanero.pdf.

Colanero, K. (2022). 'The Nature-Knowledge-Values Framework as an Assessment-for-Learning Tool in Transdisciplinary Education', in *Teaching and Learning Innovation EXPO 2022*. The Chinese University of Hong Kong. https://www.cuhk.edu.hk/eLearning/expo2022/. Oral presentation accessible at https://cuhk.ap.panopto.com/Panopto/Pages/Viewer.aspx?pid=4272ac94-1fe7-4a79-82e5-af8d003016af&id=fc5d20c6-61c1-48ae-8a60-af7b0097a0a0&advance=true.

Dewey, J. (1916). *Democracy and Education*. New York: Macmillan.

Erduran, S. and Z. R. Dagher (2014). 'Reconceptualizing Nature of Science for Science Education', in *Reconceptualizing the Nature of Science for Science Education. Contemporary Trends and Issues in Science Education*, Vol 43. Dordrecht: Springer. https://doi.org/10.1007/978-94-017-9057-4_1.

Erduran, S., E. Kaya, and Z. R. Dagher (2018). 'From Lists in Pieces to Coherent Wholes: Nature of Science, Scientific Practices, and Science Teacher Education', in J. Yeo , T. Teo, and K. S. Tang (eds), *Science Education Research and Practice in Asia-Pacific and Beyond*. Singapore: Springer. https://doi.org/10.1007/978-981-10-5149-4_1.

GEF, CUHK (2021). *General Education Foundation Programme Webpage*. https://www.oge.cuhk.edu.hk/index.php/en/2011-06-22-08-12-11/programme-content.

Gilson, K. (2021). 'Science Can't be Pākehā or Māori, it's Just Science', *Reader Report in Stuff*, 2 August. https://www.stuff.co.nz/stuff-nation/125940471/science-cant-be-pkeh-or-mori-its-just-science.

Hodson, D. (2014). 'Chapter NOS in the Science Curriculum', in M. R. Matthews (ed.), *International Handbook of Research in History, Philosophy and Science Teaching*. Springer, 911–70.

Hodson, D. and S. L. Wong (2017). 'Going Beyond the Consensus View: Broadening and Enriching the Scope of NOS-Oriented Curricula', *Canadian Journal of Science, Mathematics and Technology*

Education, 17(1): 3–17, https://doi.org/10.1080/14926156.2016.1271919.

Kampourakis, K. (2016). 'The "General Aspects" Conceptualization as a Pragmatic and Effective Means to Introducing Students to Nature of Science', *The Journal of Research in Science Teaching*, 53: 667–82. https://doi.org/10.1002/tea.21305.

Kiang, K. M., D. H. C. Cheung, and A. K. L. Ng (2018). 'Nurturing Scientific Literacy for All Undergraduates via Science Classics', *Proceedings of the International Science Education Conference 2018*, 102–20.

Kiang, K. M. and K. Colanero (2020). 'A Classics Reading Approach to Nurture Epistemic Insight in a Multidisciplinary and Higher Education Context', in *Science Education in the 21st Century – Re-searching Issues that Matter from Different Lenses*. Singapore: Springer Nature.

Kiang, K. M., A. K. L. Ng, and D. H. C. Cheung (2015). 'Teaching Science to Non-Science Students with Science Classics', *American Journal of Educational Research*, 3(10): 1291–7. https://doi.org/10.12691/education-3-10-13.

Kiang, K. M. and W. M. Szeto (2021). 'Teaching Traditional Chinese Science as a Part of a NOS Curriculum in Hong Kong', *Science & Education*, 30: 1453–72.

Matthews, M. R. (2015). *Science Teaching: The Contribution of History and Philosophy of Science*, 2nd edn. Routledge.

McComas, W. F. (2020). *Nature of Science in Science Instruction*. Springer.

McPhail, G. (2020). 'Twenty-First Century Learning and the Case for More Knowledge About Knowledge', *New Zealand Journal of Educational Studies*, 55: 387–404. https://doi.org/10.1007/s40841-020-00172-2.

Miller, J. D., E. Scott, and S. Okamoto (2006). 'Public Acceptance of Evolution', *Science*, 313: 765–6.

Osborne, J. (2017). 'Going Beyond the Consensus View: A Response', *Canadian Journal of Science, Mathematics and Technology Education*, 17: 53–7. https://doi.org/10.1080/14926156.2016.1271920.

Pieterse, A. L. and M. C. Noah (2007). 'A Socialization-Based Values Approach to Embracing Diversity and Confronting Resistance in Intercultural Dialogues', *College Student Affairs Journal*, 26(2): 144–51, https://eric.ed.gov/?id=EJ899388.

Richardson, N. and T. Gallagher (2011). *Education for Diversity and Mutual Understanding: The Experience of Northern Ireland*. Peter Lang.

Romero-Maltrana, D. and S. Duarte (2022). 'A New Way to Explore the Nature of Science: Meta-categories Rather Than Lists', *Research in*

Science Education, 52: 239–57. https://doi.org/10.1007/s11165-020-09940-y.

Taber, K. S. (2017a). 'Reflecting the Nature of Science in Science Education', in K. S. Taber and B. Akpan (eds), *Science Education*. Sense Publishers.

Taber, K. S. (2017b). 'Science Education as a Field of Scholarship', in K. S. Taber and B. Akpan (eds.), *Science Education*, 3–19. Sense Publishers.

Taber, K. S. (2017c). 'Beliefs and Science Education', in K. S. Taber and B. Akpan (eds), *Science Education*, 53–9. Sense Publishers.

PART V

Language, Technology and Inclusivity

The theme for this part is the importance of exploring diverse viewpoints in knowledge creation and education, particularly in the context of evolving technologies like AI and autonomous systems. The authors engage with the challenge of how to create a more open and inclusive future for knowledge creation and education and make suggestions about how to make use of opportunities we already have such as the teaching of languages in schools.

Puzzles we can explore are as follows:

- AI-assisted searching: We share a prototype of what a future search engine might look like. As we move towards the next stages of development, it is important to have in mind that every transaction we do with AI can reveal something about ourselves – so what might interacting with this new tool convey?

- Can we design educational approaches that encourage dialogue about complex issues across cultures and perspectives? What roles can technology play to help to facilitate inclusivity?

- There are risks that AI and autonomous vehicles might reinforce existing power structures and exclude marginalized communities. If our goals are to have inclusive approaches to technology, how can learning about languages help to prepare future generations to navigate this complex landscape?

Key ideas

1. **The limitations of current search engines in answering 'Big Questions':** By relying on popularity as a ranking factor, traditional online search engines can limit our access to diverse perspectives and insights on significant questions. This can lead to the false perception of popular opinions as 'correct' answers, deterring intellectual curiosity and exploration.

2. **The pedagogical and ethical need for broader perspectives in education:** Now that we are becoming more aware of our own sociocultural contexts, we have an incentive and opportunity to rethink our perspectives and engage with the future of knowledge in ways that acknowledge and integrate diverse viewpoints.

3. **Rethinking knowledge acquisition and representation in the age of AI and automation:** The case study explored in this chapter highlights the need for new ways of thinking and communicating to avoid excluding marginalized groups and fostering wider inclusivity. The author argues that limitations in language and thought can hamper progress in fields like AI and autonomous vehicles, necessitating more diverse perspectives and innovative approaches to knowledge creation and utilization.

Statement of support

Epistemic insight – essentially 'knowing how we know' is of immense importance in our information-rich age. In school and university education we need to encourage the breakdown of barriers between different subjects and areas of knowledge thus enhancing pupils'/ students' ability to synthesize in order to see the bigger picture. This will better equip them for solving the complex problems that pervade our world, including global poverty, food shortage and climate change.

Epistemic insight is also important outside the specifically educational context. We are all constantly bombarded with information via the media, via our devices and so on but we need to be able to judge its reliability. Some claims are false, others are exaggerated or sensationalized. How can we tell? The 'Ask for Evidence' campaign run by Sense About Science is one approach to this problem, but I suggest that developing epistemic insight (which may include asking for evidence) is more widely applicable across a range of subject areas.

However, we need to know how best to develop and encourage epistemic insight. Thus, I commend LASAR for developing this initiative. The potential contribution, both within 'formal' pedagogy and in society at large, to enhancing our ability to integrate our knowledge and skill sources to solve current problems and to meet global societal targets, is very significant.

John Bryant, Professor Emeritus of Biosciences,
University of Exeter, UK

10

Building a Smarter Search Engine

Aryn Litchfield

Introduction

Search engines have been widely used and publicly available since the mid-1990s, and as this technology became readily accessible in the classroom there was an exponential rise in its use as an educational tool. Though the medium of delivery has evolved slightly, offering broader ways to connect to search engines through technology such as smart phones, the basic operation of a search engine remains relatively the same. As powerful and useful search engines are, as a tool, they can also reintroduce knowledge silo's that lead to informational gaps, limiting a student's potential in developing more insight and research agency. Low, Yeoh and Lau (2008) state that using the internet may give students 'the sense that they have the world's knowledge at their fingertips, but it does nothing to the critical thinking ability which is essential for conducting effective research'. The research and development of our own epistemic and pedagogical tools is directly concerned with facilitating critical thinking and encouraging epistemic insight to develop in students; in this sense we see search engine technology as an obvious yet challenging area to develop.

Identifying problems with conventional search

Research agency is an area we felt search engines were, to a degree, failing students, and while factors of search engine literacy are important to develop, it is broadly recognized that the following areas are problematic, namely:

1. Convenience is often favoured over being research-engaged, that is, the first few answers are usually accepted (Morrison 2016).

2. A search engine like Google, despite having the ability to source some sixty trillion (and counting) pages, does not imply that users interact with the data on such a grand scale; it has been well documented that the majority of users rarely make it past the second page (Morrison 2016).

3. Fisher, Goddu and Keil (2015) suggest that knowledge acquired through a search engine potentially creates bias which 'may endow children with an adaptive confidence that their understandings are well grounded'. Firth et al. (2019) build on this idea by referring to the notion of 'illusion of greater than actual knowledge', implying that sometimes users greatly overestimate what they have learnt through their limited search context.

4. Knowledge retrieved from a search query is often limited to a particular silo of knowledge.

Point 4 is where we saw a direct barrier to developing insight. For example: if a user inputs the search query 'why is the sky blue?' into Google search, the knowledge base that is returned relates to explanations of why the sky is blue from a physics perspective – with explanations of wavelength diffraction dominating the first five or so pages. Such explanations are not wrong, that is, the search engine has successfully provided a relevant body of knowledge according to the user input. The trouble is that this body of knowledge is an answer, but not the only answer or approach, for example, nowhere on the first few pages are we provided with a biological perspective, or a philosophical explanation, and certainly theological perspectives are not found without dramatically altering the search query itself. In other words, the content retrieved by a search engine is often limited to a particular silo of knowledge, and sometimes that disciplinary silo is not actually identified, further obfuscating a pathway for the agent to be able evaluate the nature of the content itself.

In a sense, even if the user follows 'good' search practices, they are ultimately at the mercy of the internal logic of the engine itself, even when questions of sponsorship and profiling are set aside. The fundamental problem is that if users are normalizing their expectation to believe that the technology is 'the researcher', users are at risk of presuming that the returned answers are (1) correct and (2) comprehensive.

While it may certainly be suggested that search engines can be improved to 'not only offer web documents' but also 'make explicit the *map* of knowledges or structural semantics used to come at them' (Morrison 2016). We felt the impetus for change should directly include mechanisms that help develop the epistemic insight of the agent. Insofar that we recognize that increasing technological literacy in using a search engine is very important, but also argue that developing an 'epistemic insightful search' helps students to better refine their search query and evaluate it; both work in unison to develop research agency. The point being made here is that search literacy and lack of epistemic insight present barriers in search agency, therefore both would need to be addressed, and we felt the best way to address this was to develop a 'smarter search engine' model (SSE) that could be used to help educators.

New developments in search

Many technologists are pointing out the potential of AI search tools such as GPT3 possibly revolutionizing 'search'. While such technology offers new and interesting ways to interact with 'search', our own experiences with it reveal similar issues we saw occurring in conventional search. The fundamental issue is that a powerful tool like ChatGPT (likewise conventional search) works far better when the student has already developed higher-level thinking which we call here 'epistemic insight'.

We asked ChatGPT (2023) a series of questions and quickly discovered that while the answers it provides are generally useful, they do not overcome knowledge silos. The following question with ChatGPT's response is a good example of this:

> In the discipline of science, addressing how we live better with water, what are the key questions, methods, and norms of thought. Provide an answer suitable for a 12-year-old please:
>
> When addressing how we can live better with water through the lens of science, the key questions to ask include: How does water cycle through the environment? What impact does water pollution have on ecosystems? What strategies can be used to conserve water resources?

The methods used to answer these questions include making observations, conducting experiments, and testing hypotheses. The norms of thought involve developing theories based on evidence and using a systematic approach to analyse data.

The question itself underwent an evolution of changes as we observed that ChatGPT, like most interactive technologies, operates better when the question is refined. Despite its answer being acceptable, it is important to recognize that it is contextualized through, what appears to be, the lens of environmental science and ecological concerns. The environmental context is obviously a highly relevant and contemporary one, but it is somewhat limiting in approach, in recognizing this we decided to evolve the question further:

> Through the disciplines of chemistry, biology, and physics, addressing how we live better with water, what are the key questions, methods, and norms of thought. Provide an answer suitable for a 12-year-old please: *When addressing how we can live better with water through the lenses of chemistry, biology, and physics, the key questions to ask include: How is water chemically composed? How does it interact with organisms and the environment? What physical properties of water affect its use and availability?*
>
> *The methods used to answer these questions include making observations, conducting experiments, and testing hypotheses.*

The norms of thought involve developing theories based on evidence and using a systematic approach to analyse data.

ChatGPT has provided a more robust answer that recognizes numerous discussion points and factors, so in that sense it is being more 'insightful', interdisciplinary and interconnected with science as a broader discipline. However, it got to that point because we pushed it in that direction using our own 'research agency', the issue here is that nowhere in the first response do we see a direct pathway for a potential student to follow the same process as we underwent without prior scaffolding. The general concern here is that a potential student might assume that 'how can we live better with water?' in the discipline of science is answered solely through areas connected to environmental science if using the first reply as the content source.

Our general observation is that ChatGPT is a different way to interact with content, though we do not believe it necessarily overcomes knowledge silo's from forming. That said, such a tool, if implemented in the right way, specifically one that develops research agency and encourages insight, has a lot of potential.

Designing a Smarter Search Engine

Our design philosophy for a Smarter Search Engine (SSE) is directed at encouraging research agency and insight. We believe that one way to achieve this is in helping students develop an understanding regarding the interdisciplinary nature of knowledge and making 'search' more transparent in identifying the lenses through which content is sourced. We want the student to have their agency empowered through a search tool, not simply supplied with more content. Such a prerequisite indicates that students need to be encouraged to search insightfully, which is one of the primary reasons behind the design choice of using the Discipline Wheel (Figure 10.1) foregrounded rather than hidden behind the algorithm.

The aesthetically pleasing design, beyond providing a visual aid, is fully customizable, allowing for multiple disciplines to be searched. Users can also assign custom disciplines, with different colours and

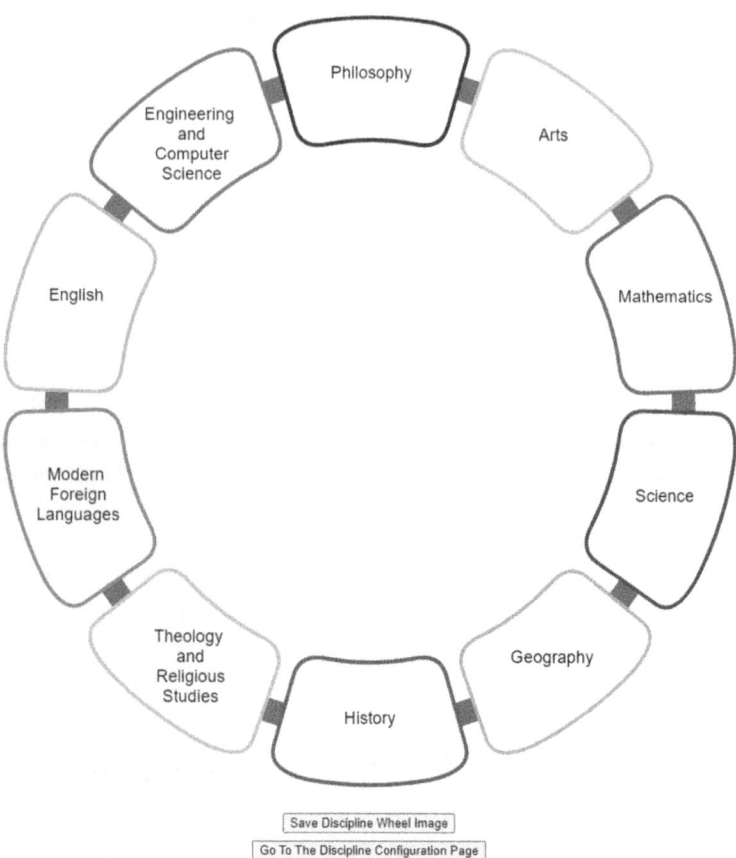

FIGURE 10.1 *EI Discipline Wheel in the foreground of the search engine.*

save them as templates for future use and/or download as an image for dissemination; the design layout is meant to be as intuitive and 'playful' as possible inviting its use.

How it works

A potential classroom exercise could be to direct students to: Enter a search term into the search bar > select the disciplines they wish to retrieve content on > indicate the number of results they want per page > Select search.

BUILDING A SMARTER SEARCH ENGINE

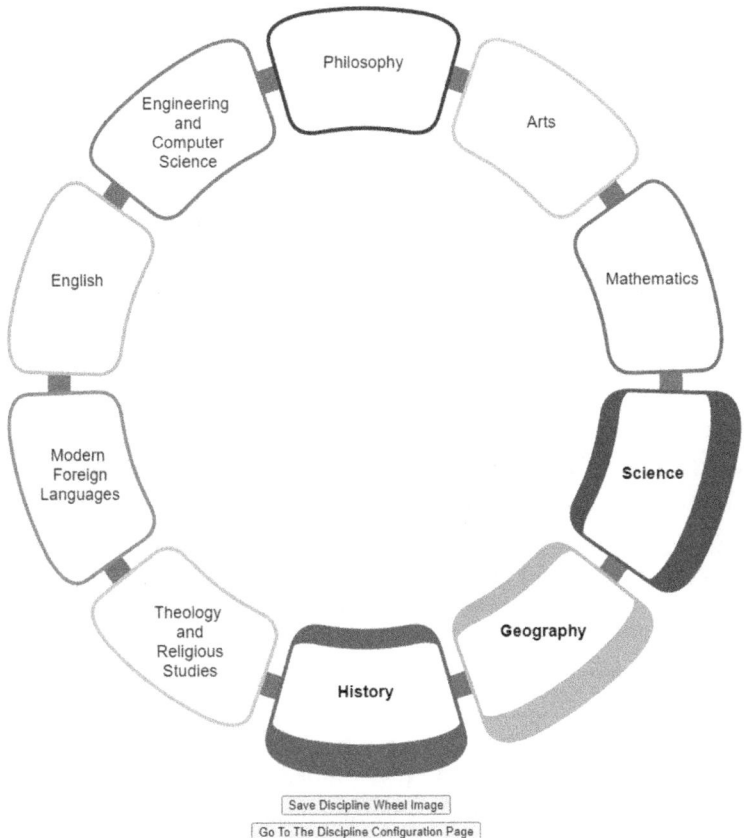

FIGURE 10.2 *Selecting disciplines to search 'How can we live with water better?'*

In Figure 10.2 we have used the search term 'how can we live with water better?', selected science, geography and history as our disciplines, and highlighted that we want three results per discipline. In the current state of our 'Smarter Search Engine', a predefined and preloaded set of results will then be shown to the students.

The 'playful' nature of our epistemic tool provides a direct experiential and tangible interaction. We view this type of engagement as being integral to helping students develop and reinforce epistemic knowledge. In essence, the student takes control of the search parameters and can directly explore the nature of the question set by the teacher through multidisciplinary lenses. By encouraging students' epistemic curiosity in this way, there is potential for students to develop a greater understanding of not only the interconnected nature of knowledge, but also a clearer understanding of how knowledge can be refined.

By using the 'Smarter Search Engine', students are directly experiencing how the parameters of search affect the outcome, this essential critical interaction extends beyond 'tool literacy', that is, knowing how to use the tool, but rather it directly encourages 'epistemic literacy'. In other words, creating the space for insight and critical inquiry to flourish.

As conventional search engines cannot reliably 'make explicit' the map of knowledge (Morrison 2016), students would need to be up-skilled considerably to develop semantic awareness in refining their answers. While such a skill set should be developed to the highest degree, there is still no guarantee that conventional search engines would return content that helps identify multidisciplinary discussions. Furthermore, in our experience, there is no guarantee (depending on the nature of the search query) that semantic refinement would produce appropriate content suited to the classroom; search engines return content in specific ways. For example, Heersmink notes: 'just because many hyperlinks point towards a website, is no guarantee that it contains epistemically useful information' (2018). There are further implications that go beyond the discussion outlined here, for example, the realities of 'Web 2.0' and user-generated knowledge bases further problematizes how students access content. Therefore, we consider it important that EI thinking is also presented in terms of search practices.

Using our 'Smarter Search Engine', the search process is far more transparent, and students get to see exactly how each discipline relates to a specific body of knowledge. We see these as beneficial processes, but ultimately, we want this epistemic tool to help encourage epistemic insight – we have based the design of the tool on classroom exercises and workshops we have conducted, including past research of using the Discipline Wheel. Acknowledging this, we feel confident that our SSE can be used to facilitate/encourage epistemic insight.

Current limitations

In the future, it is hoped that our 'Smarter Search Engine' can be connected directly to search engine results and technologies such as ChatGPT, through the development of a filtering algorithm. However, the current implementation of our 'Smarter Search Engine' is focused on providing educators with a pedagogical tool that can be reliably controlled and scaled according to their needs, without having to be concerned with any problems that occur when using 'search' more broadly.

Pre-loading search results

As stated, our 'Smarter Search Engine' is fully customizable, and this extends to search results too. Educators/teachers using this tool can set their questions, determine how many disciplines (customize them) they want to work with and then import into the engine the results they want students to see for each discipline. This type of control allows teachers to construct their lesson/workshop around specific themes and scale it according to age groups.

Alternatively (depending on age group), it is also possible to begin with a static Discipline Wheel and present students with the opportunity to develop the search results guided by the teacher. In such a way, KS5 students could be tasked with this approach and develop the results to be used for, as an example, KS3.

How do students perceive it?

We held an exhibition at the Royal Society of Chemistry (September 2022). Among the scholars, experts and educators present, we invited twenty-four students and their tutors from four schools, one of which comprised international students. The exhibition itself showcased several projects related to epistemic insight, including the 'Smarter search engine' (details of the event are located at our 'Future of Knowledge' homepage: futureofknowledge.com).

We saw this as a direct opportunity to gather some feedback from students regarding the search engine itself. To achieve this, we provided the students with a survey to complete at the end of the day which captured their thoughts and feedback. At the time the 'Smarter Search Engine' existed as a proof of concept with only limited functionality. This meant we were able to demonstrate how it works and provide examples of what it can achieve to the students. However, the 'playful' component was missing, as students were not able to directly interact with it and experiment themselves. They could pose questions and explore the tool with the research team, while the research team would draw comparatives/differences between the tool and conventional search engines to help develop discussions of a critical nature. The students responded positively to the search engine, and the types of discussion we observed them engaging in highlighted many of the areas covered in this chapter so far.

Exploring their answers

We asked the students two questions directly related to the search engine:

- Q7 – If you could add functionality to an existing search engine, what would that be?
- Q8 – Here is a screen shot of a prototype search engine designed to display knowledge from different disciplines. Would that be useful, why or why not (*the image displayed is similar in design to the one in this chapter*).

Student responses to Q7 communicated themes of interdisciplinarity, a desire to see multiple perspectives and categorizations present in search. The following are some examples of their responses:

- 'Variety of perspectives: to avoid (or minimize it) subjectivity'
- 'from different insights (disciplines)'
- 'Ensure accuracy and filter more'

- 'More accuracy'
- 'Filter by topic'
- 'Go into certain ideas and search by the sciences – like the smarter search engine'
- 'I would add an option to filter search results by certain categories'
- 'Results that are suitable for different academic levels e.g. university or secondary school.'

The exhibition may have helped develop these types of critical considerations, but we nevertheless saw it as very promising that these students were introducing a number of core features our 'Smarter Search Engine' is doing into their own suggestions of how 'search' can be improved. It was also interesting to see a student highlight 'scalability' as a point of interest. Another student responded in a similar way by stating:

> I would want to add an option to select the academic level at which search results are written for when researching topics for my GCSE, I often find university-level documents and it is very irritating to scour for results at my intellectual level.

As already indicated, one of the benefits in using our 'Smarter Search Engine' is that it can be scaled and customized to suit specific skill levels, and it is hoped that in the future we can develop this further. For example, we would envisage our 'Smarter Search Engine' being customized to connect to specific knowledge repositories, such as BBC Bite Size and similar.

Student responses to Q8 were also promising with 16/16 (responses we received) indicating they saw it as a useful inclusion. The following are some examples of their responses:

- 'Really useful, as it gives us more data to consider and broader view on the topic that we are searching.'
- 'Yes, because depending on the subject scope you decide to filter your information different websites will appear.'

- 'Yes, mainly because sometimes questions are really broad and ambiguous, so this new search engine would help with it.'
- 'Yes! As a student I very often have research works to do; therefore, such tool is a necessity.'
- 'Yes, for similar reasons as the previous question. I may look up topics for one discipline and receive topics for others, so this would be incredibly useful for me as a student.'
- 'Yes, it can be useful to search for something within a specific discipline or across multiple disciplines.'
- 'Yes, as you can draw parallels from different perspectives. For example using philosophy ideas about logic to approach questions about quantum physics "convergence of thinking"'
- 'It sparks curiosity to click on different disciplines and see different results.'

As can be seen, many of the students indicate that the ability to filter more specifically is important to them. This option gives students the agency from the outset to determine what specific area they are researching within. While we consider the ability to refine search parameters from the outset one of the defining features of the 'Smarter Search Engine', it is this idea of 'sparks curiosity' that the one student indicated as being the type of response we hoped to see. In essence, at the heart of research agency is the spark of curiosity; when students can be encouraged to channel that type of curiosity, they are one step closer to achieving that 'Aha!' moment in epistemic insight where they are able to make multidisciplinary connections with big questions and real-world problems.

Next steps

Our 'Smarter Search Engine' is a developing project, so we expect it will evolve in terms of capabilities and scope. In its current state (at the time of writing) our 'Smarter Search Engine' offers a great deal of utility that educators can use to help develop EI thinking in the context of 'search' and beyond. As the 'Smarter Search Engine's' capabilities expand we intend on retaining its ease-of-use design approach and 'playful' elements, while at the same time adding additional layers of use that expand its utility in educational settings.

The rapid expansion of AI-driven search technologies offers the future a great deal of new and exciting ways in which we can engage with content. We are keen to see the future of 'search' directly encourage epistemic agency, critical inquiry and epistemic curiosity to develop, and one way that we believe can help facilitate this is by using epistemic tools such as our 'Smarter Search Engine'.

References

ChatGPT (2023). https://openai.com/blog/chatgpt/ (accessed January 2023).

Firth, J., J. Torous, B. Stubbs, J. A. Firth, G. Z. Steiner, L. Smith, M. Alvarez-Jimenez, J. Gleeson, D. Vancampfort, C. J. Armitage, and J. Sarris (2019). 'The "Online Brain": How the Internet may be Changing our Cognition', *World Psychiatry*, 18(2): 119–29.

Fisher, M., M. K. Goddu, and F. C. Keil (2015). 'Searching for Explanations: How the Internet Inflates Estimates of Internal Knowledge', *Journal of Experimental Psychology: General*, 144(6): 74–87.

Heersmink, R. (2018). 'A Virtue Epistemology of the Internet: Search Engines, Intellectual Virtues and Education', *Social Epistemology*, 32(1): 1–12.

Low, C. K., K. H. Yeoh, and T. Lau (2008). 'Will the Internet Replace Libraries? An Exploratory Study on University Business Students' Perceptions in the Electronic Environment', in Abrizah Abdullah, et al. (eds), *ICOLIS*, University of Malaya, Kuala Lumpur, 137–46.

Morrison, R (2016). 'Surfing Blind: A Study into the Effects of Exposing Young Adolescents to Explicit Search Engine Skills', *Conference: The Australian Association for Research in Education* AARE (Australian Association for Research in Education), Melbourne.

11

A Sociocultural Understanding of Epistemic Insight

Towards an Imperative of Interdisciplinary Teaching and Learning

Dana L. Zeidler

Introduction

Thinking about what meaning 'Epistemic Insight' holds for education, I am reminded of what Aristotle referred to as Eudaimonia – the Greek notion for human flourishing. This idea of human flourishing presupposes that children are born with an innate predisposition to wonder about the natural and social world in which they dwell. Unfortunately, there exist many times where the structure, organization and pedagogical practices of schools are at loggerheads with that presupposition. More often than not, our conventional explicit, implicit, hidden and null curricula (Flinders, Noddings and Thornton 1986; Flinders and Thornton 2022) stamp out that predisposition – we compel our students to stay within prescribed lines, reside within certain curriculum boxes and we myopically assess only those predetermined, prescribed outcomes from our external points of reference. Contrary to this, is the encouragement of promoting big ideas that necessarily cut across discipline boundaries and cultivate epistemic insight by tapping into the student's natural abilities, talents and curiosity. In doing so, we are proactive in creating opportunities for children to ask questions about the world that might, at first blush, seem inconvenient to us. But it is precisely those kinds of questions that excite students, and in providing opportunities to wonder, we provide an opportunity to fulfil their own potential, and begin asking, and re-asking questions, as they investigate both the natural and the social world around them.

The development of a sociocultural context for epistemic insight

For epistemic insight to flourish, at least in the sense that I advocate, requires certain kinds of immersive academic experiences that are fundamentally sociocultural in nature. Those experiences are inescapably humanistic in that the focus of education is turned inward on the developing child in such a way that they become an active participant in their own learning, rather than being passive recipients of predetermined bundles of knowledge. That such a progressive vision of schooling had been advanced well over a century ago is both ironic and surprising, inasmuch as Dewey (1897) advanced a pedagogic creed that, among other things, viewed education as an essential method of social progress and reform. The importance of sociocultural elements that connect to progressive education are brought into view when Dewey writes: 'If we eliminate the social factor from the child we are left only with an abstraction; if we eliminate the individual factor from society, we are left only with an inert and lifeless mass. Education, therefore, must begin with a psychological insight into the child's capacities, interests, and habits' (Dewey 1897: 6).

The reasons that we are still talking about how progressive views of education are warranted are primarily political and nuanced in nature. There is, for example, undue emphasis on 'teach to the test' because educators and principals feel accountable to political pressures that seek external markers based on standardized tests. Politicians want to hold educational institutions accountable to those tests to curry favour with their constituents, many of whom have children in school. The problem lies in the fact that educational mandates are top-down and generated by parties without having the pedagogical knowledge or background to understand what it means to cultivate epistemic insight among children. Furthermore, they don't seem to have a sense of students' curiosity and interests, wanting everybody to uniformly achieve a certain point on a test, which is, in my mind, fairly arbitrary, rather than getting students to really engage in important questions that interest them. As a result, education has become quite siloed (Zeidler 2016). What we're trying to do with advancing epistemic insight is to engage children in the kinds of big questions that matter to them, and matter to the world around them ... including the biological world, the physical world and the social world.

To allow for the genesis of big questions, we must break the cycle of structuring all education from the myopic point of view that we teach from content-specific domains of specialization. Accordingly, we must shift away from compartmentalized academic content, find opportunities to connect to students' creativity and make clear that to wonder is perhaps the most important starting point for the development of scientific habits of mind and critical learning to have its day. To make this point transparent, let us examine the question of why we tend to teach 'proxies' or substitutions of critical learning? More specifically, consider the following questions: Why do we teach

- Algebra as a proxy for symbolic and abstract thought?
- Geometry as a proxy for logic?
- History and Social Studies as a proxy for conflict, social processes and change?
- Literature as a proxy for human behaviour and self-expression?
- Science as a proxy for inquiry and scepticism?

In contrast, why not immerse students in the practice of abstract thought, logic, conflict and social change, self-expression, and inquiry and scepticism through authentic, meaningful learning experiences? Such experiences are directed at tapping intellectual, social and physical immersive academic experiences which provide an engaging context for not only learning subject matter but for learning to question, think, reason, explore and reflect as active participants in the social construction of knowledge.

The work on the role of epistemic insight (Billingsley 2017; Billingsley et al. 2018) and its focus on interdisciplinary learning is synergistic with the scholarship that has been advanced by the socioscientific issues (SSI) framework (Zeidler 2014; Zeidler, Herman and Sadler 2019; Zeidler and Sadler 2023), in terms of their common goal of allowing the educative experience for children to be one where they can become immersed in pedagogical activities that promote human flourishing. The SSI framework posits four main ideas: (1) SSI are, by nature, controversial and ill-structured dilemmas in their make-up that require evidence-based reasoning; (2) SSI require the deliberate use of scientific topics that compels students to engage in dialogue, discussion and argumentation; (3) SSI tend to have implicit and explicit ethical components and require some degree of moral reasoning; and (4) SSI aim at the formation of virtue/character as a long-range pedagogical goal. The underlying premises in both approaches are that human relationships lie at the heart of the learning process and are fundamental to improving developmental and sociomoral outcomes for all students. We argue that science rarely, if ever, exists apart from milieu of ethical, political and social judgements. Failure to recognize the primal role that a sociocultural lens brings to education brings about a result where learning becomes a routine practice devoid of originality, passion and authentic interest.

So, the advancement of epistemic insight requires a kind of educative imperative whereby children are provided with the conditions necessary to think for themselves, and to think about their own thinking, what we refer to in education as metacognition (Perry, Lundie and Golder 2019). It allows students to understand and explore problems and issues from diverse perspectives and multiple points of view. It also encourages students to utilize and practice socioscientific reasoning which is needed for the negotiation and resolution of many kinds of SSI. The dimensions of socioscientific reasoning require students to understand and utilize the following cognitive skills: complexity, inquiry, perspective taking, scepticism and affordances and limitations of science (for more detail see Sadler, Barab and Scott 2007; Zeidler, Herman and Sadler 2019). These types of scientific competencies are directed towards exploring moral or ethical issues that connect to not only science but a spectrum of disciplines. It is important to recognize that SSI have a certain level of complexity that goes beyond the surface structure of that problem. To reason well, as it were, requires multiple perspectives or multiple points of view. We want students to understand that there's a need for ongoing inquiry as new information and evidence arise. Decisions about what ought to be done and what ought not to be done are always open to revision with the advancement of new knowledge as we gain access to information that was originally not considered in a prior decision. Deriving an answer doesn't end there. It typically raises more questions to investigate. Such is the nature of science.

Because we don't live in boxes and silos in the real world, students should be encouraged to examine issues from historical points of view, scientific points of view, an art-based points of view, sociological points of view (etc.) – tapping a plethora of frames of knowledge. This gives them a more robust understanding of those problems, and more tools in their tool belt to ask reasonable, researchable questions to tackle that problem. Thus, we need to create a sense of open-mindedness for students, a central intellectual virtue. Open-mindedness, in the sense that the SSI framework proposes, provides a rich breeding ground for revisions to students' own personal belief systems. Confronted with new information, new perspectives and new ideas, students can re-evaluate what they think they already know, and try to work through the process of subsuming variant ideas into a more holistic worldview, which at its essence is the expression of a more democratic worldview.

The twenty-first century that now envelops us has come to be a kind of post-fact, post-truth society (Malcolm 2021) where scientific tenets are regularly called into question in a whirlwind of 'alternative facts' ranging from misconceptions to conspiracy 'theories'. While the notion of education as a means of promoting democratic worldviews is not new (see Dewey 1916), we might argue that the promotion of epistemic insight is not just an education imperative, but a moral imperative. To counteract the ubiquitous assault on truth, drawing on the affordances that interdisciplinary domains of expertise provide, offers a viable path towards reasoning about reasoning (i.e. metacognition). This requires the willingness to explore a given topic from multiple disciplines.

I can remember quite distinctly time spent in a secondary classroom observing a biology teacher and overheard a student ask an inquisitive, clarifying question relating biology to the chemistry of life. I was taken aback when the teacher responded 'Well, that's chemistry. This is biology. We don't talk about chemistry in biology class!' My thought at the time was, how could you talk about biology without chemistry? By the same token, how can you talk about biology without talking about some connection to the world around you? My next instinct was to think about how to connect the scientific material to issues that impact the world as well as the lives of students. These kinds of questions reside in the wheelhouse of the kind of SSI that facilitate epistemic insight as we tap into the use of moral and ethical issues that affect our students, their friends, their parents, their community, societies that are interconnected to those communities, as well as possible extended global implications, since such questions permeate physical and intellectual borders (Lee, Lee and Zeidler 2019). We can leverage those moral and ethical issues to engage students in discourse and argument to explore more deeply the many faces of such issues to resolve, or at least come to a consensus on what still needs to be done relative to those questions. Doing so necessitates an interdisciplinary approach to education.

Some extend this idea to the notion of transdisciplinary learning – which aims at erasing traditional boundaries among subject matter even further to focus on the harmonizing of certain meta-skills (e.g. research skills, critical thinking skills, communication skills, social skills, etc. (Lang et al. 2012; Osborne 2015)). Such meta-skills may be linked to what was described above as actions aimed at bringing about and advancing human flourishing (e.g. social justice and equity, empowerment and community building, sustainable production and reproduction, etc. (Pezzoli 1997)). Such aptitudes and actions are representative as those that certainly transcend ordinary discipline boundaries and are acknowledged as central in confronting challenges of a global nature, both in future science education research and in practice (Abd-El-Khalick and Zeidler 2016). Interdisciplinary and transdisciplinary approaches like these also advance more informed views of the nature of science (Lederman and Lederman 2019) and develop a sense of praxis where the scientific community values and engages in the free exchange of ideas – which is, after all, the hallmark of participatory democracy (Zeidler and Abd-El-Khalick 2017).

Considerations of epistemic insight for practice

What does this mean for practice? How might it look if we choose to implement a sociocultural understanding of epistemic insight in our classrooms. Here, I extract and summarize some points and examples from work over the last decade found in the extant literature. This work connects to the central educative ideas underlying the SSI framework and its related epistemic insight practices and invite the reader to examine these resources more closely (Dolan and Zeidler 2009; Dolan, Nichols and Zeidler 2009; Kahn 2019; Kahn and Zeidler 2016; Sadler, Foulk and Friedrichsen 2017; Sá-Pinto et al. 2022; Zeidler, Applebaum and Sadler 2011; Zeidler and Kahn 2014; Zeidler and Nichols 2009). My intent here is to simply call attention to pedagogical issues related to the contextualization of science in context (Bencze et al. 2020) and present a small sample of teacher and classroom considerations. Note that there is no one 'method' or prescribed sequence of procedures to follow in a lock-step manner. The teacher needs to understand the developmental talents and limitations of their own students and have an awareness of students' interests, as well as the prescribed curriculum from which to instantiate content and concepts into an authentic meaningful sociocultural and environmental context. Having said that, consider a few generalized elements.

- *Developing your own epistemic curriculum and practices*: There are many resources to help find current (and historical) topics of interest that can be found by reviewing newspapers, books, internet sources, professional science education journals, televisions and movies and so on. There are many global controversies connected to almost any science topic. Consider just a sampling: Genetically Modified Foods, Offshore Oil Drilling, Alcohol Consumption, Space Settlements, Exotic Animals as Pets or in Zoos, Satellite Tracking and Privacy, Animal Research, Artificial and Selective Breeding Practices, Vaping, Locating Landfills, Bicycle Helmet Laws, Pharmaceuticals, Competing Forms of Energy. There is virtually an endless number of interdisciplinary and transdisciplinary issues to connect the scientific topics and content under review to issues that impact students' lives and the broader environment.

- *Collect resources that represent a wide range of viewpoints*: Look for sources that reflect a diversity of viewpoints. Most controversial issues have multiple viewpoints and perspectives that represent various stakeholder interests and concerns. It is acceptable to include resources that may represent opposing views or even biased positions. This provides an opportunity for students to attempt to analyse the material as 'objectively' as possible. It also presents an opportunity for teachers to discuss different ways students may evaluate evidence. Consider using a relatively simple but effective (with practice) tool for students using the heuristic CARS: (C)redibilty – examine author credentials, position of expertise held, reputation, peer-review controls; (A)ccuracy – consider if material is relatively current, comprehensive, consistent with other research trends; (R)easonableness – evaluate if the material is fair and whether attempts made to present information has been done in a straight-forward or 'objective' manner; (S)upport – determine the extent sources of information and support for a given position have been corroborated and/or documented through peer review or other references related to the research.

- *Use a 'hook' or an advanced organizer to prepare students for discussion*: Introduce contentious questions that will help drive interest and inquiry of the topic(s) at-hand (e.g. 'Should schools or markets charge a fat-tax for unhealthy but enjoyable foods?'). Introducing questions that help drive the lesson and subsequent inquiry allow for the identification of possible misconceptions and a baseline of prior knowledge that can be revisited after the unit if finished. Doing so helps to immerse students into what will be an exciting investigative unit of exploration. It is also important to set (or derive with the students) ground rules for class discussions, arguments, debates and so on. Again, it is important to emphasize the use of evidence (where possible) to support personal opinions and encourage students to examine the sources of their own personal (epistemic) beliefs about stances they take.

- *Encourage evidence-based reasoning and formal instruction when necessary*: For older students (Middle, Secondary, College) in particular, it may be prudent to extend the CARS heuristic above to consider a research-focused assessment or evaluation the empirical nature of resources and studies found. For example, thinking about the design and methodological features of studies themselves can be quite beneficial in understanding the strength and vigour of research. Considering methodological feature of things like the quality of the data (e.g. Was the data gathered appropriately and does it specifically address the research questions? Is there clarity of methods whereby procedures are fully articulated? Is the analysis transparent? Is there a high degree of instantiation (e.g. validity, reliability for quantitative studies; credibility, trustworthiness for qualitative studies)? Are the findings, conclusions and claims by the author(s) supported by the research?)

- *Facilitate group and informal activities but include formal instruction when necessary*: It is always sound to present subject matter in a variety of ways. Inquiry laboratory investigations, research projects, survey research by students to gage opinions and stances, place-based field trips, guest speakers, class discussions, town-hall type meetings and debates, among other group approaches, are useful tools to investigate various SSI-type problems. All these approaches are meant to problematize the issues for deeper exploration.

However, what I advocate in the spirit of a progressive approach is not meant to exclude formal lectures and presentations, particularly when students need to better understand the conceptual content that underlie the issues under investigation. Formal lectures, after all, do not preclude the use of probing questions, interesting metaphors, use of integrated knowledge from other fields and the like, to maintain student focus and engagement.

Conclusion

In summary, the cultivation of epistemic insight is a human endeavour that requires the co-construction of knowledge among students with guidance and purposeful planning by teachers. There are many moving parts with this approach, which is why a 'one-size-fits-all' approach is a phantom image. Teachers will always need to be reflective about their own approaches and willing to modify instruction to suit the ever-shifting demands of their charge. After all, epistemic insight applies not only to students thinking about thinking, but to those in the teaching profession as well. While the extant cited above is replete with empirical support and overlapping mutually supportive approaches to the development of epistemic insight, its application can be made infertile by infertile minds. If one buys into the necessity of a sociocultural context for learning, then the pursuit of interdisciplinary and transdisciplinary subject matter connections becomes an essential part of teaching. Arguably, it is a moral imperative because in doing so, teachers are nurturing the conditions required for a predisposition to question, discuss, challenge, find common ground, maintain an open mind and wonder about the world we inhabit.

References

Abd-El-Khalick, F. and N. G. Lederman (2023). 'Research on Teaching, Learning, and Assessment of Nature of Science', in N. G. Lederman, D. L. Zeidler, and J. S. Lederman (eds), *Handbook of Research on Science Education*, Vol. III, 850–98. New York: Routledge.

Bencze, J. L., C. Pouliot, E. Pedretti, L. Simonneaux, J. Simonneaux, and D. L. Zeidler (2020). 'SAQ, SSI & STSE Education: Defending and Extending "Science-in-Context"', *Cultural Studies in Science Education*, 15: 825–51. https://doi.org/10.1007/s11422-019-09962-7.

Billingsley, B. (2017). 'Teaching and Learning About Epistemic Insight', *School Science Review*, 365: 98, 59–64.

Billingsley, B., M. Nassaji, S. Fraser, and F. Lawson (2018). 'A Framework for Teaching Epistemic Insight in Schools', *Research in Science Education*, 48: 1115–31. https://doi.org/10.1007/s11165-018-9788-6.

Dewey, J. (1897). *My Pedagogic Creed*. New York: E.L. Kellogg & Company.

Dewey, J. (1916). *Democracy and Education: An Introduction to the Philosophy of Education*. New York: The Macmillan Company.

Dolan, T. J., B. H. Nichols, and D. L. Zeidler (2009). 'Using Socioscientific Issues in Primary Classrooms', *Journal of Elementary Science Teacher Education*, 21(3): 1–12.

Dolan, T. J. and D. L. Zeidler (2009). 'Integrating Argumentation into Elementary Classrooms', *Science and Children*, 48(3): 20–3.

Flinders, D. J., N. Noddings, and S. J. Thornton (1986). 'The Null Curriculum: Its Theoretical Basis and Practical Implications', *Curriculum Inquiry*, 16(1): 33–42.

Flinders, D. J. and S. J. Thornton (2022). *The Curriculum Reader*, 6th edn. New York: Routledge.

Kahn, S. (2019). *It's Still Debatable! Using Socioscientific Issues to Develop Scientific Literacy, K-5*. Arlington, VA: NSTA Press.

Kahn, S. and D. L. Zeidler (2016). 'Using Our Heads and HARTSS*: Developing Perspective-Taking Skills for Socioscientific Reasoning (*Humanities, Arts, and Social Sciences)', *Journal of Science Teacher Education*, 27(3): 261–81.

Lang, D. J., A. Wiek, M. Bergmann, M. Stauffacher, P. Martens, P. Moll, M. Swilling, and C. J. Thomas (2012). 'Transdisciplinary Research in Sustainability Science: Practice, Principles, and Challenges', *Sustainability Science*, 7(1): 25–43.

Lederman, N. G. and J. S. Lederman (2019). 'Teaching and Learning Nature of Scientific Knowledge: Is it Déjà vu All Over Again?', *Disciplinary and Interdisciplinary Science Education Research*, 1(6). https://doi.org/10.1186/s43031-019-0002-0.

Lee, H., H. Lee, and D. L. Zeidler (2019). 'Examining Tensions in the Socioscientific Classroom: Students' Border Crossings into a New Culture of Science', *Journal of Research in Science Teaching*, 57(5): 672–94. https://doi.org/10.1002/tea.21600.

Malcolm, D. (2021). 'Post-Truth Society? An Eliasian Sociological Analysis of Knowledge in the 21st Century', *Sociology*, 55(6): 1063–79. https://doi.org/10.1177/0038038521994039.

Osborne, P. (2015). 'Problematizing Disciplinarity, Transdisciplinary Problematics', *Theory, Culture & Society*, 32(5–6): 3–35. https://doi.org/10.1177/0263276415592245.

Perry, J., D. Lundie, and G. Golder (2019). 'Metacognition in Schools: What Does the Literature Suggest About the Effectiveness of Teaching Metacognition in Schools?', *Educational Review*, 71(4): 483–500. https://doi.org/10.1080/00131911.2018.1441127.

Pezzoli, K. (1997). 'Sustainable Development: A Transdisciplinary Overview of the Literature', *Journal of Environmental Planning and Management*, 40(5): 549–74, https://doi.org/10.1080/09640569711949.

Sadler, T. D., S. Barab, and B. Scott (2007). 'What Do Students Gain by Engaging in Socioscientific Inquiry?', *Research in Science Education*, 37(4): 371–91.

Sadler, T. D., J. A. Foulk, and P. J. Friedrichsen (2017). 'Evolution of a Model for Socioscientific Issue Teaching and Learning', *International Journal of Education in Mathematics, Science and Technology*, 5(2): 75–87.

Sá-Pinto, X., A. Beniermann, T. Børsen, M. Georgiou, A. Jeffries, P. Pessoa, B. Sousa, and D. L. Zeidler (eds) (2022). *Learning Evolution Through Socioscientific Issues*. EuroScitizen COST Action Network. Publishing House of the University of Aveiro (UA Editor).

Zeidler, D. L. (2014). 'Socioscientific Issues as a Curriculum Emphasis: Theory, Research and Practice', in N. G. Lederman and S. K. Abell (eds), *Handbook of Research on Science Education*, Vol. II, 697–726. New York: Routledge.

Zeidler, D. L. (2016). 'STEM Education: A Deficit Framework for the 21st Century? A Sociocultural Socioscientific Response', *Cultural Studies of Science Education*, 11(1): 11–26.

Zeidler, D. L. and F. Abd-El-Khalick (2017). 'Science Education Research Thrives in an Open, Global Community', *Journal of Research in Science Teaching*, 54(4): 437–8.

Zeidler, D. L. and S. Kahn (2014). *It's Debatable: Using Socioscientific Issues to Develop Scientific Literacy, K-12*. Arlington, VA: National Science Teachers Association Press.

Zeidler, D. L. and B. H. Nichols (2009). 'Socioscientific Issues: Theory and Practice', *Journal of Elementary Science Teacher Education*, 21(2): 49–58.

Zeidler, D. L. and T. D. Sadler (2023). 'Exploring and Expanding the Frontiers of Socioscientific Issues: Crossroads and Future Directions', in N. G. Lederman, D. L. Zeidler, and J. S. Lederman (eds), *Handbook of Research on Science Education*, Vol. III, 899–929. New York: Routledge.

Zeidler, D. L., S. M. Applebaum, and T. D. Sadler (2011). 'Enacting a Socioscientific Issues Classroom: Transformative Transformations', in T. D. Sadler (ed.), *Socio-scientific Issues in Science Classrooms: Teaching, Learning and Research*, 277–306. The Netherlands: Springer.

Zeidler, D. L., B. C. Herman, and T. D. Sadler (2019). 'New Directions in Socioscientific Issues Research', *Disciplinary and Interdisciplinary Science Education Research*, 1(11): 1–9. https://doi.org/10.1186/s43031-019-0008-7.

12

Get Ready, Steady, Allez? ¡Vamos!

Martin Pickett

The educational setting

My school, St Olave's Grammar School, Orpington, is very much like any other school in the UK, in terms of timetabling and allocating different subjects to the school day under the auspices of the Department for Education. The experience of the end-users (i.e. school children) involves going to different classes on a set day during the week when period 1 involves one subject, let's say English, and then moves to French, then to maths, then to geography.

Each subject lesson will have its objectives, terminology, methods, lesson plans and routines. In perfect isolation, each school discipline makes perfect sense. However, does the pupil at school moving from one class to the next make sense of the educational system? Does their experience reflect the real world outside of school where the worlds of business, English, modern languages, science and maths mix in a hotch-potch of human activity without much rhyme or reason?

For the student, whose intention is to learn so many subjects and become curious about the world they inhabit, their experience is somewhat confused unless they totally embrace that this is the way 'school' works and this is how the real world exists. Indeed, as all those who have been to school will testify: one day, you will find out that getting good grades in a certain subject may not be 'the be all and the end all' of your learning achievements.

In fact, you will have to negotiate and learn new skills. Work or university will demand other knowledge and competences. The realization could occur after school, after university and/or after a mid-life crisis. Nonetheless, you need to realize that although what you learn at school *is important*, it is not obvious how all these different disciplines will help form your character, your knowledge, your learning and progress your career to multiple job opportunities.

For policy makers, there is also a demand that language tuition and schools be more relevant to the world outside of school (be it work or research and development). This can be evidenced from the Dearing Report (2007) and numerous language reviews which showed that total numbers of students learning French, Spanish and German (the preferred language options in UK schools) were declining. This does not bode well for the delivery or take up of modern languages at school.

In spite of the inevitable rise of AI and instant digital translations, teachers today have to understand, show and discuss why Modern Foreign Language (MFL) specialists exist and the reasons why language students should take their language acquisition further and join more science-related teams. MFL informs us that the target language people spoken – in their communities and/or geographical areas – contains words and phrases that reflect their lives, cultures, preferences and aspirations. Knowing this information is extremely useful to commercial markets and governments as well as academia. As a result, one can anticipate different scenarios and problems that the linguist can solve.

The theory behind the proposed solutions

The theoretical underpinning of this research has come from studies of motivation in industry, educational research and other psychological investigations (Pickett 2009). Thus, motivation is defined as the impetus to create and sustain intentions and goal-seeking acts (Ames and Ames 1989). Motivation is important because it determines the extent of the learner's active involvement and attitude towards learning.

Understanding the motivating factors allows educators and policymakers to predict whether and how the foreign language learning being offered will respond to future demand and needs. For example, Julkunen in Finland focused on task-specific motivation and context. He stated that there were a variety of different levels to scrutinize, for example, physiological (the need to receive/respond to impulses, explore the environment, master performance). Learning tasks needed to be 'meaningful' in the mind of the learner, and this personal measure would affect the amount of effort produced. One example of this could be the meaningful task of creating driverless machines for world markets.

Ever since the first general curriculum for the Finnish comprehensive school (1970), motivation has been conceived as one of the didactic principles directing the organization of the instructional processes and the teaching/learning situation. Learning requires energy that stimulates/creates and directs it. The factors that stimulate and maintain goal-directed behaviour are called motivational factors and the resulting state motivation (Julkunen 1989: 23). Julkunen advanced the notion of epistemic curiosity, that is, the need-to-know factor; in other words, learning through novelty and surprise, then through interests and activities.

This idea of epistemic curiosity chimes with EI. The need to ask pupils big questions that science disciplines have never asked or are unable to answer is a novel way to motivate the linguist. Billingsley (2017) has questioned the assumption that science knows best or that there is only one valid way to answer the question. Questioning is to be encouraged. And then, by looking for solutions to these 'problems' of language and culture, one overcomes major communication barriers.

Moreover, Barnes (2015) supports the idea of cross-curricular learning and students' need to recognize multiple viewpoints – that is, key principles to the MFL discipline. A multilingual and multicultural arena will always produce multiple viewpoints. Sometimes, individuals may wish to listen passively, other times interaction is necessary for the purposes of negotiation and persuasion. The MFL communicator will be in their element to deal with real-life experiences.

The Pearson Report (2014) highlighted the skills gap of UK students and argued that schools need to equip them with 'broad cognitive skills'. In short, EI accentuates the importance of how these different disciplines interact (Billingsley and Nassaji 2019) and, by pursuing this crossover, we (teachers, students, business, policymakers) can all benefit.

The case study that sheds light on the need for language specialists in a scientific context

The case study we explore here is the challenge of optimising the design of a driverless car and our hypothesis is that students have not before considered the way that science and modern foreign languages (MFL) – as two different and distinctive disciplines – can shine different lights onto the same problem. If two disciplines or subjects have been regularly isolated in a metaphorical silo within the school curriculum, then MFL and science are arguably placed in such a silo.

For example, do UK students wanting to specialize in science and/or technology understand why MFL experts and MFL expertise are needed in the future?

MFL is a discipline which recognizes that people are currently speaking languages other than English around the world. Some scientists and engineers may suppose that the priority is to create and test the technology, the software, coding and data needed for the car to sense and respond to the physical world. And then, when they encounter 'problems' of language and culture, address them by adding a fix to the generic, universal system they have designed when testing in the field. However, a more efficient solution would be to include a linguist in the design team (Figure 12.1).

Consider the question of how our AV should interact with the colours it encounters in its environment. Let's suppose that we begin with a presupposition that 'traffic lights' are a 'universal feature' of roads here and overseas (wherever 'here' is!). It turns out that how

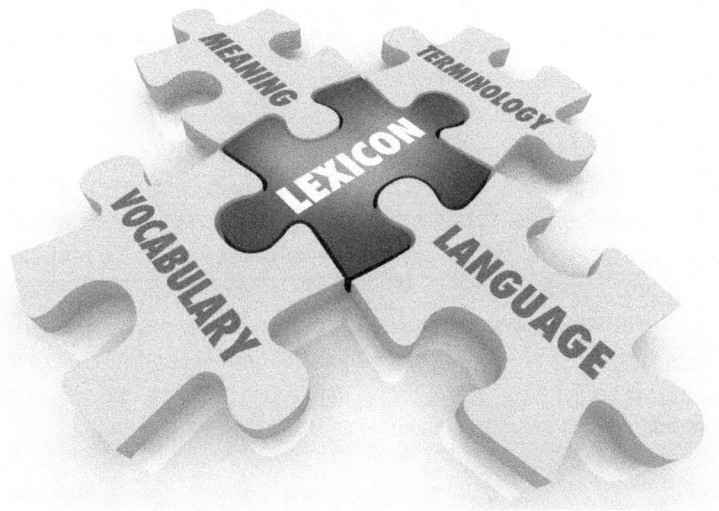

FIGURE 12.1 *Role of the linguist in the design team.*

people perceive and talk about the colours of traffic lights is not as translatable as some people might imagine.

A case in point is the 'green light', which is embedded in our psyche as the colour that tells us to 'go'. However, and possibly only once testing in the field begins, it will become apparent that the Japanese do not refer to red, amber and green traffic lights on their roads but rather to red, amber and blue. Correspondingly, the hue of the light is also bluer than the green light in the UK.

Therefore, in an engineer's AV scheme, the systems used would cover sensors, perception plus planning and control of the machine. Autonomy is viewed as a critical enabler of safer transportation, providing greater comfort and more efficient transportation.

Irrespective of language and culture, Operational Domains (ODs) are constructed in terms of weather (temperature, rain, snow, visibility etc.), scenery (roads, intersections, infrastructure) and traffic (other vehicles). The dynamic OD is expected to predict and make safe different combinations in known and unknown scenarios. Engineers spend their time testing and re-testing, recording and collecting data, predicting behaviour, generating combinations of realistic scenarios with the goal of optimizing their processes. From observation and simulation, they create a framework that deals with novelty and criticality. Further probes will then calculate the probability of such and such a scenario.

As soon as companies have become satisfied with their engineered processes and solutions, they will need the public to *accept* and *trust* their new AV product. Once again, the MFL specialist can participate in the marketing campaign by choosing the correct turn of phrase, or *mot juste*, to counter negative media stories or public attitudes. Therefore, not only can one imagine that the multilingual scenarios will need to be properly simulated, but the AV will have to be 'sold' to the target market in *their language*. Without this communication, trust and acceptance, there is no viable product that the company can sell.

The context – can we afford valuable curriculum time, effort and resources to deliver MFL?

The language curriculum at school should be designed to nurture curiosity (Julkunen 1989), enhance motivation (Dörnyei 2005; Pickett 2009), helping students become independent learners. Nevertheless, looking at the official literature on the National Curriculum and UK examining bodies, the instructions to teachers are vague and more akin to guidance rather than direction. In KS3, there is a focus on creating a strong scaffolding of linguistic skills, that is, the building blocks, on which pupils can build and develop over time.

In terms of the National Curriculum, MFL affirms the importance of the four language skills (speaking, listening, reading and writing in the target language). To ensure that pupils are confident in using a foreign language, they must be able to express themselves accurately using the correct vocabulary, syntax and grammar. Furthermore, MFL exists as a discipline to equip students with the skills and cultural linguistic knowledge with the aim of communicating, opening doors to other cultures and understanding the world outside of the UK.

From Key Stage 3, pupils should know that they are learning a foreign language for the following reasons:

1. Language is for communication.
2. Language is for identity.
3. There is intrinsic value in knowing/speaking a foreign language.
4. There are cross-curricular benefits and links to other subjects like economics/business, the English language, literacy and computer coding.
5. One should even ask the big question: Is it advantageous or disadvantageous to be monolingual?

School MFL schemes of work build on what students may have already learnt or not at KS2 but cannot take it for granted that students have a reason or a history of language learning prior to secondary school. It is up to the teachers and the schools to address key questions of motivation and the choice of target language to study. Of course, there should be progression to KS4 and GCSE but teaching staff may need to be more explicit on reasons why it is worthwhile to learn a foreign language when everyone supposes that 'all people in the world speak English'.

An opportunity to create novel solutions to future technological problems

On 28 September 2022 at the EI workshop, the year 10 Spanish students from my school enjoyed the opportunity to discuss their ideas on designing AV's with students from other schools at the Royal Society of Chemistry. Scientists and students listened to why there is a need for students to discuss real-life sociolinguistic problems in the AV context.

The pupils showed how machines are likely to interact with humans demonstrating potential language and cultural problems. They prepared a presentation on the subject with examples to show

how non-English speakers will become confused. This confusion could lead to safety issues and accidents. In turn, this could lead to a lack of trust and social acceptance for the AV. The group considered how the Discipline Wheel (Figure 12.2) could be adapted to incorporate all those school subjects necessary for understanding the future of autonomous vehicles. The range of subjects expanded to ten!

It is understood that scientists and engineers will create the technology, the software, coding and data needed to work in the physical world (Figure 12.3). Nevertheless, are we going to give all instructions to the car in English? Imagine the US user – on a UK holiday – commanding their car to 'go on the pavement'. How unsafe

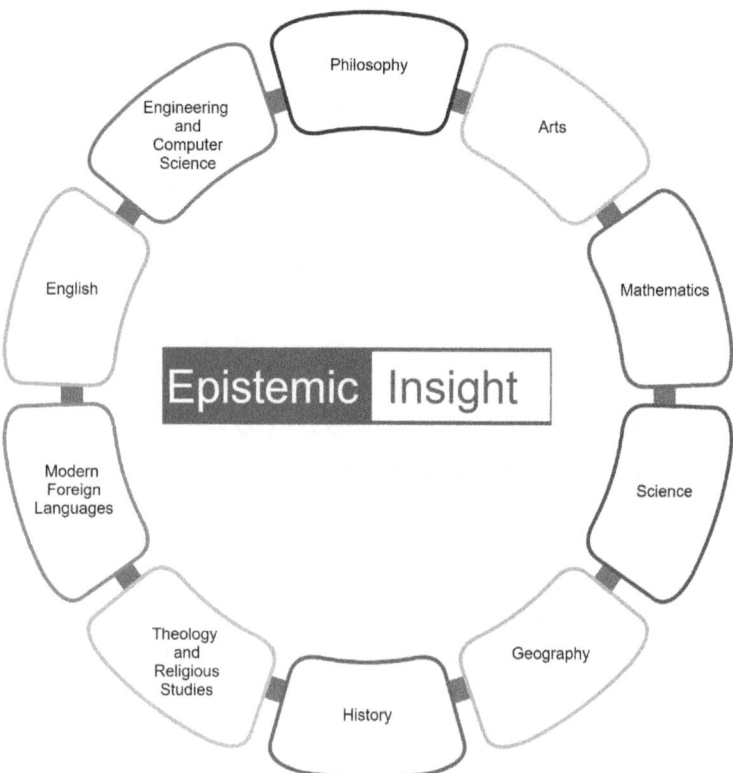

FIGURE 12.2 *EI Discipline Wheel (adapted).*

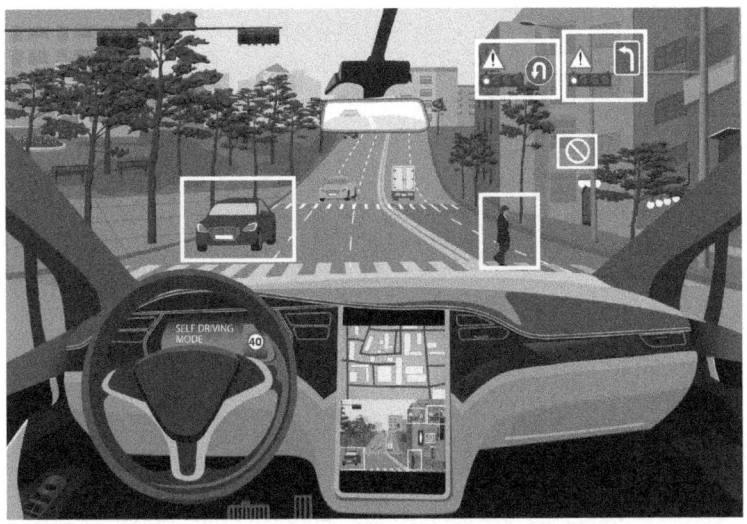

FIGURE 12.3 *Example view from a driverless car.*

could this be for those unlucky pedestrians on the *sidewalk* (UK pavement)!

A linguist would instantly inform the engineer that words can have different and contradictory meanings, even in the same language. Indeed, is it reasonable to expect that all the world must understand and command their new cars in English, especially when there are so many Spanish speakers in the United States?

Our hypothesis is that students have not before considered the way that different disciplines can shine different lights onto the same question – a key tenet in epistemic insight (EI). For some, learning a language is considered a talent, a gift, an inherited skill, even a luxury to speak. At first glance, scientists and engineers may not see the link or the advantage of having a multilingual communicator on their team. Nevertheless, they will avoid elementary mistakes by listening to an MFL communicator. In fact, business investors may save money by employing the linguist to anticipate communication problems in different cultures. Thinking and working in a different language brings real tangible benefits.

Conclusion

This chapter has studied why it benefits students to explore how different disciplines interact (Billingsley and Nassaji 2019). The EI Workshop exemplified the need to broaden the inquiry to include other disciplines such as geography, economics and psychology. We have argued that there are immediate benefits for students taking part, together with longer-term benefits for society: technologies that are more cost-effective, safer and more culturally sensitive.

In the short term, in addition to gaining epistemic insight, students who see themselves as scientists first can feel confident and motivated enough to continue language learning as they can expect their efforts to be recognized and remunerated in due course. Students who supposed that they would need to make a choice between 'languages or science' when choosing their options can feel reassured that their employability is likely to be enhanced rather than diminished if they decide to continue with both.

The coming together of subjects from different schools is a great way to fuse and diffuse information similar to any conference in the adult world; the pupils find that they have a lot in common. They are still in school learning these various disciplines and not knowing exactly how they might be useful in future life. Yet, they are thinking and learning, asking new questions. For instance, in one session at the workshop, we witnessed the merging of psychology and MFL when asking what do we want a 'pet robot' for? Could it be a pet dog? What is its use? Companionship, exercise aid, status symbol perhaps? However, are engineers and psychologists aware of the fact that dogs are viewed as 'dirty animals' in many parts of the world and are thus not considered 'cute' good friends or instantly appealing!

Here, to conclude, we have a platform to link these three subjects of MFL, psychology and engineering to ask big questions and sustain curiosity from childhood into adulthood without the call for reinventing school subjects or creating a completely new curriculum. Can we not link other subjects to more scientific and technological questions?

As educationalists, our intention is to show students wanting to pursue science that there is no reason to ignore or drop a subject like MFL. Indeed, their academic portfolio is preparing them for the world of work which could include at least one MFL subject. Moreover, one can imagine strong economic and engineering reasons why businesses and governments will want – or *need* – multilingual workers with such an appealing array of skills to solve real human problems in the global economy.

Equally, students should feel confident and liberated enough to pursue the MFL option, knowing that they are improving their career prospects, rather than hindering them. Ultimately, it should never be a false choice between MFL and the sciences. Both disciplines need each other. Students benefit from their different approaches to solve complicated communication, engineering and cultural challenges in a more diverse multicultural business context. The green (or blue) light is on, all systems are go!

References

Ames, C. and R. Ames (1989). *Research on Motivation in Education*. New York: Academic Press.

Anderson, R. (2014). *Careers 2020: Making Education Work*. Pearson Report.

Barnes, J. (2015). 'An Introduction to Cross-Curricular Learning', in P. Driscoll, A. Lambirth, and J. Roden (eds), *The Primary Curriculum: A Creative Approach*. 2nd edn, 260–83. London: SAGE Publications Ltd.

Billingsley, B. and M. Nassaji (2019). 'Exploring Secondary School Students' Stances on the Predictive and Explanatory Power of Science', *Science and Education*, 28(1): 87–107.

Dearing, R. (2007). *Languages Review*. Nottingham: Department for Education and Skills.

Dörnyei, Z. (2005). *The Psychology of the Language Learner*. London: Lawrence Erlbaum.

Julkunen, K. (1989). *Situation and Task Specific Motivation in Foreign Language Learning and Teaching*. Joensuu: University of Joensuu.

Pickett, M. D. (2009). *In a Situation Where Enormous Numbers Learn English for International Communication, what are the Motivations for English Mother-Tongue Speakers to Learn Other Languages?* Doctoral dissertation, University of Portsmouth. https://ethos.bl.uk/OrderDetails.do?uin=uk.bl.ethos.523585.

PART VI

Science, Imagination, Interdisciplinarity and AI

This part wonders about the future of science and science education and explores ways that epistemic insight is helping students, educators and scholars to engage with science in a multidisciplinary and responsible way. Science is one of the most widely recognized and influential ways of creating and organizing knowledge in the modern world. But for all of its rigour and apparent inflexibility as a way to test and validate knowledge claims, science is a human endeavour, which thrives on leaps of imagination, creativity and curiosity. The strength of science lies not only on a pursuit of truth but also on the willingness of scientists and science educators to be open-minded about their discipline's strengths and limitations. The section explains ways that science has been enriched by other forms of knowledge and expression, particularly science fiction, art and philosophy. The point being made is that new technologies and other ways of knowing can stimulate our imaginations and critical thinking and encourage us to step into different scenarios and perspectives.

Some of the puzzles that we will address in this part are as follows:

- Are there ways to teach science that go further to foster curiosity, creativity and critical thinking, and which connect science to other disciplines and domains?

- Can we use science fiction to enrich the education of astronomers and other scientists, and if we try, how do participants react?

- How can we evaluate and regulate the use and impact of artificial intelligence companions, or artificial friends, and decide whether they can actually be friends in any meaningful way?

Key ideas

- **The nature of science and science education is changing in a world of rapid discovery and innovation:** As such new pedagogies and approaches that can engage and inspire learners and educators are needed. Epistemic insight can help them to understand how science creates and organizes knowledge, and how it relates to other disciplines and domains.

- **Science fiction can be a powerful tool:** It will support the education of astronomers and other scientists, as it can stimulate their curiosity, creativity and critical thinking, and expose them to different scenarios and perspectives. Epistemic insight can help them to evaluate and communicate their findings and arguments, and to appreciate the similarities and differences between science and fiction.

- **Artificial intelligence companions, or artificial friends, pose ethical and practical challenges and opportunities for the future of knowledge:** They can influence and affect human behaviour and decision making. Epistemic insight can help us to consider whether these products can actually be friends in any meaningful way, and what are the motivations and consequences of using them. It can also help us to reflect on the meaning and value of knowledge, and how we use it for good.

Statement of support

I have been following with great interest the earlier activities of the LASAR Centre and the Epistemic Insight Initiative, and I am highly impressed by the quality of its research, and the reputation it has acquired in the science education community internationally. I am further excited by the new initiative on the 'Future of Knowledge'. I believe science is entering a new era of discoveries and innovations that are extraordinary, exciting and challenging to us as humans. It is indeed important that we ask: 'what do we want to know?' and 'what does this knowledge mean to us?' For all these reasons I am delighted to lend my support to the Epistemic Insight Initiative and the LASAR Centre.

Nidhal Guessoum, Professor of Physics and Astronomy, American University of Sharjah, United Arab Emirates

13

Science Education, Interdisciplinarity and Critical Thinking

Nidhal Guessoum

Are We, Science Educators, Achieving Our Goals?

First things first: what are the goals of science education? What are we, science educators and society more broadly, trying to achieve by teaching science generally, and those chosen topics more specifically? Do we want students to know some amount of science, what exactly and how much? Or is science education a way to develop some way of thinking, to be applied more broadly? If so, what kind of thinking is that, and how does one develop it?

Science education does aim to raise students' scientific knowledge, to learn some basic but important facts about the world, for example, how big is the earth, what gases are in our atmosphere, what are atoms and genes and so on. It also aims for some understanding of the phenomena that we observe, for example, why the sky is blue during daytime, why the sun turns red at sunrise and sunset, why water falls from clouds sometimes in droplets and sometimes as hail and so on.

But science education also aims at developing an understanding of *how* we go about discovering the world (how do we know that the air around us is made of nitrogen and oxygen, mainly, in some proportions) and what processes in nature produce those phenomena (red sunset, etc.). At a higher level, science education tries to impart to students an understanding of the nature of that (scientific) knowledge, its methodology, its limitations, uncertainties and so on. In other words, this is what has been called 'epistemic insight' (EI), that is, 'knowledge about knowledge' (Billingsley and Hardman 2017).

And last but not least, through science education we want students to develop a scientific way of thinking, that is a systematic, evidence-based, bias-free way of analysing different kinds of problems in various areas of life. At the very least, we want students to learn to distinguish between evidence-based explanations and opinions.

Unfortunately, we science educators are far from achieving the above goals at any satisfactory level.

In their recent paper titled 'Students' performance in the scientific skills during secondary education', Fernández et al. (2022) find that at the end of elementary school, start of secondary school and at higher grades, students fail to identify the problem being investigated and confuse it with the experimental design and the conclusions that are reached in a given study. In other words, students do not have a clear conceptual idea of how to formulate a question (to solve or address a problem), and even less so what method or map will lead to proper conclusions. Worse still, the most recent PISA test results (below) found that 90 per cent of the fifteen-year-old students that took the test could not distinguish facts from opinions in reports they were asked to read. This raises questions about how science is being taught and what students are learning in the process.

Recent TIMSS and PISA results

TIMSS (Trends in International Maths and Science Study) is an international Maths and Science test given every three years to Grade 4 and Grade 8 students in dozens of participating countries around the world. The 2019 edition was given to 580,000 students from 64 countries and 8 regional entities, including 10 Arab countries (Bahrain, Egypt, Kuwait, Jordan, Lebanon, Morocco, Oman, Qatar, Saudi Arabia and UAE). A score of 500 is the expected average for student cohorts, with a 'normal' statistical distribution around that mean.

At the top of the results were the usual high achievers: Singapore, Hong Kong, Japan, Taiwan, South Korea, Russia and Scandinavian countries. Regionally, for my part of the world, all Arab states had results below the international averages in both Maths and Science and at both levels (Grades 4 and 8); some came very close to the 500 mark (UAE and Bahrain), and several have made significant improvements, but a few were well below the average.

An important section of the report was devoted to students' attitudes towards Maths and Science. Attitudes were generally positive and correlated with scores, but the numbers of pupils who liked learning Maths and Science and valued these subjects declined significantly between Grades 4 and 8. This rings alarms about how Maths and Science are being learnt and perceived – apparently in ways not very appealing to the students.

PISA (Programme for International Student Assessment) is a similar international test given every three years to fifteen-year-old students in Reading, Maths and Science. The (most recent) 2018 edition was given to 600,000 students from 79 states. The highest performers included the usual high achievers but with a few surprises; in Maths: China (only a few provinces participated), Singapore, Hong Kong, Chinese Taipei, Japan, Republic of Korea, Estonia, the Netherlands, Poland and Switzerland; in science, mostly the same countries: China, Singapore, Estonia, Japan, Finland, Republic of Korea, Canada, Hong Kong, Chinese Taipei, Poland and New Zealand. From the Arab world, only six countries participated in 2018: Jordan, Lebanon, Morocco, Qatar, Saudi Arabia and the UAE; they averaged 397 in Maths and 405 in science, ranging from 366 and 377 (Morocco in Maths and Science) to 435 and 434 (UAE in Maths and Science). The PISA report claimed, 'The world is no longer divided between rich and well-educated nations and poor and badly educated ones', but this does not seem to reflect the results (with the quick highlights I just gave).

Most importantly, in what concerns us here, the PISA 2018 report had the following stunning and highly worrisome piece of information: only 10 per cent of the students that were surveyed (600,000 15-year-olds from 79 countries) were able to distinguish between fact and opinion when reading about an unfamiliar topic. This again points to a serious deficit in the development of critical thinking, in teaching science and maths, or in reading and writing.

Critical thinking: Goals and methods

It is widely accepted and frequently stated (e.g. Bailin 2002) that critical thinking is an important goal of science education. For example, the US National Science Education Standards (1996: 23) include various items that focus on critical thinking: 'identification of assumptions, use of critical and logical thinking, and consideration of alternative explanations'; 'analysis of firsthand events and phenomena as well as the critical analysis of secondary sources; testing reliability of knowledge they have generated' (1996: 33); and 'the critical abilities of analysing an argument by reviewing current scientific understanding, weighing the evidence, and examining the logic so as to decide which explanation and models are best' (1996: 175).

In education, developing 'critical thinking' skills in students means making them able to (a) examine the thinking/argumentation presented in a given text or presentation; (b) examine the evidence being given in support of any statement or claim being made; (c) avoid biases and fallacies in drawing conclusions and making judgements.

In his article 'Let's Apply Critical Thinking Outside the Classroom' (2022), Steven Mintz writes:

> intuition and snap judgments can result in correct decisions in some circumstances, but misdirect us in others. It's better, whenever possible, to base our judgments and decisions on critical thinking: the reasoned, logical and open-minded analysis and evaluation of relevant evidence and conflicting arguments. We need to identify, evaluate and question the information before us. We must reflect upon the implications, including the ethical consequences, of our judgments. We must recognize our implicit biases.

Science education should, in principle, help develop such reasoning and critical thinking skills because students should, by the end of elementary school or at the latest by middle school grades, be able to identify and distinguish scientific facts (the earth is round, living organisms are made of cells, genes are big molecules, sunlight gives us energy, which can be converted to electricity etc.), models (simplified versions of systems under investigation), hypotheses (proposed explanation for a phenomenon being explored), laws (relations, usually mathematical, between physical quantities such as temperature, pressure and volume, or force, mass and acceleration) and so on.

Bailin (2002) stresses the fact that the development of critical thinking in science education can take a variety of approaches, including practical projects that teach students how mistakes are made, particularly if based on intuition and untested common sense, the testing of competing hypotheses for a given phenomenon, examining which claims or conclusions are or are not supported by evidence, weighing the strength of the evidence being provided, proposing plausible alternative explanations for an observation and so on.

Combining science and reading/writing is an excellent way to develop and sharpen students' critical thinking skills. For example, analysing reports about research being done on a given problem is a good way to train students in identifying the problem, the method being used, the results being presented, the conclusions being drawn, the evidence that the claims are based on and so on.

Interdisciplinary topics, those that bring together science, ethics, society, history and so on, are even more interesting and fruitful, as they require understanding ideas and arguments from different fields and disciplines, and those arguments are often of different types (quantitative vs. qualitative, instrumental measurements vs. human surveys with questionnaires, different types of references etc.).

In her article 'Enhancing critical thinking through interdisciplinary teaching and learning', Shuang Wang (2019) writes:

> Empowering students to be independent and critical thinkers is considered one of the most important educational goals of higher education. . . . Critical thinking needs intellectual and academic

tools. It has been observed that an interdisciplinary approach of teaching and learning promotes critical thinking (Newell 1992; Howlett, Ferreira and Blomfield 2016). . . . [By being introduced to different fields, students learn] how each discipline asks a distinct research question, carrying out inquiries using its disciplinary methodology, and generating different kinds of material and knowledge.

Interdisciplinary trends

Calls and programmes for the integration or at least the bridging of science education with other fields of knowledge, such as art, design, engineering and humanities, have multiplied in recent years. Beyond Science Education, we now have STEM (Science, Technology, Engineering and Maths), STEAM (adding Art), STE2AM = STEAM + ESD (Education for Sustainable Development), Holistic Science Education and more.

In their article 'The World Needs Students with Interdisciplinary Education', Bear and Skorton (2019) write:

> Over the past two years, we had the opportunity to examine this trend in higher education in the context of a National Academies consensus report, *Branches from the Same Tree: The Integration of the Humanities and Arts with Sciences, Engineering, and Medicine in Higher Education*, that explored how approaches to teaching and learning that integrate across disciplines might better prepare students for work, life, and citizenship.

These authors note that science and engineering students often resent and reject the idea of having to take courses in writing and history (even history of science), not to mention ethics and the humanities; they believe that they should be focusing on courses that will directly prepare them for jobs and successful careers after graduation. Bear and Skorton (2019) respond that surveys and studies of the work environment show that 'holistic education that integrates the arts, humanities, sciences, and engineering will make students more attractive candidates for employers and more successful in their future career – or, more likely, careers'. They add:

> An online survey conducted by Hart Research Associates found that the majority of employers say that both field-specific knowledge and a broad range of other kinds of knowledge and skills are important for recent college graduates to achieve long-term career success. The skills they rated most important include the ability to communicate clearly, both in writing and orally, teamwork, ethical decision making, critical thinking, and the ability to apply knowledge in complex, multidimensional, and multidisciplinary settings.

Understanding different disciplinary approaches and bringing disciplines into conversation and using them to understand science, facts and methods is also a goal of 'epistemic insight' (EI). Indeed, in addition to 'knowledge about knowledge', EI has been defined as 'knowledge about disciplines and how they interact' (Billingsley et al. 2018). And as we shall see (below) in the 'experiment' I conducted in my Astronomy course, bringing literature, art and humanities more generally (including, occasionally, some philosophical and religious considerations) into a science (Astronomy) course can be helpful for the goals of science education and critical thinking that I outlined above.

A small experiment: Astronomy, art and writing

I have been teaching a standard Introduction to Astronomy course at my university for some twenty years, not to mention somewhat different versions of the course (in Arabic, for instance) at other institutions in my previous academic life.

I have always included in my Astronomy course(s) a number of historical segments, as I believe that the astounding development of Astronomy is best appreciated when each milestone is placed in its historical context. But I have also insisted on substantial reading and writing, by asking students to write website reviews and, most notably, having a term paper at the end of the course. From time to time, philosophical ideas pop up in my class, such as when considering the place of humans in an unimaginably huge cosmos, the very short history of humanity (a few hundred thousand years) compared to the billions of years that Earth and the Universe have existed, the possibility of highly intelligent and inconceivably advanced aliens (we have only existed for a short time and been technologically 'advanced' for a few centuries; compare that to aliens who may have appeared elsewhere millions or even billions of years ago) and so on. In fact, even religious questions are sometimes asked by students when astronomy intersects with, for instance, the Islamic calendar or the scientific scenario of earth's, life's and humanity's evolution, and so on. I do my best, in all such instances, to teach the students how to distinguish scientific from other questions, how to answer the science parts (the facts and methods needed there) and how to go about addressing other (religious or philosophical) aspects of their questions, that is, who are the experts in those fields, how to find appropriate references and so on?

Between 2005 and 2011, I added science-fiction novels (and when available, movies) to my arsenal of astronomy teaching tools. I first made *Rendezvous with Rama* by Arthur C. Clarke (first published in 1973) required reading, partly because I consider it one of the best, relatively short and most fascinating sci-fi novels ever written, but mainly because it contains a great amount of science and engineering. Thus, I integrated this novel into the course and its assessment tools, including questions in the homework assignments ('Discussion Questions') and the term paper ('Essay Questions').

However, many students resisted and resented this 'non-science' component of the course and found the whole idea of reading a novel – and carefully enough to answer questions about it, in relation to what was being learnt in the course – too demanding and challenging. It then occurred to me that a good sci-fi novel from which a movie had been made could be a good solution: watch the movie together, thus be familiar with the story and its elements, then read the novel, slowly over a semester. So, I turned to *2001: A Space Odyssey* (a classic, first published in 1968) and *2010: Odyssey Two* (its sequel, first published in 1982).

Before I give a short list of the questions that I asked for each novel, both 'discussion questions' (in homework assignments) and 'essay questions' (to be addressed in term papers), I must explain the rationale and objectives behind this exercise/experiment, and how it can be adapted and adopted by other instructors.

The idea is to draw the students' attention to the science that one sometimes/often encounters in various fields of knowledge and areas of life, but how one must be 'critical' to ensure that what is being presented is indeed correct. For instance, in *Star Wars*, deflecting or blocking laser beams would require one (the Jedi) to move faster than light. In *Star Trek*, calls are made between planets (sometimes in different parts of a galaxy) with instant communication! Thus, learning astronomy, and the basic physics needed for it helps one develop an understanding of how the world/universe works, and movies and novels present us with opportunities to think critically while enjoying the stories.

Below, and for space limitations, I only present five questions in each set ('Discussion' and 'Essay' questions) that I posed to the students.

Discussion questions for Rendezvous with Rama:

- Describe Rama's cylindrical sea.
- Describe the 'biots' and other Rama 'creatures'.
- Draw sketches of the various parts of Rama, especially inside.
- What propulsion system did Rama use to travel between stars and planets?
- What futuristic predictions (between the twentieth and the twenty-second centuries) does Clarke make that you found reasonable, and which ones did you find surprising and unreasonable?

Essay questions for Rendezvous with Rama:

- Find at least three instances in the novel that show that instantaneous communication is not possible. Did this fact

- help or hinder the actions of the protagonists. Generalize this to deep-space travel and determine its consequences.
- Describe how gravity plays an important role in the novel; find at least three examples.
- Describe the colonization of the solar system as imagined by Clarke in the twenty-second century.
- Comment on the amount, depth and accuracy of the science used in the novel. Provide examples. Do you think the author 'overdid' it? Do you think science-fiction novels should be that 'hard' (accurate)?
- What conclusion can one draw from the novel about the place of humans in the cosmos? Do you agree with the author's general philosophy? Why/why not?

Discussion questions for 2001: A Space Odyssey:

- What is the main idea of Part 1 – 'Primeval Night'? What is the main characteristic of the 'man-apes'? What was the effect of the monolith on them?
- What is hibernation? Why was it used on Discovery?
- What propulsion techniques were used by Discovery to reach Saturn (in the novel)?
- What happened to Floyd when he went into the monolith? What is a 'wormhole'?
- What is the white dwarf mentioned in the 'Reception' chapter?

Essay questions for 2001: A Space Odyssey:

- In your view, what is the scientific message of the book and the movie?
- How realistic is the voyage to the moon and to Jupiter in view of science and of today's technology?
- How realistic is the beginning plot of the book, humanity being visited by some space intelligence?

- Is the 'Alien Sky' at the end of the novel observed by *Discovery* realistic?
- Is the artificial intelligence of HAL realistic? If yes, how could it be used in future space flight? If not, why not?

Discussion questions for 2010: Odyssey Two:

- What is the inner Lagrange point – the parking spot of Discovery near Jupiter?
- Who is or what is 'Tsien'? What was its mission and how did it complete with 'Leonov'? What manoeuvre did it use to rendezvous with Europa? Why did it land on Europa?
- Where was life found in the Jupiter system (planet and moons)? In what form?
- What warning did Floyd receive? From whom? Why was that problematic for the Leonov? What solution was found to depart for home before the opening of the 'launch window'?
- What name was given to the new 'sun'? What effect does it have (over the long term) on the moons of Jupiter?

Essay questions for 2010: Odyssey Two:

- What were the planned Discovery II's mission primary objectives? How do they compare with today's mission goals to the planets?
- What is meant by 'Jupiter is a star that failed'? Under what conditions would it not have failed, and what would have been the consequences for us here on Earth?
- How can planets propel spacecraft through the solar system?
- Describe the moons of Jupiter and the possibility of their harbouring life.
- Explain methods that can or are used to discover extra-terrestrial life, either intelligent or primitive.

Results of my 'experiment'

As I briefly mentioned above, asking students to read (any) texts nowadays is tantamount to torturing them! Imagine asking them to read a novel in a science course (and I discovered that many students do not like science fiction, though some changed their minds in the process)! Watching the movies that were available (for '2001' and '2010') before reading the novels did help the students follow the story, but this solution is not always possible.

On the other hand, the 'Discussion questions' were very useful in ensuring that the students were indeed reading on a steady pace and were guided on the main ideas and milestones in each novel (What propulsion techniques were used by the spacecraft in making it to Saturn? How big was the monolith near Jupiter?, etc.)

Some students engaged well with the novels; some were in fact startled by that fact/realization. Fellow science educators may not be surprised that some students got more interested in the science of the course (gravity, orbits, radiation, physical conditions on various planets and moons) and were more willing to explore it when these topics were part of a novel/movie/story. Students certainly learnt to examine elements of a story more critically (factually, based on the science they were learning) and to distinguish scientific ideas from fictional ones. The exercise was not clearly helpful in digesting the 'nature of science', that is, how science comes to learn things about the world and how that knowledge is checked, ascertained and (if possible) established. Perhaps some other exercises (I have mentioned reading real-world scientific reports, hopefully not too technical) can help us science educators develop that understanding in students.

Still, the experiment was a big challenge to both me as the instructor and guide and to many of the students for whom this was too unusual and rather difficult. One suggestion that has been made to me is to pair my Astronomy course with an English/Writing course, to team-teach it with a colleague from the English/Writing department and perhaps to make the novel(s) more central to the Astronomy, that is teach the science *from* the novel(s).

One question that I have been asked is how this exercise could be conducted in a 'workshop' setting, which is in a few-hour session. Obviously, this would have to be limited to the movie part, unless participants were asked to read the novel in the days/weeks preceding the workshop. If the relevant movie is watched, say, the evening before the workshop, either in a group or individually, then the 'Discussion questions' can form the basis of a collective conversation, and the 'Essay questions' can be an individual-writing segment that students/participants are asked to undertake at the end of the workshop.

Concluding thoughts

One important idea is to always keep in mind that science education aims at raising students' scientific knowledge as well as digesting the scientific process/method and to apply it more widely in various areas of life. Both evidence-based knowledge of the world around us and the systematic process of reasoning and investigation can help us address many issues and problems in various domains. Science is both knowledge and tool to be used widely.

Another important objective of science education is to train students to distinguish between evidence-based explanations and opinions on any issue they read or hear about. It was indeed shocking to learn from the PISA 2018 reports that only 10 per cent of fifteen-year-old students could do that (in topics they were not already familiar with). This should become a primary objective of science education (and education more broadly).

Finally, interdisciplinary topics and approaches can be very useful in achieving the above objectives, as those topics require understanding ideas and arguments from different disciplines and realizing that science does connect to many other fields of life and social relevance.

References

Bailin, S. (2002). 'Critical Thinking and Science Education', *Science & Education*, 11: 361–75.
Bear, A. and D. Skorton (2019). 'The World Needs Students with Interdisciplinary Education', *Issues in Science and Technology*, 35(2): 60–2.

Billingsley, B. and M. Hardman (2017). 'Epistemic Insight: Teaching and Learning About the Nature of Science in Real-world and Multidisciplinary Arenas', *School Science Review*, 365: 57–8.

Billingsley, B, M. Nassaji, S. Fraser, and F. Lawson (2018). 'A Framework for Teaching Epistemic Insight in Schools', *Research in Science Education*, 48(6): 1115–31.

Clarke, A. C. (1968, 2000). *2001: A Space Odyssey*. Logan: Perfection Learning.

Clarke, A. C. (1973, 1977). *Rendez-Vous with Rama*. NYC: Del Rey / Ballantine.

Clarke, A. C. (1982, 1997). *2010: Odyssey Two*. NYC: Harper Voyager.

Fernández, G. E. A. et al. (2022). 'Students' Performance in the Scientific Skills During Secondary Education', *EURASIA Journal of Mathematics, Science and Technology Education*, 18(10): em2165.

Howlett, C., J. Ferreira, and J. Blomfield (2016). 'Teaching Sustainable Development in Higher Education: Building Critical, Reflective Thinkers Through an Interdisciplinary Approach', *International Journal of Sustainability in Higher Education*, 17(3): 305–21.

Mintz, S. (2022). 'Let's Apply Critical Thinking Outside the Classroom', *Inside Higher Ed*. https://www.insidehighered.com/blogs/higher-ed-gamma/let%E2%80%99s-apply-critical-thinking-outside-classroom (accessed 10 March 2023).

National Academy of Sciences. (1996). *National Science Education Standards*. Washington, DC: National Academy Press.

Newell, W. (1992). 'Academic Disciplines and Undergraduate Interdisciplinary Education: Lessons from the School of Interdisciplinary Studies at Miami University, Ohio', *European Journal of Education*, 27(3): 211–21.

PISA (Programme for International Student Assessment). (2019). *2018 Results (Vol. I): What Students Know and Can Do*. Paris: OECD Publishing. https://doi.org/10.1787/5f07c754-en.

TIMSS (International Results in Mathematics and Science). (2019). https://timssandpirls.bc.edu/timss2019/international-results/ (accessed 10 March 2023).

Wang, S. (2019). 'Enhancing Critical Thinking Through Interdisciplinary Teaching and Learning', *Teaching and Learning Connections*, 10. https://www.cetl.hku.hk/teaching-learning-cop/enhancing-critical-thinking-through-interdisciplinary-teaching-and-learning/(accessed 10 March 2023).

14

Philosophy and Artificial Friends

Greg Artus

Introduction: Science and philosophy

The burgeoning contemporary field known as Machine Ethics is a perfect illustration of where philosophy and the sciences meet and shape each other.

Science and philosophy have always been tightly interwoven, whether it be in the way that the work of scientists is shaped and directed by the conceptual, epistemological and metaphysical assumptions they bring to their enquiries, or in the ethical, social and political implications of the innovations and discoveries that the sciences have unleashed on the world.

Epistemologically, when embarking on any empirical enquiry, one can never simply 'look', one must always look 'for' something. And what one looks for, what one thinks is knowable or discoverable, or what one thinks must exist, depends upon the framework of assumptions about reality that one brings to the task – what one looks *for* depends upon where one looks *from*. And these assumptions are fundamentally philosophical. For example, questions about the nature of thought – what thinking and understanding actually are – are largely conceptual, philosophical issues in the first instance, and if one embarks on one's empirical enquiries assuming that thinking is computational, and that what we do is simply a vastly more complex version of what machines can do, then one will try to build thinking machines in a particular way. If one believes, however, that what we do is something other than computation, then one will approach one's research from within a different frame.

Similarly in the case of more ethical concerns, what one researches is dependent upon what one thinks is important and what one thinks will improve the world and people's lives, and this depends upon one's assumptions about what a human being is, what they need and what is the right thing to do. Nobody just does science. Everyone does it for a reason, and what they explore is related to who they are, what they believe and how they understand the world. For example, some scientists might feel that certain areas of research, such as chemical and biological weapons, ought to be off-limits, while others might believe that science should be free to explore anything and everything, and that the pure researcher cannot be held responsible for the technological applications of their discoveries. These are philosophical, not empirical matters.

In these ways and many others, science and philosophy have always been inseparable, feeding off each other, with the work of scientists being shaped by the philosophical milieu in which research is carried out, and the work of philosophers being shaped by an awareness of the discoveries and inventions of science. Machine Ethics is perhaps the most recent, and most crucial, example of this interplay, where it is imperative that science and philosophy speak to each other and learn from each other.

Machine ethics

The tremendous recent advances in machine learning technology, and the increasing use of AI to run nearly every aspect of our lives, means that the ethical, social and political implications of this technology cannot be ignored. The sheer power of modern AI, as well as its ubiquitous reach, means that we must be aware of, and must prepare for, any problems these new tools throw up long before they happen, so that we may reap the benefits of this technology while guarding against the risks that go with it.

As with any technology, the more powerful it is and the more possibilities it creates for us, the more risks and dangers it carries with it, so the ethical dilemmas thrown up by the sheer power of modern AI are endless. Algorithms are being used not only to guide and control our online consumer choices but also to shape our online interactions with each other and even our sense of self. Should these algorithms be transparent and regulated, or should they be protected as commercially confidential secrets? Should we build autonomous battlefield robots to fight our wars for us? How would this change warfare, and us? Should people be allowed to make sexbots that are perfect simulations of a human sexual partner? Would this change human sexual relations in positive or negative ways? Should we allow machines to decide criminal cases, or run capital markets? Who ought to own the data that corporations collect from us as we spend more and more of our lives online? Just how many of the decisions that used to be made by humans can safely be outsourced to algorithms which are, at present, opaque 'Black Boxes' whose reasoning and justification for their decisions are not open to scrutiny by their designers? These and many other discussions and dilemmas are what occupy both philosophers and researchers in the field of machine ethics. Artificial friends fall within this field.

The ethics of artificial friends

Concerns about the ethical implications of artificial friends have been discussed by philosophers, psychologists, scientists and industry experts ever since the realistic possibility of them became apparent in the late 1990s (Wallach and Allen 2009; Kanamori et.al 2002; Sparrow and Sparrow 2006; Sharkey and Sharkey 2010; Friedman and Kahn 2003). Since then, continual improvements in robotics as well as advances in AI deep-learning systems have expanded these possibilities, so that machines, such as Softbank's *Pepper* and Riken's *ROBEAR*, have been introduced as companions and care-assistants in hospitals and care homes for the elderly (BBC news online 2016), while others, such as Intuition Robotics' *ElliQ*, are used in people's homes, providing companionship to the elderly who suffer from social isolation and loneliness (Engelhart 2021; Fuchs 2022). There are now numerous robotic pets available, with some, such as *PARO* and the market leader, the *Joy For All Companion Pet*, having even been purchased in large numbers by various local health departments in the United States, to be distributed to socially isolated elderly citizens (ref). Once again, the aim is to provide companionship and respite from loneliness and depression. Even in the field of psychotherapy, Chatbots, such as *Woebot*, *Wysa* and *Youper*, are specifically designed and programmed to act as therapists, and their use has increased since the pandemic, as there are simply not enough mental health professionals to cope with the growing numbers who need help (Darling 2023).

The uses of such machines are many and varied, from offering companionship, to practical nursing care, to helping around the house, to therapy. Some are human-like or animal-like in design and capable of following users around, while others are designed more as tabletop devices. Some have sophisticated language programming so they can teach, converse and interact with users, while others have little or no linguistic capability. Some are even programmed to simulate a limited range of emotional responses. What binds all these machines together, however, is that they are part of a trend that is seeing machines introduced into that most intimate and important aspect of our lives, personal relationships. They open the possibility, for the first time in human history, of our forming a personal relationship with a machine. And this is why they have raised such worries and concerns about the ethical implications of encouraging people to bond, even in quite superficial ways, with an inanimate machine that, by definition, is incapable of reciprocating any of the emotions that go with human relationships. A machine cannot be hurt or upset by you (even if it may be able to simulate it, as some can); it can never love or care for you, or feel betrayal or loyalty or trust or gratitude.

Human relationships in all their forms, from casual acquaintances to friends to life partners, are at the same time both one of the most rewarding and fulfilling aspects of life, but also one of the most risky, and, like anything truly important, the solace and fulfilment they can bring always come with the risk of pain and disappointment. They involve trust, openness, care and commitment, and in this sense, they are where we are most exposed as people. It is only because we open up and are exposed to another, however, that we gain such a sense of connection to others. If I never trust anyone enough to risk exposure, then I will never have any true friends and the joys of human connection will be denied to me. Relationships can provide a sense of belonging, a oneness with others, a sense that one is not alone in the world. But the reason many people feel uncomfortable about being so exposed is exactly because when it goes wrong and one is let down, the emotional pain can be devastating. Equally importantly, one can often discover a sense of self among others, and one frequently understands who one is in terms of one's relationships with others, helping create either positive or negative ways of understanding who one is. Consequently, how one is embedded among the world of others is intimately tied to one's identity as a person, one's deepest self-understanding. Is it any wonder, then, that people are concerned about letting machines into this area of human life? These are no longer mere tools designed for purely practical tasks, such as doing calculations, or building cars for us; these machines are being specifically designed for us to form relationships with. Their express purpose is to enter into our most intimate human world in ways that machines never have before. The question, then, is, do we actually want them there, or are the risks too great?

In the literature on artificial friends, people have worried about the risks of users becoming too attached to these machines, of coming to trust them, even care for them and becoming emotionally committed to or otherwise invested in them and, perhaps more dangerously, to come to believe that their feelings are reciprocated by the machine (Fuchs 2022). The risks of disappointment and negative feelings of betrayal and abandonment that could potentially be the result of becoming so involved with their artificial friend could clearly be catastrophic for anyone, let alone for more vulnerable individuals. For example, imagine you fell on hard times and had to sell your friend, or it was otherwise taken away from you? The machine wouldn't care one way or the other and would just go to its new home and behave as it did with you, but you would be left grieving for the loss of a friend. How would you feel? Some have even argued that the very idea of such machines is built around deception, in that these machines are designed specifically to deceive people into falling into such misunderstanding. Indeed, some manufacturers are very concerned to avoid creating this problem and go to great pains to not make the simulation too lifelike for this very reason. But how likely is this to really happen?

There is a sense in which people have always had relationships with machines and other inanimate objects because humans have always been prone to anthropomorphize the things we interact with. I sometimes see malevolence in the way my computer resists my will; a child will treat its toy as if it were alive; there have even been cases where military personnel have become so attached to their bomb disposal robot, whom they christened Scoobie, that they had a memorial service for it when it was eventually damaged beyond repair (Giilani 2012; Neal 2013). Such anthropomorphization seems quite natural to humans and seems harmless, so isn't it equally harmless to form a bond with artificial friends and machine companions? Is it really so different? When a child talks to its doll, or soldiers mourn their drone, are they really taken in? Are they so gullible as to believe the doll or drone is a real friend with whom they are in a real relationship? One would be inclined to say that they are not, and that there is a part of them that knows exactly what is going on here, and that the attachment they feel is of a very different kind to that which we form with another human being. So, would artificial friends be no more unhealthy or dangerous than a child loving its doll, or soldiers mourning their drone?

Humans seem capable of some very strange and puzzling types of relationship to others, as one can see, for example, from the field of Aesthetics and questions about the totally baffling way in which we seem to relate to fictional characters (Radford 1975). On the one hand, we become involved with them, care for them, worry for them, cry for them, hate them or love them, yet all the while we keep munching our popcorn. We relate to them almost as real people, but only *almost*. We immerse ourselves in their plight, then happily go about our business. We cry, get angry, feel scared, yet all the while are *having fun*. The popular term 'suspension of disbelief' doesn't do justice to the curiousness of this relationship, and glosses over just how odd it is. While we are immersed in their lives, we genuinely care for them, and can be deeply affected by them, so it seems to be more than mere playing – what happens to them is important to us in a way we don't really comprehend. 'Suspension of disbelief' makes it sound a lot simpler than it is. It is one of those phrases that serves more to simply side-line the problem, than to explain it. Could this be one way that we might deal with artificial friends, were we to have them? For example, some anecdotal evidence suggests that elderly and vulnerable people who have robot pets love them as pets and treat them as pets, yet are never gullible enough to believe the fiction they have woven around their bot (Fuchs 2022). We are endlessly imaginative creatures, yet we don't often fall for the fictions we create.

The motivations for deploying artificial friends

Other concerns about the use of artificial friends relate to the motivations for their use and to the social consequences of them becoming more ubiquitous. In the field of mental health, as companions to ease loneliness, or as therapists, they are often used not because anyone thinks that they will do a better job than a human, but more because the demand for carers and therapists far outstrips the supply of human carers and mental health professionals. They are a second-best alternative to genuine human companionship or a human therapist. This raises some very difficult questions. First, we must ask why so many people are socially isolated and lonely, and why so many people require treatment for mental health issues. There may be wider structural issues here about the very nature of modern life – the way our lives have changed such that families are more dispersed, that few of us live in tightknit communities and support groups than perhaps we used to; more people live alone; more people live longer and so on. These are social, political and economic issues that would require significant social change to alleviate, but if we really do believe that greater numbers of people do feel alienated, lonely and isolated, then should we simply invent a robot as a sticking plaster for the problems of modern life, or should we actually address these wider issues and try to cure the causes of the problem, such that fewer people need these machines in the future? Isn't using machines as a fix simply accepting that modern life is alienating without trying to make modern life better? And would using these robots in this way simply reinforce economic, social and political models that we are discovering to be deeply unhealthy for so many people? It can be argued that the machines are better than nothing in a crisis, but does that absolve us of the need to address the causes of the crisis?

Similarly, if the motivation to deploy artificial friends in place of carers was driven by the shortage of caregivers, could their use even exacerbate the problem? If I know that mum has an artificial friend, would I feel less inclined to make sacrifices to visit her myself, and could she not then become even more alone? And if machines became common substitutes for human social care more generally, could that lead to cuts in funding for more carers. Would social care eventually become almost totally automated, creating an even more isolated and alienated society? Once again, these are deep philosophical, social and political questions that cannot be ignored. We need to ask why we want to use machines in this way.

Furthermore, could it even be argued that the apparent crisis in mental health, for which we are treating machines as a possible solution, may be caused in part by yet other machines? What is the relation between social media and mental health? Are the algorithms which determine our online interactions creating problems which we think we can now cure by using other algorithms as therapists? And if we do use algorithms to cure problems created by other algorithms, are we not then caught in an endless arms race with our own machines, continually building new tools to fix problems created by other tools and so on? Should we not step back and take a long hard look at why the machines we have built are creating problems, rather than continually racing to catch up with our own technology?

The phenomenology of artificial friends

Phenomenology is the philosophical method which attempts to describe human experience in terms of what it means to us to *Be*; what the experience of *Being-there* (*Dasein*) is actually like from the inside. In this sense, phenomenology doesn't approach things from the same stance as the sciences or much other philosophy, which tries to describe *what a human being is*, but rather tries to describe what it is like to be one. Heidegger wrote about loneliness and depression as *moods* (Heidegger 1995). Moods differ from emotions in that whereas an emotion usually is a response to some thing or event or person and has an object towards which one feels the emotion, a mood is more like an atmosphere which pervades and colours ones every experience. In this sense it is more a state of being than an emotional response, and the use of artificial friends is often aimed at combatting or alleviating such negative ways of being as loneliness, depression and feelings of dissociation from others and the world. When one is immersed in such moods, the whole of one's experience looks and feels different and has a different, darker meaning. When one is depressed, it is difficult to see joy in anything, and the world means something completely different to you compared to when you aren't depressed – even a sunny day can seem bleak. And when one is gripped by loneliness, the company of others only makes you feel more alone because you feel disconnected from them, and their presence simply reminds you of your sense of isolation (Aho 2022). Moods shape the meaning we see in experience. They can, like loneliness, make one feel *not-at-home* in one's world, as Heidegger puts it.

The key to Heidegger's thought on these issues is that he argues that our basic existential condition in that of *Being-in-the-World*, and understanding what he means by this may help us grasp the role that artificial friends could play in human life. When Heidegger says we are *in-the-world*, he does not mean that we are an object alongside other objects – we are not in the world as I am currently inside my office. Rather, the *in* he means is more in the experiential sense that one can be *in-love*, or *in-a-rage*. It is a state of Being, not a location. Similarly, by the *World*, he does not mean the collection of objects present in the world, but a world of meanings, more like the sense in which we talk of the 'world of mathematics' or the 'world of science' or the 'world of the arts'. We are always immersed in the worlds of meaning we have created, and it is these *Worlds* which create the possibilities for us to *Be* anyone at all. If there was no world of education, then I could never have aimed at being a lecturer, but now that I am a lecturer, the way I involve myself in it shapes that world, which in turn shapes me, who in turn shapes that world and so on, in a never-ending mutual embrace between me and the worlds of meaning that create my possibilities. Furthermore, we are always looking out from within a world of meanings. As mentioned above, we never just look from nowhere, but must always look from somewhere, from within some world of meanings, which colours and shapes, and is shaped by, what we experience.

These worlds of meaning create the conditions for our own subjectivity and sense of who we are. But they are worlds that none of us can create on our own, they are shot through with the presence of others – I alone couldn't create a 'world of education'. In this sense, *Being* is always *Being-with-Others*. Our world is always a *with-world*, and together we create the conditions for each of us to develop our own subjectivity. At birth, we are *Thrown* into a world of meanings, as if we were thrown onto the stage of a play which is already up and running. There is a basic plot, characters and stage directions, but each of us must find our own way to interpret the roles we choose to embrace. These roles provide us with possibilities for acting and forging ahead into the future, embarking on projects made possible by our being on that stage.

But this world of meanings is no purely intellectual set of beliefs, but a total way of orienting oneself to experience. We give shape, structure and meaning to existence by the way we are bodily involved with it over time, so our world is lived through our bodily involvements as much as it is cognized. For example, inhabiting the world-of-science is as much a case of living bodily among scientific equipment and environments and *Being-with* other scientists as it is grasping scientific methods and understanding. *Being* a scientist is not the same as knowing things about science. Similarly, our *Being-in-the-World* is no mere intellectual set of beliefs or a form of understanding, but a way of bodily grappling with the world and *Being-with-Others* over time. Consequently, while we must recognize that the mood of loneliness is not about the spatial proximity of other people but is rather a mood whereby one can feel lonely even in the presence of others, one's *World* cannot be separated from one's bodily involved experience, so the lack of the bodily presence of others cannot be ignored as a contributor to loneliness. However, it is not the mere presence of others that matters so much as the way they are present over time; familiarity with one's world must have a historical structure. A person who lives alone and is visited by a succession of different carers with whom she has no shared past, no routines, no regular rituals, no running jokes, none of the little everyday shared nonsense that makes one part of some World of others over time, would likely just feel even more isolated, despite the regular presence of others. But could an artificial friend fulfil at least some of this role of helping to create a *World* for those who feel alone, albeit in a deficient mode? Could one not *Be-With* a robot in the sense that the daily greetings, rituals and routines of sharing a physical space together over time could create some structure, some *World* for those who have become alienated and lonely?

We worry about people becoming too emotionally attached to artificial friends, committing to them or building expectations which are likely to be disappointed, thus putting them at risk of greater damage and pain, but we shouldn't ignore the benefits of bodily *Being-With-Over-Time*, and the crucial role such *Being-With* plays for our sense of familiarity with our *World* and our sense of who we are. If we lose this sense of familiarity, we lose our viewpoint on the world and our connection to it. Without a history we cannot see where the future should go and we become trapped in a meaningless present, but could artificial friends provide a temporal structure of familiarity, a *World*, that may help people reconnect with the world in ways that help them see the future as meaningful? And could this not then make it possible for people to reconnect with others and become, once again, part of a *with-world*?

Conclusion

As we have seen, just like all other powerful technologies, our ever-expanding capacity to create artificial friends capable of sharing the most intimate and exposing areas of human life raises many difficult questions, but only by exploring the question of artificial friends from many different angles can we begin to understand how these devices might help us and how to avoid the pitfalls that may come with them. We must look at them through philosophy, psychology, the political, social and economic science, as well as from a technological point of view.

The risk of people becoming too attached is real, but we can take steps to make sure the machines in no way encourage this (e.g. they should never be able to say 'I love you', or perhaps shouldn't be too human-like in appearance). But even if people do become attached to their artificial friends, is that such a bad thing? When my dog died, I grieved for months, but I wouldn't conclude from that that I shouldn't have had a dog. Is not grieving a natural, healthy human experience that connects us to the world and others?

Would an artificial friend encourage people to withdraw from others into a world of machine fantasy friends, or is the sheer anonymity of machines the very thing that makes it safe for some people to engage and connect with them? Could they not be a steppingstone to a fuller engagement with others by providing a limited structure and meaning to people's everyday existence?

If, however, the reason we want to deploy artificial friends is simply so that we can ignore the lonely and make them the machine's problem, then surely this would be to further break down the bonds and responsibilities that make our *World* liveable as a *Being-with-Others*. If used as one way to help re-establish a meaningful *with-world*, where loneliness is no longer the dominant mode of existence for many, then artificial friends can be a valuable tool, but if they are supposed to be a technological solution to a problem such that we absolve ourselves of the need to look carefully at why loneliness is such an issue in modern life, then they become part of the problem, rather than its solution.

References

Aho, K. (2022). '"We're Protecting them to Death" – A Heideggerian Interpretation of Loneliness Among Older Adults in Long-Term Care Facilities During COVID-19', *Phenomenology and the Cognitive Sciences*, 22: 1053–66. https://doi.org/10.1007/s11097-022-09803-z.

BBC News (Technology). (2016). *Pepper Robot to Work in Belgian Hospital*. 14 June. https://www.bbc.co.uk/news/technology-36528253 (accessed 4 April 2023).

Darling, K. (2023). 'Rise of the Therapy Chatbots: Should You Trust an AI with Your Mental Health?', *BBC Science Focus*, 12 March. https://www.sciencefocus.com/news/therapy-chatbots-ai-mental-health (accessed 2 April 2023).

Engelhart, K. (2021). 'What Robots Can – And can't – Do for the Old and Lonely: For Elderly Americans, Social Isolation is Especially Perilous. Will Machine Companions Fill the Void?', *The New Yorker*, 4 May. https://www.newyorker.com/magazine/2021/05/31/what-robots-can-and-cant-do-for-the-old-and-lonely (accessed 4 April 2023).

Friedman, B. and P. H., Jr. Kahn (2003). 'Human Values, Ethics, and Design', in J. A. Jacko and A. Sears (eds), *The Human–Computer Interaction Handbook*, 1177–201. Mahwah: Lawrence Erlbaum Associates.

Fuchs, M. (2022). 'Meet the New Robots Helping to Solve the Depression and Loneliness Problem in Aging Adults', *Fortune Well*, 12 June. https://fortune.com/well/2022/07/12/robots-help-solve-depression-and-loneliness-epidemic-in-aging-adults/ (accessed 2 April 2023).

Giilani, N. (2012). 'Soldiers in Mourning for Robot that Defused 19 Bombs After it is Destroyed in Blast', *Daily Mail Online*, 4 January. https://www.dailymail.co.uk/sciencetech/article-2081437/Soldiers-mourn-iRobot-PackBot-device-named-Scooby-Doo-defused-19-bombs.html (accessed 2 January 2023).

Heidegger, M. (1995). *Being and Time*, trans. J. MacQuarrie and E. Robinson. Oxford: Balckwell (pt 1, Division1, §§ V).

Kanamori, M. M. Suzuki and M. Tanaka (2002). 'Maintenance and Improvement of Quality of Life Among Elderly Patients Using a Pet-Type Robot', *Japanese Journal of Geriatrics*, 39(2): 214–8.

Neal, M (2013). 'Are Soldiers Getting Too Emotionally Attached to War Robots?', *Vice*, 18 September. https://www.vice.com/en/article/jppy8g/are-soldiers-getting-too-emotionally-attached-to-war-robots, (accessed 1 April 2023).

Radford, C. (1975). 'How Can We Be Moved by the Death of Anna Karenina?', *Proceedings of the Aristotelean Society*, 9(Suppl.): 67–80.

Sharkey, A. and N. Sharkey (2010). 'Granny and the Robots: Ethical Issues in Robot Care for the Elderly', *Ethics and Information Technology*, 14: 27–40. https://link.springer.com/article/10.1007/s10676-010-9234-6 (accessed 4 April 2023).

Sparrow, R. and L. Sparrow (2006). 'In the Hands of Machines? The Future of Aged Care', *Mind and Machine*, 16: 141–61.

Wallach, W. and C. Allen (2009). *Moral Machines: Teaching Robots Right from Wrong*. New York: Oxford University Press.

15

Library Perspective

Closing the Book, Continuing to Grow...

Keith Chappell

The linguist Benjamin Whorf once invited his readers to enter into a thought experiment in which we were to imagine ourselves as people with a '*physiological defect of being able to see only the colour blue*' (Whorf 1956). An important part of this, he argued, is that if this were the case it would be impossible for those people to conceive of the rule that they only see the colour blue. In order to do this, they would need '*exceptional moments in which they saw other colours*'. When our perspectives and sources of knowledge are limited, then it is often hard to know that they are limited. It is only by contrast with the full spectrum of knowledge and ways of gaining that knowledge that we become alert to the limitations of what we perceive. It seems that Whorf's thought experiment is less abstract now than it has ever been. Despite a vast array of sources of information, a number of changes have happened since he was writing in the middle of the twentieth century that have led to increased compartmentalization of knowledge and ways of gaining knowledge. This can be seen in schools, especially as we reach higher levels with students frequently being limited to a few subjects and encouraged to study those that naturally group together such as the sciences, humanities, arts or languages. For example, it is a rare student who leaves an English school at the age of eighteen with leaving qualifications in Chemistry, English and Art. This said, the place of compartmentalization *par excellence* is perhaps the modern university. Here we will consider this with some special focus on the place within the university where knowledge of all sorts comes together – the library.

There have been three key moments in recent history that have proved to be seismic events regarding the compartmentalization of knowledge, disciplines becoming more siloed and the role of library and information services in supporting learning in its broadest sense. One is specific to the university; the others are more external but crucial, nonetheless.

Perhaps the first key stage has been something of an evolution over the last century or more but accelerated in the UK during the 1960s. This is the development of campus universities in which buildings and areas are clearly delineated as being dedicated to a single discipline. Some universities will even have science or health campuses that are entirely separate from the rest of the university; in some cases, this may even be in a different town or city. There are clearly practical aspects to this, such as staff being gathered around key equipment and other resources, and some efficiencies in staff in the same department being able to meet both formally and informally. The common room or coffee area has always been an important part of academic life. There is a degree of separation and indeed suspicion that can develop from such isolation and, much like a finch isolated on an island, evolution apart can take place when communities do not interact. At one university, a note was sent to staff by the dean of science instructing scientists not to walk around campus while wearing lab coats. The instruction made it clear that it was okay if they were in the general 'science area' of campus (which had never been formally designated) but that it might cause alarm to those in humanities and arts departments. I try to think of an analogous situation regarding other disciplines but can only recall an incident in which a philosophy department asked the neighbouring music department to reduce the noise of their practising.

Libraries hold a particular place here as the campus develops. While some departments may retain some small library facilities of their own, for example holding some key journals, most campus universities have developed large central libraries that are often tower blocks and the most visible building on campus. This makes the library perhaps a unique place where disciplines come together, albeit perhaps on separate floors or areas. A library is not, however, simply a building but, from the perspective of students, it can be seen as a collection of the reading lists for all tutors in the university. As such, it is a place where knowledge comes together, and a student of English may find themselves next to a physicist as they strive towards similar goals. Neither is likely to be alarmed by what the other is wearing, beyond the usual sensibilities of fashion that is. Many libraries also have regular themed displays which draw on material from around the library to give insight into topics that may be of local or wider significance. Additionally, the recent acquisitions racks provide a chance of serendipity for those inclined to browse the range of books and journals held there from all fields. All this said, the library classification systems that have developed have frequently resulted in the phenomenon of notices next to lifts and stairwells saying things such as 'Physics Floor 8' and 'History Floor 4'. At least, however, someone reading this is reminded that these other disciplines exist.

The second and more sudden event has been the Covid-19 pandemic. Several topical issues facing the world, such as climate change, have required multidisciplinary approaches but the pandemic gave such approaches a new urgency and focus like no other issue had. This global problem also presented a huge opportunity for working across traditional boundaries. Biologists working on vaccines needed to interact with specialists in refrigeration and transport while medics found themselves needing the help of psychologists, public relations professionals and religious experts, among others, to achieve the widest distribution of vaccines. This, of course, only scratches the surface of the issues raised. Knowledge creators such as scientists, educationalists, social scientists and ethicists needed to work more immediately than usual with knowledge workers such as lawyers, teachers and communicators as well as those professions that deliver outcomes in a practical way such as clinicians, drivers and food logistics. All of this has happened for a long time but rarely, outside war, have these groups actually found themselves in the room together (albeit a virtual room in most cases).

When the pandemic hit, libraries found that they had a matter of hours to shut down and try to move vast amounts of information online. This, of course, had been happening for decades in a managed and sometimes selective way, with some disciplines more disposed to using digital platforms than others. Suddenly, all disciplines needed to find ways to meaningfully communicate and store vital knowledge through digital formats. While this provided some opportunity for interdisciplinary interaction, the reality is that students and staff stopped coming into libraries and became even more siloed within their disciplines. They were neither in the building nor encountering resources on others' reading lists. It is becoming increasingly clear that we are now settling into this as our new pattern of engagement with knowledge. In my teaching, I no longer record lectures or hold seminars through virtual platforms, for which I am immensely grateful, but there is no indication that I will ever be able to send students back to the library in a physical way. Books and periodicals are now largely in digital formats, and to suggest a book that isn't is to invite a comment from the head of the department. It seems that serendipity no longer has a place in undergraduate education and in order to broaden perspectives tutors will need to actively select books that challenge their students to look beyond their silo. There is little incentive at the moment to do so.

Just as sudden and probably equally as revolutionary, perhaps more so in the longer term, is the event of artificial intelligence chatbots such as ChatGPT and their current integration into everyday software such as Microsoft 365 Copilot. Search engine algorithms and AI technology make decisions about perspectives and where valid answers come from to particular questions. Here, even the broader setting of your own subject reading list is lost as all knowledge is presented apart from any context. Answers to questions or other outputs are presented as definitive but without any sense of where the information is located within the greater body of knowledge and which disciplines or sources are given priority. Content is taken out of context, not only of the interdisciplinary and multidisciplinary context but of even the discipline that is given weight. There is no consideration of methodologies, strengths and weaknesses or veracity of individual sources nor of the nature of the discipline itself. There is a risk that the shoulders of those giants on whom we stand are forgotten because we never look there. One example of how context is important in such gathering and use of knowledge is to simply think historically. Knowledge is never fixed at a given point, there is always the history of growth in understanding to the current point and the view of the trajectory of current trends to suggest where we might best look for deeper understanding in the future. AI systems do not prevent this but are not necessarily geared towards it. Indeed, used well they could provide this perspective in a way that has perhaps not been possible before.

Another important factor to consider is that AI systems are culturally loaded. Here again, although AI can amplify existing cultural biases, once we are mindful of the challenges, AI technology can potentially be a huge opportunity for this.

Here, I think, is the value of EI and of genuinely taking time to think about the future of knowledge. Chances to take a step back and to evaluate knowledge, seeking exciting opportunities and testing for risks, need to be built-in to each of these key moments. They have each brought benefits, but it is vital to ensure that essential aspects of knowledge in its broadest sense are not lost along the way. Some of the current EI projects discussed elsewhere in this book, such as Dancing with the Digital (Chapter 7) or Building a Smarter Search Engine (Chapter 10), start to build on the opportunities presented here through breaking down traditional discipline barriers or inviting a wider perspective when seeking knowledge through online systems. What is clear throughout the chapters of this book is the need to engage in knowledge in new and innovative ways. There is no opportunity for conservatism or looking to some golden age, even if that meant being able to read in a library without the sound of phone alerts or the taping of keyboards. This book opens with concepts such as 'cultivating' (Chapter 1) and 'igniting' (Chapter 2) which capture the exciting moment in which we sit, and the opportunities presented. The global perspective of the book highlights the universal nature of the issues at play here, and the need for global perspectives to be brought to this discussion and response. We cannot afford for there to be only a western view of the future of knowledge, a view only just coming to terms with its colonial and limited perspectives. EI has embedded in its very nature the value of diversity, whether this is from subject disciplines or lived experience and it is here that its radical and lasting benefit for the future of knowledge will spring. Big questions, so often used as models for philosophy or pedagogy in this book, are 'Big' because they are not limited to a particular interest group, discipline or culture. The future of knowledge is undoubtedly big.

There are certainly opportunities for providers and funders of research and education to grasp the difficult issues at play here while we have an opportunity, an opportunity that is moving quickly. The philosopher William MacAskill argues that there are key moments in any societal shift when intervention can achieve genuine changes in the course of history, affecting the lives of billions for generations to come (MacAskill 2022). We are at one of those key moments regarding knowledge generation, and the future will reveal how we acquire, use and understand it. We can lock in a model of knowledge that leaves us separated from context and the perspective of others or we can learn from what the library used to represent, a place of coming together of minds. The key thing is, as MacAskill notes, the sooner you respond, the more difference you can make.

References

MacAskill, W. (2022). *What We Owe the Future: A Million-Year View*. London: One World Publications.

Whorf, B. L. (1956). *Language, Thought, and Reality: Selected Writings*. Cambridge, MA: Technology Press of Massachusetts Institute of Technology.

16

Teacher Notes and Resources

Epistemic Insight Initiative glossary

VOCABULARY	DEFINITION
Big questions	Big questions are complex and invite enquiry through many disciplines. They seldom have simple agreed-upon answers. 'Big Questions about human personhood and the nature of reality' are questions that stretch across discipline boundaries and across subject boundaries in schools. They are also questions on which both science and religion have something to say. Examples are as follows: 'Why do life and the universe exist?', 'Are humans significant in the universe?', 'Can a robot be a friend?' 'Why does water matter in our lives?' and 'Are you what you eat?'
Real-world opportunities and problems	Real-world opportunities and problems are practical issues to work with that you can connect to key themes such as citizenship, health and well-being and sustainability. For example: 'Where should we put a wind turbine?', 'How do we stay safe during a pandemic?' and 'Can computers make some decisions for us?'
Disciplines	A discipline is an approach to enquiry and a branch or field of knowledge. There are examples of subjects that match the name of a discipline such as science, history, geography and mathematics.

(Continued)

VOCABULARY	DEFINITION
Subjects	A school subject may focus on working with one discipline or it may cover more than one.
Discipline Wheel	A tool which has a space for a question in the centre of a wheel of disciplines. If the question is a big question like 'what does it mean to be alive?', then students could be invited to think critically about how each of the disciplines around the wheel could help them to investigate the question. Or if the question is a more focused question, students could be asked to consider which of the disciplines would be particularly important to work with.

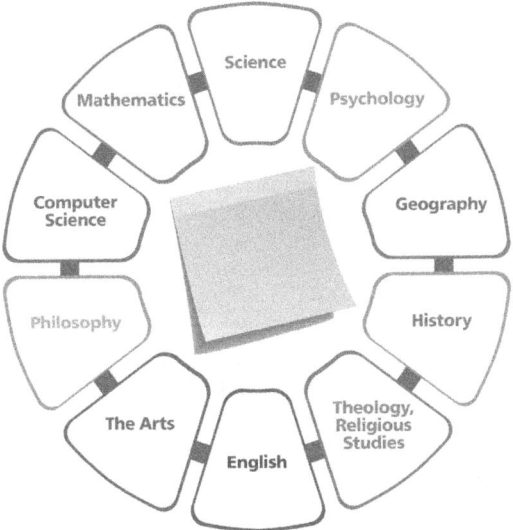

Epistemic insight	Knowledge about knowledge, particularly knowledge about disciplines, and how they interact.
Bridging question	A question that is chosen or designed by the teacher to bridge two disciplines. An example is 'Why did the Titanic sink?', which bridges science and history. A bridging question means that students can compare and contrast how two disciplines interpret and investigate the question. Bridging questions can be used by specialist teachers in secondary schools to show how their discipline connects to another discipline taught in school.

(Continued)

VOCABULARY	DEFINITION
Science questions	Science addresses questions about the natural world. Good questions for science are questions that we can investigate by gathering observations to build and test ideas. For older students we explain that scientists use many methods in their work. The scientific method involves designing investigations that generate observations which we can use to test a hypothesis. A good answer in science helps us to understand how the natural world works and is supported by repeatable observations and measurements.
Observation	Science begins with observations. When we observe in science, we are making connections between our theories and what we observe.
The natural world	Questions about the natural world deal with the building blocks of nature such as fire, water, land, air, minerals, plants and all living things. Science investigates and helps us to understand how the natural world works.
Bubble Tool	We can use this tool to decide and talk about how scientific a question is.

There are likely to be useful smaller scientific questions we can explore

Partly amenable to science

Very amenable to science

Here is a question that is a good one for science: 'How does the size of a parachute affect how quickly an object falls to earth?'

Teaching how disciplines work using the Epistemic Insight Discipline Wheel

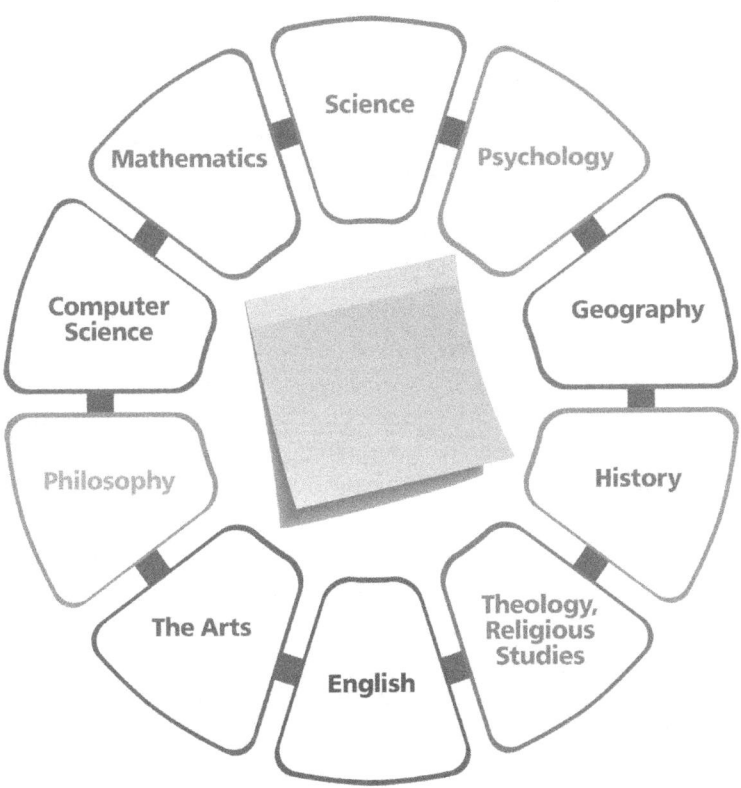

This approach builds students' epistemic insight through hands-on science, enquiry into big questions and working together to solve real-world opportunities and problems.

Session 1 – A hands-on science enquiry

We recommend starting with a question that students can investigate first-hand through a hands-on science activity. The focus will be on learning about how science can help us to get to an answer, rather than the answer itself. There are lots of handy examples in science textbooks. Here's one that's fun to do:

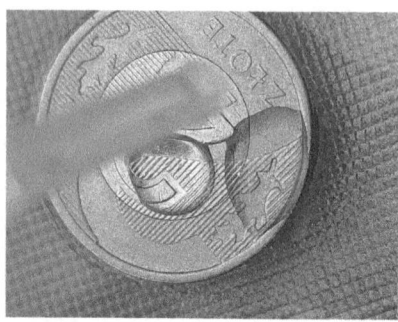

"How many droplets of water can land on a coin before the water overflows?"

To investigate this question – scientifically – we can use a coin, a straw or pipette and a small container of water.

By 'thinking like a scientist' – by making observations, predictions, testing and comparing their results – students can build their understanding of science as a discipline. This is 'epistemic knowledge' – about science. Epistemic knowledge means knowledge about a discipline. Students gain or apply epistemic insight when they discover or use epistemic knowledge in practice.

Once we have asked and investigated a question through the lens of science and learnt how to 'think like a scientist', we can next move to asking, investigating and thinking 'like a historian'?

Working around a selection of disciplines in the 'Discipline Wheel', students can learn and apply their epistemic knowledge through carefully chosen questions, one discipline at a time.

Spotlight on science:

Science helps us to ask and explore **questions about** the natural world. The **methods** we use in science focus on making observations to test ideas and predictions. In science **we say it's a good answer if** many scientists have separately repeated the investigation and have reached the same conclusion.

Session 2 – A bridging question

By exploring a cross-curricular or 'bridging question', students can build their epistemic knowledge about two disciplines and how they are similar, how they are different and how they can work together.

> ### Spotlight on 'Why did the Titanic sink?':
>
> Science helps us to ask and explore **questions about** the natural world. The **methods** we use in science focus on making observations to test ideas and predictions. In science **we say it's a good answer if** many scientists have separately repeated the investigation and drew the same conclusion.
>
> History helps us to ask and explore **questions about** what happened in the past. The **methods** we use in history focus on gathering testimonies, reports and artefacts to look at where people were, what they said and what they wanted to do. Historians say **it's a good answer if** is considered informative and credible – and justified in the context of other things known about the past.

Session 3: A real-world opportunity or problem

Working on a real-world opportunity or problem gives students insight into how disciplines can work together to create better solutions.

Students can be put into groups that each work with a particular discipline. Groups of students can come together to offer their different disciplinary perspectives on the opportunity or problem.

Characterizing disciplines

Here are some more summaries of disciplines – in terms of their preferred questions, methods and norms of thought. They can be adapted for different age groups.

Science	Science helps us to ask and explore **questions about** the natural world. The **methods** we use in science focus on making observations to test ideas and predictions. In science **we say it's a good answer if** many scientists have separately repeated the investigation and drew the same conclusion.
Geography	Geography helps us to ask and explore **questions about** people and places. The **methods** we use in geography focus on gathering observations and other kinds of data to look at where people live and how landscapes change. Geographers say **it's a good answer if** is there are many different types of evidence to support it and if the evidence is not unfairly stacked to suit one group or another.
History	History studies the past and changing accounts of the past. **History asks questions and teaches us about things that happened in the past** (sometimes referred to as the 'stuff' of history), as well as the way history is understood. This includes questions about causes and consequences, change and continuity, similarity and difference, significance and interpretations. It's a good answer if it tells us something new about a previously unknown event in the past or provides new evidence for why something in the past occurred.
Engineering	Engineering helps us to ask and explore questions about how technology can improve people's lives. The methods we use in engineering focus on testing the designs of technologies to assess how well these meet their criteria. Engineers say it's a good answer if it explains how to create technologies that are safe, ethical and reliable.
The arts	The arts help us to ask and explore questions about how to express and communicate what is in our imaginations through forms that we can share. The methods we use in the arts focus on discussing the medium, tools and techniques used, and how meanings in art are perceived by artists and audiences. Artists, audiences and art critics bring in their own views of the world to say whether a work of art or approach is a good answer.

Religious studies	Religious studies help us to ask and explore **questions about religious faith, practices and experiences.** The methods we use focus on gathering sources, texts and stories that express beliefs about human existence and purpose. Scholars in this field say it's a good answer if it is considered informative about a system, history and experience of belief – and justified in the context of other things known about a religious tradition.
Philosophy	Philosophy asks fundamental **questions about existence, reason, knowledge, values and language.** The methods we use in philosophy are based on rational inquiry, systematic thought and critical reflection. One branch of philosophy is known as epistemology. Epistemology is the branch of philosophy that studies knowledge. Another branch of philosophy is Logic which emphasizes the study of reasoning and argument. It's a good answer if, given certain premises, certain conclusions are unavoidably implied.
Economics	Economics is a discipline that studies of how people use resources and respond to incentives, it is also the study of decision making. It often involves topics like wealth and finance. Economics asks a wide range of questions like: 'Why are some countries rich and some countries poor?', 'What causes recessions?' and 'How do people respond to an increase in prices?' The **methods used in economics** involve forecasting models using quantitative analysis, as well as historical analysis. It's a good answer if it tells us something about how people make financial decisions.
Psychology	Psychology is the scientific study of mind and behaviour. Psychology includes the study of conscious and unconscious phenomena, including feelings and thoughts. As a discipline, psychology involves aspects of both the natural and social sciences. There are different types of psychology like behavioural, social, cognitive and psychoanalytic. Although each of these types will have different questions, most of the questions relate to behaviour of individuals or groups. Some psychologists use **empirical methods,** while others use more **theoretical methods.** It's a good answer if it tells us something about why people behave in particular ways.

Teacher resource: The Epistemic Insight Curriculum Framework (two formats)

Version 1 (original version) introduces epistemic insight by Key stage – upper primary, lower secondary and upper secondary.

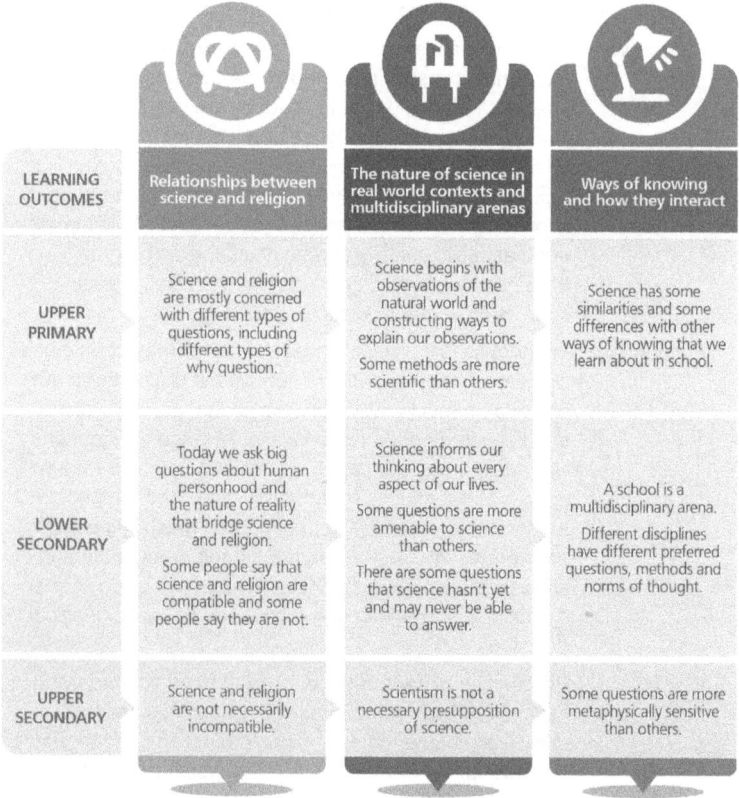

Version 2 introduces the stages of epistemic insight development as a starter, intermediate or advanced and can be accessed by learners at any stage of their learning.

TEACHER NOTES AND RESOURCES

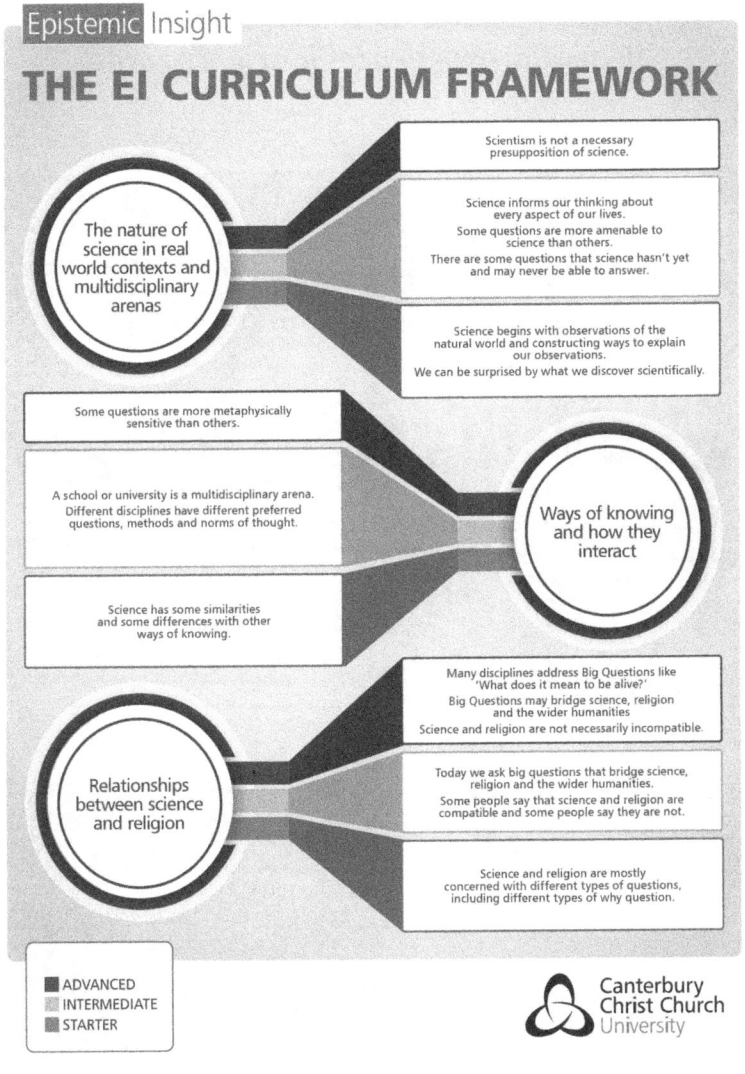

Teacher resource: Why do spinners spin?
Essential experiences in science card

Epistemic Insight

Why do spinners spin?

Essential Experiences in Science

Observe, Measure, Record

To make a spinner
Copy the template below onto a piece of paper. Fold the dotted lines and cut the solid lines. Fold the two wings in opposite directions. Make 2 spinners.

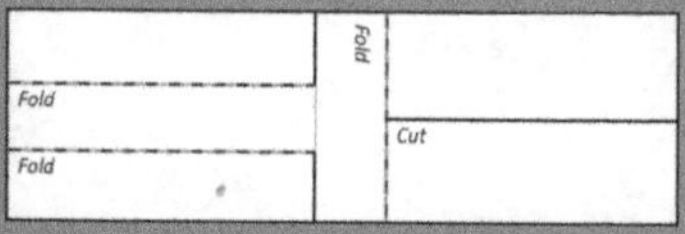

Fold	Fold
Fold	Cut

Challenge 1: Make a spinner that falls quickly. What did you do?

Challenge 2: Make a spinner that falls slowly. What did you do differently?

Challenge 3: Make a spinner that spins quickly. What did you do?

Observe and Record your results.

Paper Race

I have two same sized sheets of paper. One is flat and one is scrunched into a ball.

What will happen when I drop them both at the same time from the same height?

Which one will hit the ground first? Do you know why? Try it out!

Canterbury
Christ Church
University

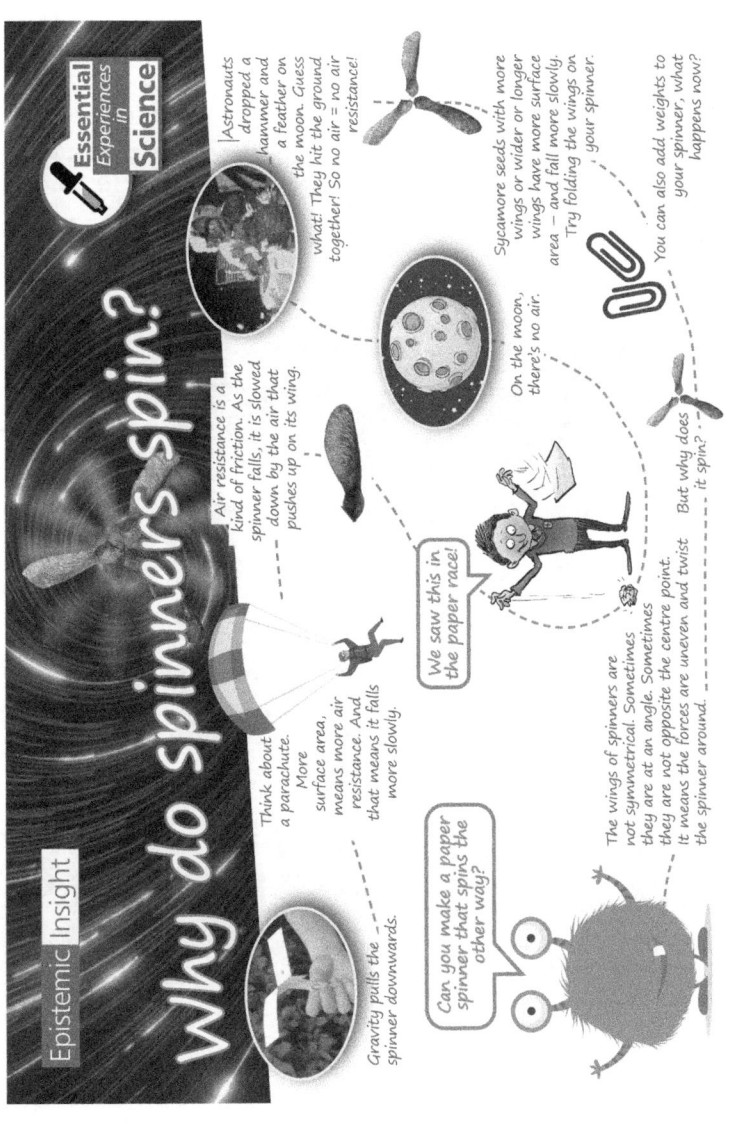

Teacher resource: Why did the Titanic sink? Essential experiences in science cards (science card)

Epistemic Insight

Essential Experiences in Science

Why did the titanic sink?

- If the ship was built to be unsinkable...
- ...how did it manage to sink?
- Was the ship too heavy to float?
- Were there too many passengers?

I went to the fruit bowl in my kitchen and picked out a grape and a watermelon, but I accidentally dropped them into my washing up bowl! To my surprise, the watermelon floated on the water. Even more surprising, the grape sank to the bottom!

Why did the watermelon float when it's so heavy?

And why did the grape sink even though it's so small?

Predict, Observe, Record

Check with an adult that you can use a bowl or the sink for some scientific explorations. Fill with water. Choose a variety of fruit to put in the water.

Which do you predict will float? Which will sink? Why?

Observe what happens to each fruit and record. Were your predictions correct?

Can you make something that floats sink? (e.g. what happens if you poke a hole in it? Can you wrap it in something e.g. an elastic band?)

Canterbury Christ Church University

Epistemic Insight

Why did the Titanic sink?

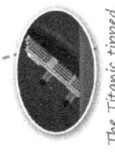
Essential Experiences in Science

Can science help us to answer this mystery?

We can make a model of the Titanic and simulate what happens when a ship strikes an iceberg.

Buoyancy is a term for how well something floats.

The Titanic struck an iceberg. It tore a hole in one side. Water began to break in.

We added some pebbles to simulate a lot of water in the front of the ship. Our model tipped up. Water flowed over the tops of bulkheads and into the other chambers.

Gravity pulls the ship downwards. Upthrust is the upwards push of the water on the ship.

Air trapped inside a ship gives it more buoyancy. Air takes up space but has very little weight.

The Titanic tipped up and sank.

The Titanic was designed to be 'unsinkable', but the bulkheads were too short to save the ship. Is the ship's designer the only person to blame?

This is our model of the Titanic!

The Titanic had bulkheads. So does our model. These are walls inside. If water breaks into one chamber it can't get into the rest of the ship. Why did it still sink?

Teacher resource: Who sank the Titanic? Essential experiences in science cards (history card)

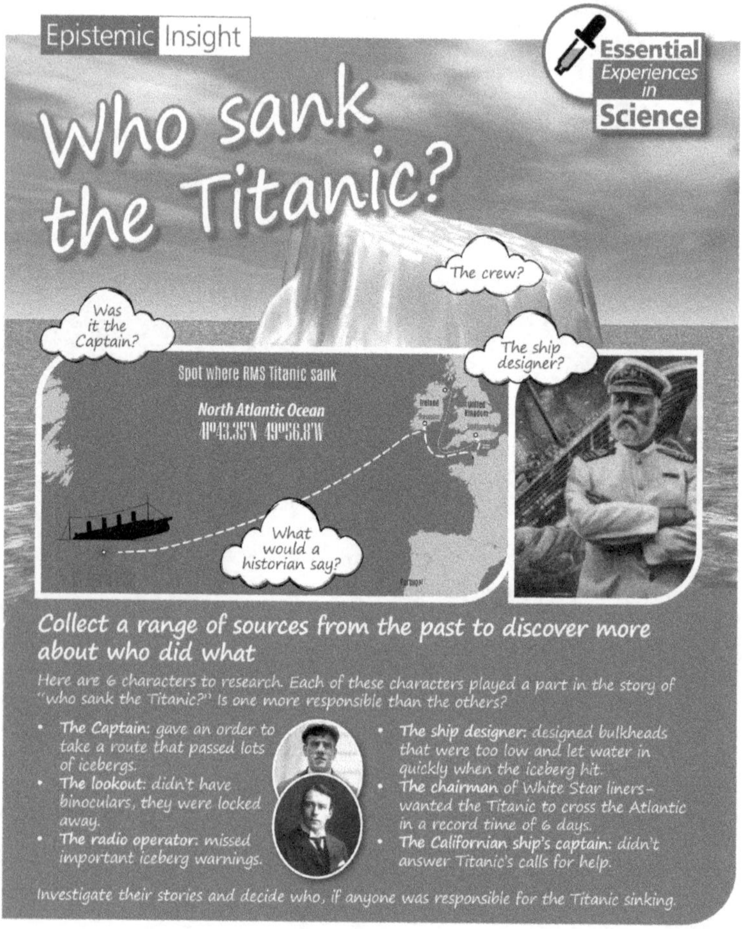

Epistemic Insight — Essential Experiences in Science

Who sank the Titanic?

- Was it the Captain?
- The crew?
- The ship designer?
- What would a historian say?

Spot where RMS Titanic sank
North Atlantic Ocean
41°43.35'N 49°56.8'W

Collect a range of sources from the past to discover more about who did what

Here are 6 characters to research. Each of these characters played a part in the story of "who sank the Titanic?" Is one more responsible than the others?

- **The Captain:** gave an order to take a route that passed lots of icebergs.
- **The lookout:** didn't have binoculars, they were locked away.
- **The radio operator:** missed important iceberg warnings.
- **The ship designer:** designed bulkheads that were too low and let water in quickly when the iceberg hit.
- **The chairman** of White Star liners — wanted the Titanic to cross the Atlantic in a record time of 6 days.
- **The Californian ship's captain:** didn't answer Titanic's calls for help.

Investigate their stories and decide who, if anyone, was responsible for the Titanic sinking.

Epistemic Insight

Why did the Titanic sink?

In April 1912, the Titanic was on her maiden voyage from Southampton in England to New York city in America.

While crossing the Atlantic ocean the ship struck an iceberg and sank. Can history help us to discover why?

What do science and history tell us together? Can we ever be sure we have solved the mystery?

History can help us to find out what people saw and did — the human side of the story.

Historians investigate the past by studying artefacts such as clothes and paintings. They also look for photos, diaries and reports by people at the time.

By drawing on historical evidence, we can construct character cards on some of the people who played a part in Titanic's story.

The Titanic was designed to be 'unsinkable' but history tells us that the actions of the crew also played part in the disaster.

The Captain, The lookout, The radio operator, The ship designer, The chairman of White Star liners, The Californian ship's captain...

If you ask me, it was the ship's designer or then again, maybe the captain. What do you think?

Essential Experiences in Science

Teacher resource: Why is the sky blue? Investigating big questions card

Epistemic Insight

Our Precious Planet

INVESTIGATING BIG QUESTIONS

Planets that are closer to the Sun than we are are hotter. Any water boils away.

On Neptune the temperature is minus 200 degrees Celsius. Too cold!

Our planet has been protected from meteor strikes by Jupiter – a giant planet that has a stronger gravitational field than ours.

Large stars have short lifetimes but our star, the Sun is the right size for a long stable life.

It means there has been enough time for complex life to evolve on the Earth.

The spiral arms of our galaxy are risky places to be – because of the risk of stellar collisions.

Luckily we are in the space in between two spiral arms.

PERFECT

Our planet is the only planet in our solar system that is teeming with life.

Scientists say that the Earth is just right for life.

Get ready to find out how perfect we are!

We live in the 'Goldilocks zone' from our star. This is the zone where water is a liquid.

Teacher resource: How do clouds stay up? Essential experiences in science card

Epistemic Insight — Essential Experiences in Science

How do clouds stay up?

Firstly we need to find out some things about water

Have you seen a spider's web looking like this one?

Or a droplet of water caught in a leaf?

What happens if two droplets run into each other?

Explore, Observe, Record

Dip a straw into a beaker of water and trap some water inside by putting a finger over the end.

Drop water droplets onto a penny. Draw or record your observations.

Canterbury Christ Church University

Epistemic Insight

Why don't clouds fall out of the sky?

Essential Experiences in Science

A cloud is made of tiny water droplets.

They are too light to be pulled to the ground.

The droplets of water join up – just as they did on the penny.

As it rains, the cloud shrinks.

Once the water is gone, there is no more cloud.

You may not see it shrinking because clouds are moving, blown along by the wind.

But you might see a rainbow!

What happens to the cloud after it rains?

The sky darkens...

Big droplets are pulled to the ground by gravity.

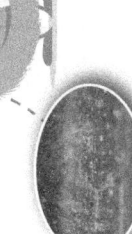

Teacher notes: Why did the spaghetti break (bridging questions)

Epistemic Insight
WORKSHOP

Why did the spaghetti break?
Thinking Insightfully about how two different disciplines address the same question

In this 'hands-on' activity, students are investigating what happens as they put more and more weight into a gondola. They load pebbles into a gondola or basket which is hanging from a spaghetti bridge.

We want to know – what is the force that breaks the spaghetti? But there's a twist. Explain to students that this activity is also a competition. Students work in groups of four. Each student puts a stone into the gondola. If they are the last person to put in a stone before the spaghetti breaks, they are the winner. But if they put in the stone that breaks the spaghetti, they lose! So – can they now use two different disciplines to investigate: Why did the spaghetti break?

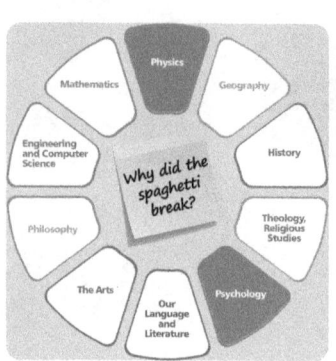

WHAT'S GOING ON?

Students are investigating two things at the same time – the behaviour of the people and the behaviour of the spaghetti. Ask them – which discipline can best help us to measure and explain the force that breaks the spaghetti?

Which discipline asks questions about the behaviour of the people and helps us to think about the tactics they use and how competitively they play the game? Do they agree that working with both disciplines together can give us a richer understanding of why the spaghetti breaks?

Canterbury
Christ Church
University

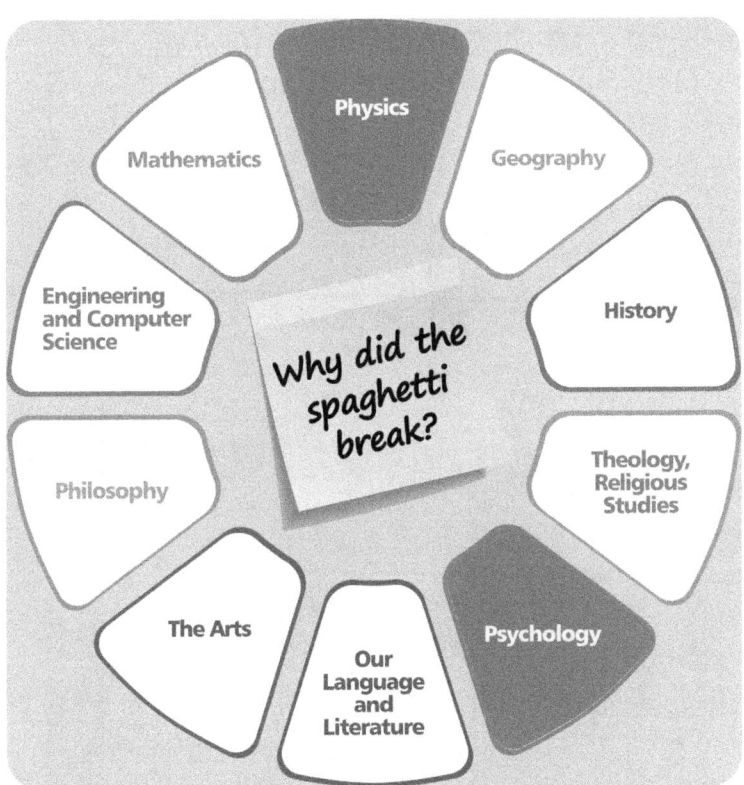

Teacher notes: Why is the sky blue? – Search engine

Epistemic Insight
WORKSHOP
Why is the sky blue?

Fun Facts and Instant Answers

The internet has an abundance of fun facts and answers to popular questions. They are like sticky treats and the most popular facts are repeated again and again - to capture our attention and reward us for staying online. But have you considered how that affects the results you see when you search?

Consider for example, *"Why is the sky blue?"* A search engine can take you directly to an answer, but what did you miss seeing on the way? In this activity we compare – searching for an answer using Google, searching in a library and searching using EI Search. More about each of these follows.

THE PROBLEM WITH POPULAR SEARCH ENGINES

Google is a wonderful way to speed up searching online. But there's a problem. If students search 'Why is the sky blue?', they will see an explanation from physics about the scattering of sunlight in our atmosphere. It's a popular question and this answer is repeated on thousands of websites.

We begin with a library:
If you use a library to research 'Why is the sky blue?' you are likely to go first to the discipline where you expect to find an answer.

Which discipline would you pick? Physics? OK, so suppose you decide to widen your search to investigate whether other disciplines also have something to say.

How could you do this if you are in a library?

So scrolling down the page of search results, the same answer is repeated again and again and again. But is this the only way to answer and is physics the only discipline that has something to say?

Canterbury Christ Church University

TEACHER NOTES AND RESOURCES 279

EI SEARCH
EI Search is a completely different way of searching – now students will need to click on a discipline to choose it. EI Search it uses a Discipline Wheel to prompt students to wonder about which disciplines can give them an answer. And it encourages them to test out disciplines they probably haven't considered.

Why is the sky blue'?
White light coming from the sun contains all of the colours. When sunlight reaches the earth's atmosphere it is scattered and the colours are separated.

Red, yellow and orange colours are scattered least. Blue light is scattered most and seems to come to our eyes from all over the sky.

Do all planets have blue skies?
Some small planets and moons have no atmosphere. Sunlight travels through empty space to the surface without scattering. When astronauts were on the moon, the sun appeared to be very bright and white. When they were facing away from the sun, they saw the darkness of space, even in the daytime!

Do other animals see colours the way we do'?
Biologists investigating this question have discovered that dogs and cats have two receptors to detect colour, where we have three. They predict that their spectrum of colours would look like this:

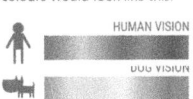

HUMAN VISION
DOG VISION

Can your mood affect how you see colours?
Some psychologists have asked this question and hypothesise that it can. It makes sense when you think of the phrase,, "looking at the world through rose tinted spectacles." Put on a happy mood and everything looks ... brighter. But if this is your theory, how do you test it?

Wising up AIs and using Tech Wisely - Now we're not suggesting that EI Search should replace popular search engines. But once they've tried it, your students will be better placed to recognise the strengths and limitations of search engines.

Index

accessible
   classroom resources and activities 16, 36, 43, 45, 49, 50, 56, 83, 91, 120, 179
agency 21–32, 43–57, 61, 82, 100–6, 128, 179–84, 190
agentic
   learning 11, 13, 16, 18, 27, 47, 49, 55, 82, 117, 130, 133
artificial intelligence (AI) xx, 4, 15, 16, 33, 81, 218, 219, 233, 253

big questions 2, 55
   bridging questions 2
   extra-curricular activities 69
   higher education 155
   primary education 43, 59, 69
   secondary education 207
   sustainability 117
   teaching with 39
boundaries
   disciplines, subjects and domains of knowledge 3, 8, 11, 25, 44, 45, 48, 53, 56, 64, 78, 81, 101, 102, 107, 111, 119, 120, 131, 144, 147, 151, 193, 197, 252, 256
bridge (s) 8, 95
   across subjects or disciplines 18, 60, 66, 73, 143, 158, 257
   bridging questions 2, 146, 147, 257, 261, 276
   interdisciplinary trends 228
   the Bubble tool 10, 127, 129, 130

co-creation 43–4, 53, 99–116
compartmentalisation 250–1
compartmentalised 4, 194
   curriculum 101, 111
   learning 49, 64
creativity 6, 11, 82, 126, 137, 143, 149, 151, 169, 194, 217, 218
critical thinking 6, 127, 131, 218, 223–36
cross-curricula(r) 207, 211, 215, 261
curiosity, *sic passim*
curriculum 22, 45, 60, 71, 99–115, 146, 158, 192, 207, 210

dance 143–53
dinosaurs 69
disciplinary knowledge 47, 48, 108, 124, 158
   learning experience in the classroom 107
Discipline Wheel 27–37, 53, 75, 90, 92, 122, 130, 183–7, 212, 259
discipline(s), *sic passim*
Discovery Bag 43, 45–50, 52, 55, 72, 73

The EI Curriculum Framework 46, 61, 264, 265
empower/ed/ment/ing 13, 18, 19, 47, 52, 54, 94, 103, 104, 183, 197, 227
enquiry/inquiry, *sic passim*

INDEX

epistemic curiosity   34, 49, 53, 56, 64, 145, 149, 186, 191, 207
epistemic insight   xviii–xxi, *sic passim*
  AI   1–8
  epistemic agency   23–32, 43–8
  higher education   59–66, 137–9, 155–71
  interdisciplinary knowledge   4, 143–5, 192–201, 217–19
  libraries   87–91
  primary education   43–57, 70–2, 259
  search engine   179–91
  secondary education   70–2, 118–33, 192, 213
Epistemic Insight Initiative, *sic passim*
epistemic knowledge   19, 185, 260–1
epistemically insightful   xx, 1, 7, 13, 50, 76, 99, 101, 104, 107, 117, 132, 141
Essential Experiences in Science   43, 44, 48, 50
  teacher resources   10, 266, 268, 270, 274
explore(s)/explored, *sic passim*

friend (artificial)   27–37, 219, 237–48
future, *sic passim*

generative AI (GenAI)   1, 3–5, 8, 81, 89–97, 138
global, *sic passim*

'Hands-on'   8, 16, 45, 50, 51, 124, 259
How do clouds stay up?   56, 57, 274

imagination   15, 217–19
inclusive   22, 47, 70, 73, 175, 176
  classroom   50

  resource   43, 45
interdisciplinary, *sic passim*
investigate/investigation, *sic passim*
investigating big questions   54, 71, 77
  teacher resources   10, 272

knowledge, *sic passim*

language   3–4, 15, 88, 110–12, 175–6, 205–15, 251
Large Language Models (LLM)   96
lens
  disciplinary/disciplines   5, 50, 78, 113, 146, 195
  of religion   70
  of science   70, 120, 182, 260
lenses
  disciplinary   1, 2, 7, 27, 35, 41, 49, 54, 55, 61, 62, 64, 119, 149, 151, 182, 183, 186
library   88–98, 250–5

machine learning   239
metacognition   139, 195, 197
multidisciplinary, *sic passim*

the natural world   45, 74, 129, 258, 260–2
nature of science   121, *sic passim*
  real-world contexts and multidisciplinary arenas   124, 127, 264, 265
norms of thought   5–7, 30, 31, 48, 53, 55, 60, 78, 109, 111, 119, 126, 129, 130, 182, 183, 261

observation/s   48, 50, 53, 70, 73, 126, 167, 227, 258
  ChatGPT   183
  engineers   209
  methods used   5, 182, 261, 262

INDEX

thinking like a scientist   260
Why do spinners spin?   45
Why do we have rainbow colours?   74
Why is the sky blue?   53–4

pedagogy/pedagogical, *sic passim*
practical
   learning and teaching   9, 11, 16, 19, 25, 43–7, 49, 50, 53, 54, 56, 59, 119, 121, 133, 139, 153, 157, 219, 227, 240, 241, 251, 252, 256
   preferred questions   5–7, 48, 78, 126, 261

religion   12, 70–3, 78, 101, 157–8
research, *sic passim*
research-engaged   78, 99, 100, 103, 104, 114, 180
robot   29–37, 70–2, 147–8, 239–48

science, *sic passim*
science questions   258
scientific enquiry   18, 43–5, 48, 128, 259
silo/s/ed   25, 27, 88, 96, 118, 133, 137, 139, 144, 179–83, 194, 196, 208, 251, 253
space travel   232–3
spinners   44, 57, 266
sustainability   14, 56, 82, 117–34
sustainable   22, 46, 118, 119, 121, 129, 132, 197
   development   11, 18, 19, 41, 228

teacher education   40, 59–66, 102, 114–15, 122, 192–202
thinking like a historian   44, 124
   Why did the Titanic sink?   52
thinking like a scientist   44, 56, 260
   Why did the Titanic sink?   50, 51
two disciplines   113, 146, 149, 208, 257
   addressing a question   7, 37, 115, 119, 132, 145, 182

water   3, 73, 100, 258
   droplets   49, 56, 260
   questions about water   8, 40, 72, 76, 78, 182, 183, 185, 223, 256
ways of knowing   10, 11, 41, 44, 47, 55, 70, 75, 130, 149, 158, 218
   how they interact   124, 264, 265
Why did the spaghetti break?   276
Why did the Titanic sink?   47, 50–2, 57, 257, 261, 268
Why do spinners spin?   44, 57, 266
Why is the sky blue?   44, 53, 72, 180, 272
wonder (s)   62, 70, 192–4, 201, 217, 241
working scientifically   48
worldview (s)   15, 119, 157, 160, 163, 196